# self-insight

## roadblocks and detours on the path to knowing thyself

DAVID DUNNING

Psychology Press
Taylor & Francis Group

NEW YORK AND HOVE

Published in 2005 by
Psychology Press
270 Madison Avenue
New York, NY 10016
www.psypress.com

Published in Great Britain by
Psychology Press
2 Park Square
Milton Park, Abingdon
Oxon OX14 4RN U.K.
www.psypress.co.uk

10 9 8 7 6 5 4 3 2

Library of Congress Cataloging-in-Publication Data

Dunning, David (David A.)
   Self-insight : roadblocks and detours on the path to knowing thyself / David
Dunning.
      p. cm. — (Essays in social psychology)
   Includes bibliographical references and indexes.
   ISBN 1-84169-074-0 (hardcover : alk. paper)
   1. Self-perception. I. Title. II. Series.

   BF697.5.S43D78 2005
   158.1—dc22

                                                        2004017285

The most excellent and divine counsel, the best and most profitable advertisement of all others, but the least practiced, is to study and learn how to know ourselves. This is the foundation of wisdom and the highway to whatever is good. God, Nature, the wise, the world, preach man, exhort him both by word and deed to the study of himself.

**Pierre Charron, French Philosopher, 1541–1603**

It's not only the most difficult thing to know one's self, but the most inconvenient.

**Josh Billings, American Humorist, 1815–1885**

# CONTENTS

# ABOUT THE AUTHOR

David Dunning is Professor of Psychology at Cornell University. He is the author or co-author of over 50 journal articles, book chapters, reviews, and commentaries. His areas of specialization center on the accuracy of self-judgment and the psychology of eyewitness testimony. He also has published work on depression, stereotypes, behavioral economics, and social perception. Much of this work has been supported financially by the National Institute of Mental Health. His work has been featured in *The New York Times*, *U.S. News & World Report*, ABC and CBS news, and NPR's *All Things Considered*. One highlight of his career was the morning his parents discovered his work mentioned in the comic strip *Doonesbury*. Professor Dunning received his BA in Psychology from Michigan State University and his PhD in Psychology from Stanford University.

# PREFACE

The comedian Bill Maher says that each person in the world has one book in him or her. This is probably my one. It focuses on an on-and-off professional obsession in my research lab through the years on the accuracy with which people view themselves.

I hope to convey to the reader what a fascinating and ever-expanding topic this is. It is a complicated and subtle matter to know one's self, and writing this book has only introduced me to more nuance and mystery related to the pursuit of self-knowledge. I hope the reader finds in the pages of this book as much surprise and intrigue as I have come across thinking about the topic.

I also hope that one subtext of the book becomes clear to the reader as he or she ambles through the pages. The bulk of the material comprising this book comes from difficult, systematic, and rigorous observation of human thought, feeling, and action taking place in psychology laboratories, as well as in survey research units and medical schools. This is frustrating, confusing, but often satisfying and illuminating work. Research psychologists are not armchair philosophers. Rather, they battle-test their ideas by collecting data under the unbending and unforgiving rules of scientific inquiry, an enterprise that constrains what the individual scientist can claim, hopefully what is most likely to be correct. It is my hope that nonprofessionals who pick up this book will gain some insight into the rigorous nature of this process.

No book is the province of one individual. Many graduate student collaborators and undergraduate research assistants have sweated over the surveys and experiments described in this volume. Their creativity, dedication, and persistence should be properly acknowledged. They have been the front-line troops in our little scientific campaigns, and their efforts are deeply appreciated. In particular, the craftwork of Emily Balcetis, Keith Beauregard, Deanna Caputo, Geoff Cohen, Joyce Ehrlinger, Nick Epley, Andy Hayes, Kerri Johnson, Justin Kruger, Rory O'Brien

McElwee, Scott Perretta, David Sherman, Lisa Stern, Amber Story, and Leaf Van Boven is in evidence across many pages of this book.

Although this book discusses research coming out of several research labs, it does feature work coming out of my own. Much of that work has been financially supported by National Institute of Mental Health Grant RO1 56072. That said, the conclusions and opinions expressed in the book are my own and should not be taken to represent the views of the institute.

Lucy Morehouse and Audra Snyder did yeoman's work tracking down articles and references for the book. David Myers and Chip Heath provided quick pieces of counsel that I believe significantly enhanced the execution of the book. Harry Segal and David Sherman provided terrific comments on sections of the book. Detlef Fetchenhauer, Debbie Prentice, and Jim Sheppard read and commented on the book in its entirety. Their counsel is greatly appreciated. Elaine Wethington's preternatural skill at knowing the answer to any question thrown at her is deeply appreciated. Finally, the intellectual curiosity, enthusiasm, and good cheer of Paul Dukes at Psychology Press are also gratefully acknowledged.

# Thales's Lament

*On the Vagaries of Self-Assessment*

I sometimes wonder what it would be like to be standing just outside the village of Namche, in the crisp and arid air of Nepal, staring up at the mountain that the locals refer to as Sagarmatha, the goddess of the sky. Rising over 29,000 feet (or 8,000 meters), the mountain fascinated the British when they first came to the Indian subcontinent. They took pains to measure it precisely, and then later gave it the name, Everest, by which it is known worldwide. Today the fascination with Mt. Everest continues unabated, with hundreds of mountaineers every year attempting to climb its ice and rock to reach the roof of the world, the highest point on Earth.

But one fact remains clear for those attempting the summit. To scale Everest, climbers had better have an accurate impression of themselves. They have to know their strengths and weaknesses as a mountaineer, their capacity to surmount all the challenges that lay ahead, and their strength of will when the body and then the mind begin to fail. Climbers have to know whether they have the courage and agility to walk in full mountain gear across rickety aluminum ladders perched over 100-foot–deep crevices of ice along the Kumba icefall. They have to know whether they have the health and stamina to walk up to the 26,000-foot elevation of Camp 4, in the "death zone," above the highest point where any rescue helicopter can reach.

And then one day, they have to know whether they have the fortitude to get up early in the morning, perhaps with little sleep or food, to walk the last 3,000 vertical feet to the summit, in an environment with only a third of the oxygen of sea level, where winds can reach hurricane force and the wind chill can drop to −150 degrees Fahrenheit. They have to know whether they have the technical skill to scale the sheer vertical treachery of the Hillary Step just 200 feet below the summit. They have to know whether they have the discipline to turn around in midafternoon, no matter how close they are to the summit, to reach camp before darkness, the clouds, and the cold envelopes the mountain.

These insights are not luxuries. Through 2001, a total of 1,496 climbers have reached the summit of Everest and returned safely, but 172 others died—a ratio of 1 to every 9—with roughly 120 of their bodies still lying somewhere on the mountain (Brunner, 2002), either lost in some unknown fissure or to be stepped over by other climbers on their way to their own fates.

This book is about the accuracy of the impressions that people hold of themselves. It focuses not on mountaineers but rather on the rest of us who face all those more mundane but no less important summits in our own lives, such as getting an "A" in that important class, getting promoted at work, raising smart and moral children, or perhaps even writing one's first book. It explores whether people have adequate insight into their capacities and their talents. It examines whether people are aware of their shortcomings. It assesses whether they have a good sense of the content of their character.

The notion that accurate self-insight is important is not a new one. One has only to go back to the classical Greeks to see the importance that they placed on accurate self-knowledge. The Oracle of Delphi, for example, was a place where kings, queens, and lesser personages went to ask questions about their lives and futures. Although their questions were important, receiving wisdom from the Oracle tended to be a tricky business. The Oracle answered questions with questions, posed riddles, or responded with frenzied *non sequiturs*. But on the building that housed the Oracle itself were two admonitions that were crystal clear in their meaning, thus indicating their importance, at least in Western thought. The first was "nothing too much"; the second was "know thyself."

This book, in essence, is about that second admonition. It addresses the extent to which people have an adequately accurate view of self. It is clear that such accurate views are helpful, if not essential, for navigating our everyday worlds. People need to know what their strengths are in order to choose, for example, the right careers and avocations. They need to be aware of their weaknesses so that they can improve upon them or, failing that, know which situations to avoid. They need to have a firm grasp of their moral character to know when they may be weak in the face of temptation, when they might transgress to commit sins they will be punished for later, either by their own guilty conscience or by the disapproval of others.

At first blush, such accurate self-knowledge would seem easy to attain. People are constantly exposed to an ongoing stream of information about their triumphs and failures, their habits and their limits. They see when they act superhuman versus when they are all too human. And, given that each of us is the most important person in our own little personal drama, one would conclude that people are motivated at some fundamental level to take such information in order to form accurate self-impressions.

In this book, however, I argue that it is surprisingly difficult to form accurate impressions of self. Even with all the time we spend with ourselves and all the motivation to achieve accurate self-understanding, we reach flawed and sometimes downright wrong conclusions about ourselves. If self-insight is a destination we all desire, we face many roadblocks and detours along the way, and each of us fails to reach that destination in some important fashion. No matter how useful an accurate self-vision would be, and no matter how motivated we are to attain it, this accuracy is a commodity that elusively remains outside of our reach.

This observation, however, is also not very new. One can again go back to the Greeks to find that accurate self-awareness was a difficult possession to obtain. As reported by Diogenes Laertes, the Greek philosopher Thales, one of the first Western philosophers whose thinking we still have records of, lamented that "knowing thyself" was one of the most difficult tasks people face—certainly more arduous than the easiest task he could think of, which was, of course, giving advice to others.

## □ Evidence of Inaccurate Self-Views

Recent evidence of psychological research gives credence to Thales's lament about the human inability to achieve accurate self-impressions. If one scavenges through the literature, one finds ample evidence that the impressions people have of themselves seem to be detoured away from realistic self-views. Such evidence comes in two forms.

### Correlational Evidence

The first form of evidence comes from studies about how closely tethered self-impressions of ability are to actual performance. Do people with lofty views of their own intelligence, popularity, and competence, in fact, display more smarts, social skill, and achievement than the rest of us?

What about people with pessimistic impressions of their skills? Are they, indeed, less smart and popular than most of their peers?

A large number of studies from many corners of psychology research suggest that, as a general rule, people's impressions of their abilities—whether arrogant or humble—are not anchored very closely to their actual level of skill. Across a large number of domains—from scholastic performance to leadership ability to clerical skills to professional knowledge—what people think about themselves can be quite distinct from the truth of their competence and expertise.

The usual way research psychologists document this fact is to compute a correlation coefficient (or $r$) between people's perceptions of their ability and their objective performance. A correlation coefficient is a statistic that indexes how tightly one variable, such as perceptions of performance, rises and falls in tandem with another variable, such as reality of performance. Correlation coefficients can range from $+1.0$ (the two variables are perfectly related) to $-1.0$ (the two variables are still perfectly related, but in a negative direction). A correlation of 0 means the two variables are completely unrelated—knowing a person's perception of his or her ability, for example, would not give you any information about the reality of his or her ability. To give a real-world example of a correlation, it is well known that gender and height are correlated, with men tending to be taller than women. The relationship between gender and height is not perfect—some women are taller than some men—but the relationship produces a correlation coefficient of roughly .7.

How does the correlation between self-impression and actual skill compare with this benchmark? A good deal of research suggests that the comparison does not paint a kind portrait of our skills at self-insight. The correlation between perception and reality is often modest to meager, if it appears at all. For example, people's ratings of their intelligence tend to correlate roughly around between .2 and .3 with their scores on IQ tests and other intellectual tasks (Hansford & Hattie, 1982). When tested in their ability to tell when other people are lying, their impressions of performance correlate only .04 with actual proficiency (DePaulo, Charlton, Cooper, Lindsay, & Muhlenbruck, 1997). When expressing emotions to others, people's estimates of success fail to be related at all to actual success (Riggio, Widaman, & Friedman, 1985).

The dissociation between perception and reality can be found in real-world areas of some consequence. The views adolescent boys have of their knowledge about condom use correlates only slightly with their actual knowledge (Crosby & Yarber, 2001). Nurses' estimates of their proficiency at basic life support tasks fail to correlate with their actual level of knowledge (Marteau, Johnston, Wynne, & Evans, 1989). Doctors' beliefs about their understanding of thyroid disorders does not correspond at all to their actual level of understanding (Tracey, Arroll, Richmond, & Barham, 1997). Family practice residents' views about their patient interviewing skills do not correlate highly (roughly .30) with what their instructors and other experts think (Stuart, Goldstein, & Snope, 1980).

Thus, the general rule is that self-perceptions of competence are generally not tightly tethered to actual performance. To be sure, self-views do have some validity. In an exhaustive review of the literature circa 1982, Mabe and West found that the correlation between perception of ability and the reality did tend to be positive—and at times it could climb as high as roughly .70, such as when college students guessed what their grades would be or when secretaries evaluated their clerical skills. In addition, the correlation dropped to around zero only occasionally, and it almost never went negative. But, when all was said and done, the typical correlation was roughly .29. That was high enough to suggest a real relationship between perception and reality, just not a very strong one. To put it in terms of an old cliché, their research suggested that the glass of self-insight was not completely empty, it just was not all that full.

Other research has also demonstrated how empty the glass of self-insight can be, at least compared with other benchmarks of insight. Almost to add insult to injury, it appears that in some very important contexts other people have more insight about our proficiencies than we do ourselves. College students do a better job at predicting the longevity of their roommates' romantic relationships than they do their own (MacDonald & Ross, 1999). What employees think of their job and social skills in the workplace tends to correlate only .36 with what their peers think of them and, perhaps more important, only .35 with what their supervisors think. However, both supervisors and peers seem to be spotting something in common, in that the correlation between supervisor and peer impressions tend to be rather high, roughly .62 (Harris & Schaubroeck, 1988).

What others see in us also tends to be more highly correlated with objective outcomes than what we see in ourselves. In a study of naval officers, self-ratings of leadership ability were not related to how often a sailor's superior recommended him or her for early promotion. However, leadership ability as rated by peers successfully predicted who would be recommended and who would not (Bass & Yammarino, 1991). Similarly, in a study of surgical residents, self-ratings of surgical skill failed to predict how well residents did on an object test of those skills. However, ratings by superiors and peers (which, of course, tended to be highly correlated with each other) successfully predicted performance on the objective test (Risucci, Tortolani, & Ward, 1989).

Indeed, perhaps the most intriguing demonstration that self-impressions carry little additional insight relative to the impressions of others comes from a study in which strangers were asked to judge a person's intelligence after having viewed only a 90-second videotape. On the tape, participants watched as the target person walked into a room, sat behind a table, read a standard weather report, and then got up to walk out of the room (Borkenau & Liebler, 1993). After seeing only this, participants' impressions of that person's intelligence correlated just as highly with the person's scores on standardized intelligence tests (around .30) as did the person's own self-impression (around .32).

In sum, the notions people have about their skills and knowledge are far from perfect indicators of their actual proficiency. Those with the most vaulted beliefs of their competence are not necessarily the most competent; those who denigrate their skills are not necessarily the least skillful. Impressions of skill are somehow decoupled from reality—perhaps not completely, but to an extent that is surprising.

## Overconfidence

But there is another set of findings that, perhaps more importantly, demonstrates that the opinions people hold of themselves are not well connected with reality or even with what can possibly be true. On average, people tend to hold overly favorable views of themselves. They overestimate their skill, their knowledge, their moral character, and their place on the social ladder. Ironically, they even overestimate their ability to provide veridical and unbiased judgments about themselves.

This overconfidence has been shown in what people say about themselves when they compare themselves with others. If asked if their skill level is "average," "above average," or "below average," too many people endorse the above average option—so much so that the average person rates himself or herself as well above average, a belief that cannot be objectively possible.

For example, in 1980, Weinstein asked college students at Rutgers University how likely they were to encounter a number of positive life events while avoiding negative ones, relative to other Rutgers students. Typically, his respondents stated that they were be more likely than the typical student to live past 80, graduate in the top third of the class, have a good job offer before the end of their senior year, have a terrific salary, and to own their own home. At the same time, the typical respondent said he or she was less likely than the typical student to have a drinking problem, get divorced, have a heart attack, get fired, contract a sexually transmitted disease, and, last but not least, suffer gum problems.

Other studies have found similar patterns of overestimation. In a large survey of high school seniors, the College Board (1976–1977) found that while 60% rated themselves as "above average," relative to other high school seniors, in athletic ability, only 6% rated themselves as "below average." On leadership ability, a full 70% rated themselves as above average, but only 2% as below average. On their "ability to get along with others," virtually every respondent described himself or herself as at least average, with 60% saying they fell in the top 10% among their peers on this skill—and 25% saying that their level of skill was in the top 1%!

Other researchers observe the same pattern of overestimation. Workers tend to think their absentee record is better than the typical employee in their workplace (Harrison & Shaffer, 1994). People think they are less susceptible to the flu than the average person (Larwood, 1978). Motorcyclists think they are less likely to cause an accident than other bikers (Rutter, Quine, & Albery, 1998). Elderly drivers tend to think they are better drivers than other individuals their age (Marottoli & Richardson, 1998). Business executives think their firm is more likely to succeed than the typical firm in their business sector (Cooper, Woo, & Dunkelberg, 1988; Larwood & Whittaker, 1977). Grocery store cashiers think they are much better than their peers at spotting which young-looking customers should be "carded" for alcohol (McCall & Nattrass, 2001). Bungee jumpers think they are less likely to meet harm than will the typical bungee jumper, a perception, by the way, that is not shared by their friends and family (Middleton, Harris, & Surman, 1996).

Indeed, such overly rosy views of self can be found among the population I could describe as the wisest, most learned, and contemplative in modern society. Namely, 94% of college professors say they do above-average work (Cross, 1977). In a similar vein, academic researchers think the manuscripts that they submit for publication possess more methodological and theoretical value than the manuscripts of others (Van Lange, 1999).

People's predictions also prove to be overly optimistic when compared with the true likelihood of events. A survey of lawyers revealed that they overestimated the likelihood that they would win cases that they were just about to try (Loftus & Wagenaar, 1988). Students in negotiation games possess overly confident impressions that the other side will accept their final offers (Neale & Bazerman, 1983). Stock pickers tend to be too optimistic that they have chosen winners—and this has consequences, in that the stocks they buy tend to do less well than the stocks they sold to purchase them (Odean, 1998).

This overestimation of self also comes in other forms. When asked to make predictions, and then to state the likelihood that these predictions will later prove accurate, people tend to overestimate this likelihood. College students answering trivia questions overestimate the chance that their answers are the right ones (Fischhoff, Slovic, & Lichtenstein, 1977;

Koriat, Lichtenstein, & Fischhoff, 1980). They overestimate how accurate their predictions about another college student's preferences will be, even when that college student is their roommate (Dunning, Griffin, Milojkovic, & Ross, 1990). They also overestimate the accuracy of their predictions about what events they will experience during the course of an academic year (Dunning & Story, 1991; Vallone, Griffin, Lin, & Ross, 1990).

Such overconfidence is also observed among people who are not college students. For example, surgical trainees overestimate the accuracy of their diagnoses after looking at x-rays of possible radial fractures (Oksam, Kingma, & Klasen, 2000). Clinical psychologists do the same in their inferences about a client after reading case study materials (Oskamp, 1965).

Such overconfidence is also observed when people are absolutely certain in their judgments. Indeed, such overconfidence is exactly at its maximum when people are *sure* of what they are saying. When people express 100% certainty in their predictions, they still tend to be wrong roughly one time out of every five, an error rate of 20% (Fischhoff, 1977). Similarly, in a study focusing on diagnoses of pneumonia, when physicians were the most confident that a patient had pneumonia, being roughly 88% confident in their diagnosis, only around 20% of the patients actually turned out to have pneumonia (Christensen-Szalanski & Bushyhead, 1981). The fact that certainty in belief does not compel certainty in outcome leads to one very interesting observation. In one study of individuals starting a business, a full 33% expressed absolute certainty that their business would succeed (Cooper, Woo, & Dunkelberg, 1988). However, best estimates indicate that more than two-thirds of small businesses will fail within four years (Dun & Bradstreet, 1967).

Other work shows that people remain overconfident even when, it could be argued, they should know better. Smokers, for instance, know that their health is more at risk than nonsmokers, but they significantly underestimate that risk (Strecher, Kreuter, & Kobrin, 1995). Students whose parents were married and divorced several times are the most confident among their peers that their future marriages will be stable and long lived (Boyer-Pennington, Pennington, & Spink, 2001). Despite the fact that people know in the past that they typically have had to scramble to get some task done before a deadline, be it a class assignment or their income tax return, they continue to believe that they will complete the task well before the deadline (Buehler, Griffin, & MacDonald, 1997; Buehler, Griffin, & Ross, 1994).

To be sure, this work on overconfidence does generate some complaints from some researchers, who at times assert that (*a*) overconfidence can be reduced to a statistical artifact, or (*b*) overconfidence depends greatly on the particular context in which it is tested (Dawes & Mulford, 1996; Erev, Wallsten, & Budescu, 1994; but for vigorous responses to these critiques, see Brenner, 2000). And although overconfidence is the general rule, people do not display overconfidence at all times. There are systematic circumstances in which people show little overconfidence, or sometimes even unwarranted underconfidence. For example, if the task at hand is particularly easy and performance is high, people tend to be underconfident in their performance (Lichtenstein & Fischhoff, 1980). If people think they are horrific at a task, such as computer programming, they exaggerate how bad they are to an unrealistic degree (Kruger, 1999). And, perhaps most important, this pervasive pattern of overconfidence, so evident in individuals in North America, often evaporates as one crosses the Pacific Ocean, in that Japanese nationals show very little tendency to overestimate their ability and character relative to that of their peers (Heine, Lehman, Markus, & Kitayama, 1999).

But overall the general tendency found in the research psychology literature is for people to overestimate themselves. Perhaps this will not come as a surprise. Each of us has seen so many examples in which other people have acted overconfidently, even foolishly, and so formal research on these types of overestimation would seem unnecessary.

Perhaps that is true, but it still could be the case that people underestimate the pervasive role that overconfidence plays in their own lives. For example, when asked, people concede that overconfidence is a phenomenon they deal with constantly in their own lives, although, truth be told, such overconfidence seems to be more characteristic of other people than it is for themselves. When directly asked, people tend to say that they are uniquely able to avoid the overconfidence and bias that other people demonstrate so pervasively (Friedrich, 1996; Pronin, Lin, & Ross, 2002). Perhaps this is true, but perhaps it is also evidence of how close to home overconfidence hits in our own lives.

## ☐ The Journey Ahead

In this book, I focus on the roads that take us away from accurate self-impressions. I describe several lines of research that explain, in part, why ratings of ability and character wander away so often from the objectively demonstrated as well as the logically possible.

In doing so, I concentrate on several different aspects of the self. In chapters 2, 3, and 4, I concentrate on skill and discuss why people so often poorly judge their competence in a number of social and intellectual domains. In chapter 2, I discuss why we cannot expect everybody to be a good judge of his or her ability. In particular, I argue that people who are incompetent are often not in a position to know that they are incompetent. Judgment of self is an intrinsically difficult task, and the incompetent just do not have the tools necessary to meet this difficult challenge, nor should the rest of us expect them to. In chapter 3, I discuss where perceptions of skill and accuracy come from, if not closely tied to actual performance. In chapter 4, I focus on why life experience and feedback do not necessarily prod people toward more accurate impressions of self.

In chapters 5, 6, and 7, I turn to perceptions of character and personality more generally. In chapters 5 and 6, I discuss why people tend to overperceive their own personal uniqueness, focusing on the circumstances that induce people to falsely believe that they are special or exceptional, or at least better than the typical person. In chapter 7, I turn to perceptions of morality specifically to discuss how and why people so often feel ethically superior to their peers. In chapter 8, I explain why mistaken predictions of self may at times have nothing to do with faulty self-knowledge, but rather may be a function of misunderstanding the situations in which we place ourselves. Finally, in chapter 9, I touch upon basic questions that undoubtedly linger from the material in the rest of the book.

You will notice as you traverse the book that no overarching theory of self-insight, or rather the lack thereof, is offered. Instead, in each chapter I concentrate on one facet of the everyday self-concept and discuss how empirical research, some done in my lab and some done elsewhere, provides some understanding of why people reach and maintain impressions of self. Thus, each chapter can be considered a campfire tale about one aspect of the self-concept, detailing the triumphs and failures of self-insight.

I think such an approach is a fruitful one for one important reason. In the social psychological literature in recent years, there has been a continuing debate about whether, in essence, the Greeks were right when they asserted that "knowing thyself" was at the core of living a happy, productive, and gracious life. Some researchers have asserted the good life does not flow from accuracy, but rather from bias. They argue that having unrealistic and positive views of self are the golden keys to the good life, that mistaken self-images are essential for generating motivation, good moods, creativity, and generosity with others (e.g., Taylor & Brown, 1988). Needless to say, this position has its discontents (e.g., Colvin & Block, 1994).

I think this debate about the value and costs of unrealistic self-impressions, although well worth having, may be premature at this moment. At this time, one cannot judge whether such biases are good or bad until one has mapped out more comprehensively the ways in which people's impressions wander toward or away from the truth. It is too early to judge the worth, whether positive or negative, of such biases until one has a more exhaustive and nuanced understanding of the psychological processes that move people toward accurate or erroneous self-impressions.

Thus, in this book, I take various facets of the self and explore why people reach the judgments they do about themselves, whether accurate or not. Along the way, the detailed lessons we encounter will speak to whether reaching an accurate self-impression is a worthwhile and profitable enterprise. Also, along the way, in lieu of grand theory, we will encounter general themes and variations in the processes that underlie the thoughts and impressions that people reach about themselves. Thus, I invite the reader to come along. The journey across any book, like any journey up a mountain, begins with a simple series of steps. I hope the minor Everest this book represents provides some provocation, intellectual stimulation, and perhaps some self-reflection along the way. I am only sorry that I cannot provide the physical rigors that mountain climbing represents, but a book can only go so far.

# Ignorance as Bliss

*Why People Fail to Spot Their Own Incompetence*

In 1896, Gabriel Anton, a medical doctor from Austria, presented a paper at a medical conference describing a set of individuals that he had come across who shared a curious trait (Redlich & Dorsey, 1945). They had severe disabilities but did not seem to know it. One of them, for example, was a 64-year-old teamster who was deaf but seemingly unaware of that fact. He failed to answer questions posed to him but did not seem to notice these failures. He complained that he had problems understanding others in conversation, but he thought this difficulty arose because other people made such a racket rather than of his inability to pick out particular voices. He asked questions of other people but then appear undisturbed when no one answered him.

Cases like this, although rare, do crop up in the medical literature for a number of people suffering from specific neurological or cognitive deficits brought on by brain damage (for reviews, see McGlynn, 1994; Redlich & Dorsey, 1945). Some people who are blind, obviously not all of them, are not aware of their blindness, complaining, for example, that they have been left in a dark cellar (Redlich & Dorsey). Some people suffering from left-side *hemiplasia*, who through brain damage experience paralysis on their left side, at times remain unaware of their paralysis. Ask them to perform some task with their left hand; they will not do it, stating afterward that they simply did not wish to (D'Amasio, 1994).

Patients suffering from Korsakoff's syndrome, an amnesia linked to alcohol-induced brain damage, typically do not appreciate the depth of their impairment (Shimamura & Squire, 1986). The same holds true for patients suffering from Alzheimer's disease, who typically overestimate their ability to remember words (Schacter, McLachlan, Moscovitch & Tulving, 1986), even though they can more accurately predict how their relatives will perform on the same task (McGlynn & Kaszniak, 1991).

Other psychiatric syndromes also display the same lack of awareness. Boys suffering from attention deficit/hyperactivity disorder (ADHD) tend not to recognize deficiencies in their academic performance, social popularity, and behavioral conduct, overestimating themselves the most when they are the most impaired (Hoza, Pelham, Dobbs, Owens, & Pillow, 2002). A World Health Organization survey found that 85% of schizophrenics deny having a mental illness (Carpenter, Strauss, & Bartko, 1973). Another survey of hospitalized patients revealed that 69% of schizophrenics denied that they needed doctor supervision or hospitalization (Lin, Spiga, & Fortsch, 1979). And these denials matter: Of those refusing to take medication for their illness, 76% denied that they had schizophrenia, whereas 40% of those taking their drugs made similar denials (Van Putten, Crumpton, & Yale, 1976).

In 1914, Babinski coined the term now used, *anosognosia*, to describe these cases in which people are physically or neurologically impaired, sometimes grossly, yet fail to recognize the depth or even the existence of their impairment (Redlich & Dorsey, 1945). Over the years, medical doctors and clinical psychologists have puzzled over how people can have these deficits and not have any insight about them. Researchers have concluded that only a few people suffering from brain damage fail to recognize the effects. The type of blindness or paralysis that is not recognized must occur on the left side, and thus involve damage to the right hemisphere of the brain, usually in the parietal or frontal lobes (McGlynn, 1994). From this pattern, medical researchers infer that certain areas of the right hemisphere are crucial for monitoring performance, or perhaps updating people's images of their physical abilities (McGlynn).

# ☐ The Anosognosia of Everyday Life

In this chapter, I take the notion of anosognosia and transfer it, by analogy, from the neurological and physical realm to the cognitive and psychological one. People suffer all types of deficits, not just ones caused by physical insults, and it is interesting and important to see whether people are aware of their intellectual and social deficits in everyday life.

A person might be a terrible proofreader, for example, or not be able to form a logically coherent argument, or make horrible choices when it comes to disciplining his or her kids. How well do people recognize their impairments in these everyday challenges?

In recent research, my colleagues and I have argued that people are often not aware of their deficits on everyday tasks. When they perform poorly as a proofreader or parent—when they display, for lack of a better term, their *incompetence*—they remain blissfully unaware of the fact, thinking they are doing just fine when they are actually doing quite badly. A student failing a course exam can believe that he or she is out-performing most of the people in the class. A lawyer can make a closing argument that the jury finds completely unconvincing, and then be bewildered when he or she loses the case. A novelist may craft a crummy book but think that the manuscript comprises the great American novel, an impression not even shared by his or her loved ones.

But, in actuality, our argument is a stronger one. It is not that people performing poorly fail to recognize their incompetence. Instead, our argument is that people performing poorly cannot be *expected* to recognize their ineptitude. They are simply not in a position to know that they are doing badly. The ability to recognize the depth of their inadequacies is beyond them. Much like certain types of brain damage prevent suffer-ers from recognizing their blindness or paralysis, incompetence places people in a state of anosognosia that makes it very difficult, and at times impossible, for sufferers to gain insight into how impaired their intellec-tual and social skills are.

The reason incompetent individuals cannot be expected to recognize their deficits is that they are doubly cursed: In many areas of life, the skills necessary to *produce* competent responses to the outside world are also the exact same skills needed to *recognize* whether one acted compe-tently. Consider the skill of constructing a logically sound argument. To produce a sound argument, one needs adequate knowledge of the some-times subtle and tricky rules of logic. One has to know what a logical argument looks like and know how to avoid the common pitfalls into which people stumble. But now consider the task of judging the sound-ness of an argument. To be an adequate judge, one once again needs to possess a comprehensive and nuanced knowledge of the rules of logical reasoning. The act of judging the logic of an argument draws on the very same skills as the act of producing an argument.

Several domains in the intellectual and social realms share this prop-erty—the skills needed to produce a correct response are also the skills needed to evaluate the adequacy of a response. In a phrase, the skills needed to perform the *cognitive* task (producing the response) are the exact same ones necessary for *metacognitive* tasks (judging the response).

A doctor's judgment of whether he or she has made the best diagnosis for a patient presupposes that his or her knowledge of medical conditions is up to snuff. The words of advice an English teacher gives to his or her students assume that he or she knows all the subtleties of standard English. A tax accountant's assessment of his advice to a client assumes that he knows all there is to know about tax law. To the extent that any of these individuals possess knowledge that is imperfect or incomplete, their assessment of their actions will also be flawed.

In short, because they lack the skill to produce correct responses, incompetent people also lack the skill to accurately judge their responses. Indeed, if they had the skill to know they were making consistent mistakes, they would also have the skill to avoid those blunders in the first place. In a sense, a common "marker" of achieving incompetence is to possess anosognosia about the faultiness of one's performance. Assuming people want to do the best job possible, any true awareness of the flaws in one's reactions would cause people to remove those flaws, nudging them more toward the competent side of the ledger.

Before continuing, I should make three notes about what I mean when I refer to a poor performer—especially in our studies—as incompetent. When describing a person as incompetent, I mean that he or she performs poorly in a specific domain, such as logical reasoning skill, interviewing a patient in an emergency room, or writing an interesting book. I am not referring to a person who appears dull-witted no matter what the task is. Instead, let me stipulate that a person who is hopelessly inept in one domain may be immensely skilled in many other domains, such as the stereotypical mathematician who is skilled at numbers but not at telling a joke at a cocktail party. This stipulation comes with a good deal of justification. Much work in cognitive psychology reveals that the intellectual skills a person has can differ dramatically from domain to domain. For example, the most skilled horserace handicappers, those who set the odds of each horse winning a race, tend not to be particularly bright when it comes to more academic tasks (Ceci & Liker, 1986).

Second, when I refer to incompetence, I do not imply that an incompetent person has limited potential and will never be competent. That may be the case, but often people are incompetent because they are inexperienced, young, or just lack proper training. Often, people who are incompetent can become competent with the proper education and practice. Children, for example, are obviously incompetent in many domains, and the law (as well as parents) takes pains to protect them from their inadequacies. Children cannot enter into contracts, sign up to race (let alone drive) automobiles, or be left responsible to decide their own alcohol intake. But with maturity, gentle counsel, and experience, these incompetents will grow into able adults.

Third, it is important to think of incompetence as a matter of degree. There is no bright line that separates out the able from those who are inept. Each person, to some degree, displays some imperfection in his or her knowledge or ability. It is in those instances in which task demands rub up against our imperfections that we are led into trouble. Some people have greater areas of imperfection, which means that they more commonly confront problems, but no person is completely exempt from the issue of incompetence.

## ☐ Awareness among the Incompetent: Empirical Studies

Do people performing incompetently fail to recognize that fact? This was the central question in a series of studies that Justin Kruger and I published in 1999. In one study, we brought college students into the laboratory and gave them a pop quiz on a basic intellectual skill: logical reasoning. After they completed the quiz, we asked them to compare their reasoning skills against those of other peers also participating in the experiment. They also estimated how many of the items on the quiz they had gotten right.

We then split people into four categories based on their performance. The bottom quartile consisted of those students who performed in the bottom 25% on the test. We next similarly grouped students into the second, third, and top quartiles, again based on their performance on the test. We then looked at how well each group thought it had done compared with how well it had really done.

When comparing their performances against those of their peers, students provided percentile estimates of their logical reasoning ability in general as well as their specific performance on the test. Figure 2.1 depicts how bottom to top quartile participants perceived their performances. The figure does not depict the specific data from the study (for that, see Kruger & Dunning, 1999), but instead represents the typical pattern of perceptions we observed in all our studies to date.

As seen in the figure, there were three findings of interest (actually four, but let us delay discussion of the fourth until later). First, on average, students saw their reasoning ability as anything but average. Whether they were describing their overall logical reasoning skill or their specific performance on the test, a strong majority of the students described themselves as above average, that is, above the 50th percentile relative to their peers. Second, there was a small, but not very strong, correlation between perceived performance and actual achievement. So far,

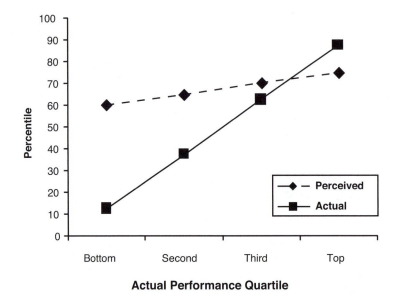

**FIGURE 2.1.** Typical relationship found between perceived and actual performance in Kruger and Dunning (1999) and follow-up studies.

these two findings should not be surprising. They merely recapitulate the results of the many studies discussed in chapter 1.

The third finding was the novel one and became apparent when we focused our attention on the perceptions of the bottom quartile. For purposes of our research, we categorized students performing in this quartile as "incompetent" and focused on how well their perceptions matched the reality of their performance. As the figure suggests, and our data confirmed, participants in the bottom quartile seemed to have little awareness that they had done so poorly on the test. Although bottom-quartile students, by definition, averaged around the 12th or 13th percentile in their performance (on average, they outperformed roughly 13% of their peers), they thought that their ability and performance fell around the 60th percentile. They also overestimated how many items they had gotten right on the test by 37%. In sum, although performing far worse than students in the top percentile, bottom-quartile students were almost as confident in their ability as their more able peers.

Subsequent studies repeated this story. In another study, we tested an important yet complicated social skill—knowing what is funny and what is not. We presented another set of college students with 30 jokes and asked them to rate each one on how funny it was. We then told students that we would compare their ratings with a set provided by an expert panel of professional comedians, as a way of objectively gauging their skill. We then asked students to compare their skill at finding humor to that of their peers, again asking them to provide a percentile ranking.

Based on how well their ratings correlated with those of our expert panel, we split students into four groups based on their performance. Again, Figure 2.1 gives an approximate representation of what we found when we compared perception to actual performance. On average, students believed that their skill at finding humor was better than the 50th percentile. There was also a stronger, but still moderate, correlation between perception of performance and the reality of performance (around .40). But, as before, participants in the bottom quartile thought they were doing just fine, placing their ability on average at around the 55th percentile, far higher than their actual percentile rank of 12.

In follow-up studies, we found that this overall pattern is just as strong when one ventures out of the laboratory and into the real world. College students scoring at the bottom on a quiz about sexually transmitted diseases think that they are outperforming roughly half of their peers (Dunning, 2003). Students performing in the bottom quartile on a college course exam think they have outperformed nearly 60% of their peers as they walk out the room at the end of the test. They also overestimate their raw score on the test by 30% (Dunning, Johnson, Ehrlinger, & Kruger, 2003). Students performing in the bottom quarter of a college debate tournament think they are winning 61% of their matches when they, in fact, win only 23% of them (Ehrlinger, Johnson, Banner, Dunning, & Kruger, 2004).

Poor performers continue to lack insight into their errors as one moves from the academic realm to the medical. When lab technicians are tested on their knowledge of medical terminology, which tests to prioritize, and on how to solve day-to-day dilemmas, those performing poorly tend to think they are doing just fine (Haun, Zeringue, Leach, & Foley, 2000). When medical residents complete an exercise in which they interview a mock patient who may have abused her child, those doing badly think they have handled the interview much better than their supervisors think they have (Hodges, Regehr, & Martin, 2001).

## ☐ Complaints

The central contention guiding this research is that poor performers simply do not know—indeed, cannot know—how badly they are performing. Because they lack the skills needed to produce correct answers they also lack the skills needed to accurately judge whether their own answers are correct. The data so far are consistent with this argument, but one could complain that there are other accounts, unfortunately less interesting, for the data.

One notable complaint against our conclusions is easy to describe and straightforward to dismiss. One can claim that incompetent participants did know or could have known that they had performed poorly, but they just did not care to be accurate in their estimates. This carelessness could have arisen for two reasons. First, participants may have known that they had performed poorly but thought the experimenter would not know. To save face, they reported that they performed well. Second, participants, if they had paid attention, would have realized that they performed poorly, but they just were not very motivated to provide accurate assessments, wanting instead to quickly jot down a careless estimate so that they could take off from the experiment as quickly as possible.

However, we have conducted an experiment that argues against these alternative explanations for our results. We gave participants a test of logical reasoning skills and again asked them to estimate how well they had done. Roughly half the participants simply provided these estimates. The other half, however, were told that they would receive $100 if they, for example, could guess exactly how many items they had gotten right, and $20 if they were off by one item. Providing this incentive did nothing to improve the accuracy of participants' estimates. In particular, bottom-quartile participants still dramatically overestimated how well they had done (I refer the reader, once again, to Figure 2.1), suggesting that they really did have little knowledge of their poor performance, even when they were given ample incentive to provide accurate assessments. (And, luckily, from our point of view, not one participant actually won the $100, though a few did win $20.)[1]

## ☐ Evidence for Metacognitive Deficits Among the Incompetent

However, the best way to rule out the previous alternative accounts is to rule *in* what we think prevents the incompetent from recognizing their condition, as well as what is causing obviously competent people to underestimate theirs.

Our explanation is that incompetence robs poor performers of the skills necessary to adequately judge performance. They are not able to accurately assess when someone, either themselves or another person, is turning in a superior or inferior performance.

## Assessing Metacognitive Skill

Past research supports this claim. When it comes to individual decisions, competent people are better at recognizing which of their decisions are likely to be right and which are likely to be wrong, relative to their more incompetent peers (although see Glenberg & Epstein, 1987; Wagenaar & Keren, 1985, for results not supporting this conclusion). Students performing well on an exam are more accurate than mediocre ones at predicting which specific test questions they got right (Shaughnessy, 1979; Sinkavich, 1995). Skilled readers are better able than less skilled readers to judge when they have or have not understood something they have been asked to read (Maki & Berry, 1984; Maki, Jonas, & Kallod, 1994). Trained clinicians have a more accurate sense, relative to their clerical staff, of when they have accurately diagnosed mental illness among children (Levenberg, 1975; see Garb, 1989, for a review of similar studies). Expert bridge players know when they have made good moves better than do novices (Keren, 1987). Physics experts can guess which physics problems will be more difficult than beginners (Chi, Glaser, & Rees, 1982). Accomplished tennis players better identify which play attempts were successful than tennis novices (McPherson & Thomas, 1989). Expert chess players know which chessboard positions they will have to see repeatedly before recreating them more precisely than do chess novices (Chi, 1978).

In our own data, we have shown that skilled people do better at a different—and perhaps more important—metacognitive task: being able to spot superior and inferior performances in other people (Kruger & Dunning, 1999, Study 3). We brought college students into the laboratory and gave them a pop quiz on grammar. After splitting students into four quartiles based on their performance, we again found that bottom-quartile participants grossly overestimated how well they had done on the test (see, again, Figure 2.1).

This study, however, contained a second phase, in which we invited every single participant in the bottom quartile and every person in the top quartile back into the laboratory a few weeks later. We handed them five tests that had been filled out by other people in the experiment, with these five tests chosen so that they would be representative of how well people performed as a whole in the experiment. We then asked each participant to "grade" each of the five tests, indicating how many items they thought each test taker had gotten right. Importantly, we did not give our graders an answer sheet. Much like real life, we called upon them to use whatever knowledge and wisdom they had brought with them to the laboratory to evaluate the performances of other people. Not surprisingly, we found that top-quartile participants provided more accurate grades than did their more incompetent counterparts—spotting who among their peers had demonstrated actual knowledge of grammar and who had not.

This finding that competent people more accurately spot the top and bottom performers among their peers, of course, needs to be replicated in domains other than grammar. The finding suggests, for example, that spotting the experts among us is not a straightforward task, that some (the experts themselves) are better able to do it than the less competent among us. Current research on decision-making within groups bolsters the observation that judging expertise among people is a surprisingly subtle and challenging task that not all people perform successfully. Auditors looking over financial statements in a group fail to recognize who among them is making important and accurate statements (Trotman, Yetton, & Zimmer, 1983). College students working on a winter survival problem fail to recognize those among them with any expertise on the issue (Miner, 1984). To be sure, groups at times do show some modest ability to judge the expertise of group members (Libby, Trotman, & Zimmer, 1987; Yetton & Bottger, 1982), but often perceived expertise is more related to how much a group member talks and displays confidence than to any expertise that member might actually possess (Littlepage, Robison, & Reddington, 1997).

I should note, however, that there is one extant finding that echoes the results of our grammar study. In the academic world, researchers submit manuscripts describing their research to journals for publication, upon which the manuscripts are studied and reviewed by two to four specialists, typically, to see if the manuscript is worthy of publication. In the late 1980s, the editor of one of the flagship research journals in social psychology, *Personality and Social Psychology Bulletin*, decided to investigate how often these reviewers agreed in their assessments of manuscripts. He found that agreement varied on several factors, including the prestige of the reviewers themselves. "High prestige" reviewers—that is, those with longstanding and highly visible research careers—tended to agree more in their evaluations of the methodological rigor of the submissions, as well as whether the manuscript should be accepted for publication, than did "mixed prestige" reviewers (Petty, Fleming, & Fabrigar, 1999). If we presume that high-prestige reviewers had earned their recognition because they had displayed high levels of competence in the past, it would make sense that these expert scholars would zero in on the true quality of the manuscripts, whether good or bad, and thus agree more often.

## Altering Metacognitive Skill

Other evidence more directly suggests that it is this deficit in metacognitive skill that explains why the incompetent think they do so well even when they are performing so poorly. Intriguingly, this evidence contains an informative paradox.

To a behavioral scientist, the best test of our "metacognitive deficit" explanation for the lack of self-awareness among the incompetent is easy: If deficits in metacognitive skill are responsible for this lack of awareness, then giving the poor performers an adequate amount of metacognitive skill should cause them to recognize just how unskilled they are. But therein lies the rub. How does one give the incompetent metacognitive skill?

According to the theoretical framework presented here, the path is clear, although it is a catch-22: The most direct way to confer metacognitive competence onto a person is to make them competent. Teach them the rules and knowledge necessary to make right decisions, and they will then be able to discern when right or wrong decisions are being made. Of course, the paradox in all this is that people can easily recognize their own incompetence only when that incompetence has been removed from them.

We decided to test this logic in a study in which we trained incompetent individuals to become competent, to see if that training also gave them the metacognitive skill to recognize just how poorly they had performed in the past (Kruger & Dunning, 1999, Study 4). Students were brought into the laboratory and given a logic test based on a particular puzzle called a Wason selection task (Wason, 1966). Some students did well on the test; others did poorly, with those doing poorly not recognizing the extent to which they had "flunked" the test (see, again, Figure 2.1). Indeed, on average, participants in the bottom quartile got every single question wrong, although they thought they had gotten about half of them right.

After completing the test, we then gave half of the participants a mini-lecture on how to approach Wason selection task problems. The other half of participants did some irrelevant filler task. Participants in the training condition took our mini-lecture seriously, and afterward demonstrated almost perfect competence in how to solve Wason logic problems. We then showed them the test they had previously completed and asked them now how well they thought they had done relative to everyone else in the experiment. Trained students who had done poorly were quite willing to admit that they had done badly on the test. Before training they had thought that their performance would put them in the 51st percentile; afterward they thought it was in the 32nd. To be sure, that was still an overestimate (their actual percentile was in the 14th), but it was a significant improvement over their first assessment. Students not receiving the mini-lecture did not change their self-ratings much between their first and second estimates.

Interestingly, trained participants also became more cautious in how they rated their overall ability at reasoning logically. After the mini-lecture, they lowered their self-rating on logic ability by over 10 percentile points (from the 55th percentile to the 44th). Of course, it must be pointed out that between their first and their second self-rating, participants receiving the mini-lecture had, if anything, become *more*, not less, skilled at thinking logically. But now armed with this new intellectual skill, participants could recognize a chink in their logical armor that they had not seen before. As a consequence, they had become more cautious in their self-evaluations even after acquiring a higher level of competence.

## ☐ Further Complaints

However, the careful reader could still harbor reservations about our characterization of the psychology of incompetence. According to our view, ignorance truly is bliss—but can that really be so?

### When People Recognize Their Incompetence

For example, the careful reader might protest the notion that incompetent people are not in a position to recognize their own limits. After all, each of us can cite pockets of incompetence, sometimes glaring ones, that we possess. Very few of us, for example, would volunteer to take part in the main event at a professional wrestling show, no matter how much we know such events are staged. Few of us would think that after getting off the couch, putting down the remote, and training for a month that we would have the slightest chance to make the U.S. Olympic track and field team. What separates these areas of insight from the ones in which people seem to fail so completely?

According to the Kruger and Dunning (1999) analysis, people fail to recognize their incompetence because the skills necessary to recognize competence are the exact same ones necessary to produce competence. This is most likely to be true when talking about intellectual skills, such as logical reasoning ability, and social skills, such as the ability to manage others in an office. However, this convergence of the skills necessary for production and recognition does not arise in all areas of life. It does not necessarily arise, for example, in athletic pursuits. The skills crucial for producing a good golf shot (e.g., good hand-eye coordination) are not the same ones needed to judge the quality of a shot (e.g., adequate eyesight).

Given this, it comes as no surprise that people produce much better estimates of their athletic skills, with the mean correlation between perception and objective performance averaging around .47, than they do of intellectual and social skills, where the convergence of skills needed for cognitive and metacognitive success is greater (Mabe & West, 1982). Similarly, the impressions football players have of their physical skills agree much more with their coaches' evaluations than their impressions of their "football sense" (Felson, 1981).

People are also likely to recognize their incompetence in areas where they know they cannot come up with any plausible response at all. For example, if someone asked me to rebuild the carburetor on his car, I know I am not the man. Similarly, if someone needed a quick heart transplant, I would reach for the phone to dial 911 rather than a scalpel to start the incision. However, if people have just enough knowledge to believe that they can conjure a plausible response to a task (more on this in chapter 3), they can develop blindness to gaps in their knowledge.

## The Burden of the Highly Competent

A careful reader might have one last question about our analysis of mistaken self-assessments. A glance at Figure 2.1 shows one last pattern that we found in our studies: Top performers consistently underestimated their achievement relative to their peers. How could this be, if top performers have the skills essential for accurate metacognitive judgment?

Top performers underestimate themselves because they suffer a special burden that differs from the one borne by the incompetent. Unlike the incompetent, top performers have a fairly accurate sense of how well they are doing on a given test. In a phrase, they get themselves and their performances right. What they get wrong is other people. Because top performers do so well, they just assume that other people are doing well, too. As a result, they do not believe their performances to be that unique or special, leading them to underestimate their percentile ranking of skill relative to their peers. In short, top performers suffer from a *false consensus effect*, which refers to the tendency for people to overestimate the commonness of their own responses and experiences (Marks & Miller, 1987; Ross, Greene, & House, 1977). Top performers, being knowledgeable, overestimate how knowledgeable their peers are.

The psychological literature reports many instances that support this analysis of top performers, in that knowledgeable people consistently overestimate how common their knowledge is. One example of this bias is found in work on the *hindsight bias*, which is also known as the *knew-it-all-along* effect. The bias occurs once people are informed about a fact, such as an answer to a trivia question. After learning the fact, people overestimate how likely they, or anyone else, would have been able to deduce it without being told, such as that Wyoming is the least populous state in the U.S.A. (Fischhoff, 1975, 1977). People also overestimate how well they or anyone else could have predicted an event once that event takes place (Christensen-Szalanski & Willham, 1991).

Other studies directly show that knowledgeable people misperceive how much other people share the same knowledge. Several studies have asked participants to answer questions, like identifying landmarks in New York City, everyday objects (like musical instruments and car parts), or answering questions about sports or history. In each, when participants knew the answer, they tended to overestimate the percentage of other people who would also know the answer (Fussell & Kraus, 1991, 1992; Nickerson, Baddeley, & Freeman, 1987).

In our own studies, we find evidence for similar biased perceptions among top performers, in that they misperceive how common their stellar performances are. Indeed, across a number of studies, we found that top performers, on average, overestimated the typical performance of their peers by 26%. Incompetent performers, paradoxically, provided more accurate estimates of how well their peers performed (Ehrlinger, Johnson, Banner, Dunning, & Kruger, 2004).

We have conducted a direct test of the false consensus account of underestimation among top performers. If top performers underestimate themselves because they overestimate how well their peers perform, then showing them the performances of others, and thus showing them how poorly other people tend to do, should disabuse them of their undue modesty. Recall the "grading" study described previously in which we asked bottom and top performers on a grammar test to grade the performances of other participants (Kruger & Dunning, 1999, Study 3). There was one last phase of that study, in which we handed back to participants their own grammar tests and asked them to re-rate their own performance and ability, now that they had seen how other people handled the test.

Consistent with a false consensus account, top performers raised their self-ratings after looking over the tests of others. Presumably, they raised their estimates because they became aware of just how distinctive their own performance was after seeing just how poorly other participants in general had done on the test. Beforehand, they had rated their skill and ability at just over the 70th percentile. Afterward, their estimates rose to around the 80th.

In effect, this experiment had captured for top performers an experience I used to have when I taught a course in Cornell's summer school. To assist me in that course, I would hire the best undergraduate I could find, usually a spectacular one, to serve as a teaching assistant. About a day after the assistant began grading the first exam in the course, he or she would run into my office to have what I later came to call "the conversation." In the conversation, the assistant would breathlessly begin to talk about how amazingly bad students were doing on the test—that students did not know the material, or could not form a logical argument, and that some of them could not even spell! How, the assistant would ask, could students be so lousy? I would then assure the assistant that students could, indeed, be that lousy, and that the assistant really did not know how terrific he or she was. I would then admonish the assistant not to get a big head.

For bottom performers, seeing the responses of others did nothing to cause them to correct their self-estimates. Before the grading exercise, they thought their skill placed them in roughly the mid-60s; afterward, they still thought their skill lay in the mid-60s. In effect, their experience captured a story told to me by a colleague, Dick Neisser, who once had a student who was incredulous that a paper for a course had only received a "C." After a long, circuitous, and inconclusive discussion, Dick showed the student the best paper that had been turned in for the course, in the hope that the student would see why he did not get an "A" once he saw a proficient paper. The student dutifully studied the A paper, and then proclaimed that after seeing this other, obviously excellent paper, he was even more mystified because he saw no real difference between the two papers.

In short, the grading study showed that observing the performances of others helps the competent to achieve more accurate views of themselves, but does not necessarily help the incompetent. This basic pattern has been replicated elsewhere in the medical domain. In one study, medical students completed a standard exercise in which they interviewed a patient under difficult circumstances. They then were shown videotapes of how five other students had handled the interview, with the interviews selected to show a wide range of skill. After seeing these interviews, top performers raised their self-estimates, and their revised ratings more closely agreed with how their teachers had rated them. Seeing the interviews did not significantly help bottom performers to achieve more accurate self-ratings (Hodges, Regehr, & Martin, 2001).

# ☐ Other Processes That Interfere with Self-Insight

So far, we have laid the blame for the lack of self-awareness of the incompetent at the feet of the double burden that they suffer: Their lack of skill means they can neither produce nor recognize competence. However, the reader may have approached this book with an entirely different notion for why the incompetent fail to recognize the flawed nature of their performance, and the reader might be surprised that this notion does take a front-and-center position in this chapter.

## Denial

The notion is that, at some level, the incompetent really know, or at least suspect, that their performance is lacking. However, to admit to poor performance either to themselves or other people is an action that they are motivated to avoid. That is, the incompetent are actively engaged in denial. They just refuse to recognize their errors; they deliberately short-circuit any awareness they may have of their mistakes. Instead, they consciously try to collect whatever shards of evidence they can gather that would show that their decisions are really good ones.

I am not one to deny denial. The social psychological literature is replete with examples of how people avoid, distort, or spin information to reach favorable conclusions about themselves and their abilities (for reviews, see Baumeister & Newman, 1994; Dunning, 2001; Kunda, 1990). Thus, there might be a significant dose of denial in the self-assessments provided by the incompetent.

In fact, isolated research examples show that people bolster their decisions as accurate ones after those decisions have been made. This was the central finding of Brehm (1956), when he presented participants with a long list of household appliances and asked them to evaluate them. After they completed their list, Brehm offered participants their choice of two appliances as a free gift—with the twist being that participants had to choose between two appliances that they had rated rather equally. After deciding, participants rated their chosen appliances more favorably than the ones they had rejected. This finding was echoed by Knox and Inkster (1968), who discovered that gamblers became more confident that their horse would win just after they placed their bets relative to their confidence 30 seconds before placing it (for similar results, see Blanton, Pelham, DeHart, & Carvallo, 2001).

However, these demonstrations may reflect a general tendency that all people share and not a specific habit among the incompetent that explains why they are especially ignorant of their deficits. That is, in the research just cited, there were no attempts to see if the incompetent were especially prone to bolster their confidence out of a need to protect self-esteem. Such a special tendency may exist, but there is no research work revealing it.

Thus, active denial of incompetence may exist, but then again it may not. However, until the role of denial is finally nailed down, Kruger and Dunning (1999) made an important statement about the role of denial among the incompetent. The incompetent do not have to be in denial to fail to recognize their shortcomings. They can fail to recognize their short-comings even though they may be trying hard to honestly assess their talent. Unfortunately, they just do not have the cognitive tools necessary to reach accurate assessments. They might be quite willing to admit that their talents are rather meager if only they were in a position to recognize how paltry their talents are. Indeed, when the incompetent are placed in a position to recognize their errors in our training study, they were quite willing to lower their impressions of themselves—indeed, to make rather negative statements about themselves (Kruger & Dunning, 1999, Study 4).

Thus, when spotting an incompetent person who thinks too much of him- or herself, one need not assume that that person is in denial. Incompetence itself is a sufficient reason for the person not to recognize the error of his or her ways. Such a person is not in a position to recognize his or her true level of ability.

## Errors of Omission

Indeed, upon reflection, it is clear that any individual—competent or incompetent—is only rarely in a position to accurately assess his or her performance or ability. No one has all the information necessary to reach a correct impression. The reason for this is contained in just one English word. That word is *spontaneous*.

When I was a child, I loved to play a word game in which I took some longish word, such as *spontaneous*, and worked to see how many other English words I could squeeze out of the letters contained in the target word. For example, if staring at *spontaneous* long enough, one sees that the words *tan*, *neon*, *us*, and *tone* can be pulled out of the letters comprising *spontaneous*. My favorites are *sonnets* and *peanuts*.

If one played this game with *spontaneous* for an hour, one could pull out a great number of words. Let's say that one could pull out 30, 40, maybe 50 words. How good is that performance? What grade should we give it? Clearly, any evaluation depends on the obvious statistic of how many words the individual found in the target word. But any evaluation also depends on another statistic, one that is difficult to determine: the number of words the individual could have pulled from the target but missed. If there were 60 possible words in *spontaneous*, we would be more impressed with a person's performance than if there were 200.

This word game reveals one fundamental problem in self-judgment that plagues both competent and incompetent people alike. One is given a problem that requires coming up with one or several solutions. For example, one might have to come up with some comforting words when a friend suffers a loss. Or upon the birth of a child, one must realize that it is time to childproof the house. The fundamental difficulty one faces in tasks of these sorts is that although one may be quite aware of the solutions one reached and the actions one took, one by definition is completely unaware of all the possible actions one could—and should—have taken but did not.

In a phrase, people are not aware of their errors of omission. They have no magical insight into the numbers of solutions they could have reached but missed. The word *spontaneous* contains more than 1,300 English words within its letters, and very few people have any intuition that so many possible solutions are hiding among the letters of that word.

This problem is not constrained to this particular word game. In many areas of life, people cannot be expected to reach accurate views of their ability because they cannot be expected to have accurate knowledge of their errors of omission. For example, as Stephen Fatsis (2001) says in his book, *Word Freak*, about the curious world of people scratching to make a living playing the board game Scrabble:

> In a way, the living-room player is lucky … He has no idea how miserably he fails with almost every turn, how many possible words or optimal plays slip by unnoticed. The idea of Scrabble greatness doesn't exist for him. (p. 128)

But the true importance of this issue was highlighted in an answer to a question once posed to Secretary of Defense Donald Rumsfeld as he discussed the difficulties the U.S. military had against the threat of terrorism. As he discussed the range of threats against the United States, he noted,

> There are things that we know that we know. There are [also] known unknowns—that is to say, there are things that we now know we don't know. But there are also unknown unknowns. There are things we do not know we don't know. So when we do the best we can

and we pull all this information together, and we then say well that's basically what we see as the situation, that is really only the known knowns and the known unknowns. (Kamen, 2002, A25)

What was left unspoken, obviously, was that it was the unknown unknowns that presented the greatest danger to the United States and its allies.

In a sense, when people judge themselves, they know what they know, but they have little, or no, awareness of their own personal "unknown unknowns." They are not aware of their gaps in knowledge, or the errors of omission that they make.

In a series of studies, Deanna Caputo and I (in press) decided to test whether people had any awareness of their own personal "unknown unknowns" when they evaluated their performances and abilities. Keeping with the spirit of the example that inspired this research, we began our investigations with a word game. We brought college students into the lab and asked them to play Boggle. In Boggle, participants are given a 4 × 4 array of letters and are asked to find as many words as they can by chaining adjacent letters together. Words must be at least three letters long (and no proper names, please). Participants were given three different Boggle puzzles and asked to find as many words as they could. We then asked them to evaluate their performance on the puzzles, as well as their general ability at the game.

Not surprisingly, the more words they found, the more favorably they judged their performance to be, as well as their Boggle-playing ability in general. However, and central to our hypothesis, their evaluations gave no weight to how many words they had missed. Participants admitted that such errors of omission were important and that they would have given them weight if they knew how many of those errors they had made; they just did not have any insight into what those errors may have been. True to their word, when we informed them about the number of words actually contained in each puzzle, participants gave significant weight to the number of words they had missed. In fact, they gave as much weight to their errors of omission as they did to the number of solutions they had found. Overall, participants lowered their evaluations of their performance and ability, and this was strikingly the case among participants who had turned in the worst performances relative to their peers.

Follow-up studies replicated these basic findings (Caputo & Dunning, in press). For example, we quizzed graduate students in psychology departments on their knowledge of research methods by asking them to spot methodological problems we had inserted into descriptions of several psychological experiments. When informed of the problems they had missed, students tended to lower their self-ratings of skill, particularly those who had done poorly on our quiz.

In one final study, a lack of awareness about omission errors also had an impact on decisions participants later made about their performances (Caputo & Dunning, in press, Study 5). Participants once again played Boggle. After finishing the last puzzle, they were given $2 and told that they could bet any or all of that money that they had outperformed some other person in the room on the last puzzle they had dealt with. One group of participants, the "informed group" was told how many total words there were in all the puzzles they had confronted. Another group of participants, the "uninformed" group, was not told. When it came time to bet, the informed group, aware of their errors of omission, bet significantly less than the uninformed group.

In sum, these studies suggest that people possess no magical insight into their errors of omission, even though they recognize that such errors were relevant and factor such errors in their self-evaluations once they know about them.

However, although these studies showed how the inability to recognize errors of omission prompts imperfect performance evaluations, they also likely underestimated the magnitude and pervasiveness of this problem in real life. In everyday life, the real problem is not that people do not know about their errors of omission, the real problem is that often such errors are *unknowable*. Such errors are unknowable because the tasks people typically face in everyday life are not well structured, with a finite set of solutions as well as well-defined procedures with which to find them. Real-life tasks rarely have the well structured properties of a math problem, such as calculating the volume of a cylinder, in which there is a set equation that one can use to get to an obviously correct answer.

Instead, the tasks people typically face are ill structured, with no established set of solutions, or universally accepted procedures to get to them—indeed, no set criteria to use to judge when one has gotten to a right or at least acceptable answer (Newell, 1969; Reitman, 1964; Simon, 1973). For example, there is no structured algorithm one can use to write a poem celebrating true love, achieve perfect *feng shui* in the living room, negotiate the best deal from an employer, deliver a funny after-dinner speech, write a great novel, raise happy and successful children, or save enough money for retirement. There are strategies people can try, some better than others, but there is no one perfect solution to any of these problems, or any absolute way to know when one has constructed the best solution.

Thus, with ill-structured tasks, one makes errors of omission, but the set of omission errors is not well defined. For example, a person might succeed in saying comforting words to a friend who is feeling down, but one will never be in a position to know whether those were *the best* words that could have been said. One might write a book about, let's say, self-insight, but one will never know if the observations made in the book were the *best* set of observations that could have been made on the topic.

In short, with ill-structured tasks, people are never really in a position to know just how well they have done with the solutions they reached. They may have done well, they may have done poorly, but reaching a precisely accurate assessment necessitates knowing about solutions that were possible but missed. Because people by definition possess no awareness of these solutions, they are not in a position to provide precisely accurate evaluations.

In a sense, this conclusion may explain an observation made about how well elementary school children assess their classroom performances. The assessments students make of themselves agree much more closely with their teachers' assessments in math and science classes rather than in English or social studies classes (Falchikov & Boud, 1989; see also Rolfhus & Ackerman, 1999). This finding makes sense if we presume that math and science classes present students with well-structured problems that have well-defined solutions. In that situation students may be better able to know when they have reached the right solution or have failed to reach all possible solutions to a task. In other types of classes that involve ill-structured tasks, students have less clear criteria against which to judge their performance and also less guidance concerning their errors of omission.

# ☐ Concluding Remarks

It seems every six months or so, some news organization releases a story about how unknowledgeable Americans are on some important topic. In early 2002, the National Science Foundation surveyed Americans on their knowledge of scientific principles and found that less than half knew that lasers work by focusing light rather than sound waves, or that electrons are smaller than atoms. Over half thought that humans had lived at the same time as the dinosaurs, which may be true in the *Flintstones* but not in the real world (mankind missed the dinosaurs by 60 million years). Less than a third understood the crucial role played by control conditions in scientific experiments (National Science Foundation, 2002).

What makes news stories like this interesting is that readers are often shocked by the level of ignorance displayed by other people. We understand that not everybody will know where Iraq is, but the level of ignorance is often far higher than we would ever imagine. We may even titter self-assuredly about how much more knowledgeable and learned we are than these respondents.

The material in this chapter, however, suggests that we may be even more surprised if some researcher burst into our house, apartment, or dorm room and presented us with a clipboard containing a test on science, geography, financial planning, or nutrition. If we are proficient on these topics, that quiz would only affirm that perception. However, if we are not proficient, we may never know. We might think we have done just fine even if our answers tell the researcher that there is yet another juicy news story to write about American ignorance.

Philosophers and social commentators since the Greeks have noted that the knowledge each of us possesses has many more boundaries than we know. As Socrates noted, "The only true wisdom is to know that you know nothing." A sentiment echoed 20 centuries later when Detective Harry Callahan of the San Francisco Police Department noted that "A man's [and presumably a woman's] got to know his limitations."

What the material in this chapter suggests is that knowing those limitations may be far more difficult than we could imagine. If we have absolute faith in our ability to know our limits, that may very well be evidence that we do not.

# ☐ Endnote

1. A lengthy footnote is necessary at this point. One could also complain that our findings (see Figure 2.1) are a simple statistical artifact, coupled with the fact that people tend to rate themselves as above average (Krueger & Mueller, 2002). The key to this complaint is the statistical truism of *regression to the mean*. Whenever two variables are correlated with one another, the correlation tends to be imperfect. The height of parents, for example, is imperfectly correlated with the heights of their offspring. To be sure, tall parents tend to produce tallish children, but the relationship is neither complete nor exact.

   This fact of imperfect correlation creates an obvious set of circumstances when one examines individuals who produce the most extreme scores on some measure. The scores of these extreme individuals on some other measure tend not to be as extreme. The tallest parents, for example, will not have children who are as tall as they are. Turning to our data, one could argue regression to the mean would guarantee that the poorest performers would overestimate themselves. Perception of performance is imperfectly correlated with actual performance (see chapter 1). Thus, if one selects, as we did, the most extreme poor performers, their impressions of their performances simply could not be as low.

   Importantly, two variables can be imperfectly correlated simply because they are both measured imperfectly. In our studies, for example, we could have taken flawed measures of actual or perceived ability. Indeed, such flaws are almost guaranteed: Any single test will be an imperfect representation of an individual's skill, which will mean that his or her test scores will tend to bounce around a little bit from test to test, sometimes showing him or her to be incredibly skilled and sometimes only so-so. Such measurement errors guarantee an imperfect correlation between two variables and thus will ensure regression to the mean.

In short, one can claim that the results depicted in Figure 2.1 do not reveal anything about our participants' incompetence, but rather only ours (see Krueger & Mueller, 2002). We might have presented participants with imperfect measures of ability, thus guaranteeing an imperfect correlation between actual ability and perceptions of that ability.

However, we have collected data that argues against this regression-to-the-mean account. Statistically, it is possible to estimate how imperfect our measures were, to correct for that imperfection, and then see if our incompetent participants still overestimate themselves. When we do that, we find that poor performers continue to overestimate themselves. In fact, correcting for measurement error reduces the amount of overestimation by bottom-quartile participants by only two to three percentile points. The same goes for top-quartile participants: They continue to significantly underestimate their performances even after correcting for measurement error (Ehrlinger, Johnson, Banner, Dunning, & Kruger, 2004; Kruger & Dunning, 2002).

# Clues for Competence

*Imperfect Meta-Cognitive Cues of Good and Bad Performance*

Just to get the blood flowing and the neurons crackling, let's start this chapter with a little pop quiz on world geography. The central point of this quiz is not whether you get the answers right. Rather, it is on *how* you arrived at your answers. With that, as you answer the following questions, be sure to make mental notes on how you reached those answers.

*Question 1*: What is the capital of Australia?
*Question 2:* Which of the following countries is the leading producer of olive oil: France, Italy, Romania, or Spain?
*Question 3*: Which city lies farthest north: Philadelphia, Pennsylvania, or Rome, Italy?

## ☐ This Chapter's Agenda

With that pop quiz now complete, we can turn to the central point of this chapter. The material in the previous chapter (chapter 2) left us with a quandary. That chapter focused on why people fail to recognize their own incompetence, and in doing so focused exclusively on what *does not* happen: What prevents people in general from forming accurate self-views? What are the impediments in their path to accurate self-knowledge?

However, in focusing on what does not happen in self-judgment, chapter 2 completely left open the question of what *does* happen. What prompts people to think they are competent, incompetent, or indifferent in their skill? People tend to have some ideas, sometimes firm or even unshakable, about whether they are good or bad at certain tasks. They walk out of their exam room, away from their first date, or after giving a public speech with a definite notion that they have triumphed, caused a fiasco, or defined mediocrity. The simple question of where these self-perceptions come from is left open in chapter 2.

Therefore, chapter 3 focuses on the sources of people's self-judgments. It examines the cues people rely on to decide whether they have done a terrific or a lousy job. Across the psychological literature, there are three general classes of cues that people use to judge their performances.

First, people often have specific *reasons* to back up their decisions and judgments. When someone tells you that it is smart to have snow tires on your car during winter, that it is time to plow into the stock market in a big way, or that they know which country to go to for the best olive oil, they can usually articulate some rationale why that suggestion is a wise one. Second, people can rely on *fluency* cues, focusing on how much they can respond to a question in a quick, facile, and familiar way. If an answer is fluent, that is, it comes in an instant, people tend to be quite confident in their answers. Finally, people can rely on *top-down* clues to assess their performance. They can overlay abstract, preconceived notions about themselves, such as whether they are intelligent or socially skilled, to guide their estimates about how well they have done on any specific performance.

At first blush, these three sets of cues would seem to provide a quite reasonable basis for deciding whether one should be confident in one's actions. And to provide fair full disclosure, these cues can often be sensible indicators of a job well or poorly done. However, these cues are not foolproof and relying on them can prove problematic. Thus, the theme of this chapter is that people face a vexing predicament as they examine the potential accuracy of their answers. People do not reach their decisions haphazardly. They have a basis for the choices they make and for the confidence they imbue in those choices. However, the basic problem is that ambling one's way to a wrong answer often looks very much like approaching the right one—and so it is difficult to know when one is in the former circumstance versus the latter.

This similarity between arriving at wrong answers and getting to right ones, as chapter 2 drove home, is that the cues people use to evaluate their decisions are often tantamount to the material they use to arrive at those decisions in the first place. Perhaps Koriat (1993) put it best when he said that the self-evaluation process is "parasitic" upon the processes used to generate answers. They frequently are the same processes, drawing on the same knowledge and wisdom people use to solve the puzzles they face. As such, when people base a correct decision on some bits of information that they can bring to mind, those clues will also prompt them to have appropriate confidence in their decision. However, when those clues steer people toward an erroneous conclusion, that rationale will also lead them to harbor misplaced confidence.

Koriat (1993) showed the parasitic nature of evaluative processes directly in an experiment in which he asked people to memorize letter strings, such as *SRVB*. When participants were asked if they could remember a particular string, their answers depended on how many of the four letters they could remember. If they could correctly remember three of the letters (e.g., *SRV*), they were fairly confident and, indeed, at a later time they did commonly remember the entire string. However, if people remembered three letters, but did so incorrectly (e.g., *SBL*), they again were confident in their memory, even though they frequently recalled the string incorrectly at a later time.

Koriat (1995; see also Koriat, 1976) also replicated this finding in a more real-world demonstration. He asked college students in Israel to answer general knowledge questions, measuring how often participants had some information in their head that led them to an answer, but also noting how often that information led them to correct or incorrect conclusions. When participants had accessible information that guided them to a correct answer (such as for *What is the name of India's "holy" river?* which is, of course, the Ganges), they were usually quite confident and accurate in their responses. However, when whatever information they had in their heads led them astray (as it does for *The Mediterranean island of Corsica belongs to what country?*), they tended to show some confidence even though they typically got the answer wrong (the correct answer is *France*).

## ☐ Basing Confidence on Explicit Reasoning

People frequently base their decisions on thoughtful and rigorous deliberation. A personnel director thinks hard about the qualifications of job candidates before deciding who should be hired into the office. A psychiatrist ponders over the many characteristics of his depressed client to decide whether he is likely to commit suicide. A mechanic tries out many hypotheses to determine what is wrong with her car. In each case, the decision-maker gathers all, or at least some of, the facts and figures he or she can to address a decision, and applies systematic procedures to reach a conclusion. Often, this thinking can lead to the right decision as well as a reasonable level of confidence in that decision.

People are quite adept at using such deliberation to evaluate how sound their decisions are. They have at their disposal millions of facts that can be applied to decisions in a wide variety of domains. They know that $2 + 2 = 4$, that Arnold Schwarzenegger was a big movie star in the 1980s, that taxes are due on April 15, and that republicans tend to be more conservative than democrats. The list is almost endless. Awash in all this knowledge, how could people ever get a decision wrong without knowing that they ran the risk?

In some sense, people are often unknowingly wrong precisely because they have all this knowledge. When faced with a question, they can draw on this vast storehouse of information to rationalize their way into an acceptable answer that later proves to be invalid. There are a number of ways that the information we have—even when it is bona fide—can steer us into wrong conclusions that we consider terrific. Three are of particular interest.

## Our Knowledge Is Accurate, but Incomplete

When faced with a puzzle, we can often think our way into an answer. The answer has a rationale behind it, but it leaves out important information that we may not know we do not have. In an informal survey, I asked 20 people the "olive oil" question that begins this chapter, and found that 55% of them thought that the correct answer was *Italy*. They had a sound basis for their answer: Italian cuisine makes liberal use of olive oil, and it makes sense that the country that uses the stuff should produce it in the first place. The only glitch here is that Italy is the wrong answer. Of the countries listed, which has more arable land and a favorable climate upon which to grow the crop? *Spain* is the leading olive oil-producing country in the world, having more suitable land with which to cultivate the crop, but only 20% of the survey respondents correctly identified Spain as the answer.

A similar issue arises for the question about Philadelphia versus Rome. Thinking it through, it seems reasonable that the correct answer would be *Philadelphia* (as did 55% of respondents in the survey described above). Here are two bits of information in support of that conclusion: (a) Philadelphia lies toward the north of North America, whereas Rome is in the south of Europe, and (b) winter temperatures are demonstrably colder in Philly than in central Italy. All true, but incomplete. What people generally do not recognize is how much farther north Europe as a whole is compared against North America. And because of this, Rome turns out to be the more northern city, although it is close.

## Our Knowledge Is Largely Accurate but Has a Few "Bugs"

At times, our prodigious knowledge base may contain "bugs," glitches that steer people away from the right choice. Some of these bugs might be factual. Consider, for example, children trying to solve math problems. Children might reach wrong conclusions in multiplication problems if they erroneous believe that $7 \times 8 = 54$.

Other bugs might be procedural (VanLehn, 1990). For example, children learning subtraction for the first time commonly reach this erroneous conclusion (VanLehn, 1986):

$$33 - 17 = 24 \tag{3.1}$$

At first blush, this error may seem inexplicable, until one realizes the glitch in the child's understanding of subtraction procedures. The child does not realize that he must subtract the 7 from the 3 by carrying a 1 over from the 3 in the tens column. Instead, the child believes that he should subtract the smaller 3 from the larger 7, resulting in an incorrect, in some sense, but reasonable answer.

These examples suggest that errors can often be as *rational* as correct decisions. Errors are not arrived at differently from correct responses. They are based on fact and some systematic understanding of procedure. The only difference is that the person has his or her facts wrong or does not realize that the procedure he or she follows is incorrect. However, errors often have a factual and logical base, and within that base those errors are reasonable and seemingly well supported.

Of course, this suggestion presents a metacognitive predicament for anyone deciding whether his or her responses are correct ones. People making errors might be just as deliberative, thoughtful, rigorous, and systematic in their thinking as those who achieve accuracy. Those making errors consider facts and apply cognitive rules just as carefully as those reaching accurate conclusions. They may have just as much of a "sound" basis for their decisions as their more accurate counterparts. As a consequence, people who make these errors might be just as confident in their responses as those giving the correct response. And distinguishing the former circumstance from the latter might be quite difficult.

The problem with social life is that these types of bugs, both factual and procedural, can be common. There is lots of room for people to know facts or believe in procedures that are either irrelevant, or worse, misleading.

# Our Knowledge Is Only "Pseudorelevant"

The lesson here is that people often have enough knowledge about the world in their heads upon which to base a decision. Enough of the time, these thousands of bits of facts and figures may help to reach a right answer. But all of this information can mislead people into a confident answer that is wrong.

This issue is particularly pressing because people are typically awash in information they can draw on to reach any sort of conclusion. But which specific information to rely on? Which is the most relevant? For example, imagine that you were a business manager trying to determine whether your employee had stolen company property. You confront him and he denies it—but is he lying? Here are six different types of behaviors you could focus in on; which three behaviors would most accurately suggest that he is, in fact, being deceptive: (a) avoids eye contact with you, (b) does not smile, (c) shifts his body posture a lot, (d) responds to you in short utterances, (e) responds to you in a way that contains a good deal of irrelevant information, and (f) has both pupils dilate when responding?

Past research suggests that the last three behaviors listed are associated with lying, although not all the time or with everybody (DePaulo, 1994). The first three behaviors listed are *not* associated with lying even though people tend to believe they are (DePaulo, Stone, & Lassiter, 1985). In fact, there is evidence that people who lie tend to make *more* eye contact, not less, when they attempt to deceive (Riggio & Friedman, 1983). That said, lack of eye contact, no smiling, and lots of body posture shifting just seem like they should be associated with lying. Of course, a person who is lying would feel ashamed and nervous, at least a little, and would thus avoid making eye contact and would feel no reason to smile. This would seem to be the case; it just is not.

A little informal data affirms this disconnect between perception and reality in detecting deception. In an informal survey of 20 people, I found that 80% thought that avoiding eye contact was associated with lying, and that 90% thought the same for shifting body posture, even though both these behaviors are not connected to lying in reality. Indeed, respondents endorsed these indicators more than they did valid ones, such as keeping responses short (25%), providing irrelevant information (60%), and having one's pupils dilate (45%).

One major problem that people face in everyday life is that, being awash in so much information, people confront information that could plausibly be relevant when it is not, such as eye contact and body shifting seems to be relevant to lying. The information, in a word, is *pseudorelevant* (Gill, Swann, & Silvera, 1998). Regrettably, people rely on pseudorelevant information in many different circumstances, leading them to confident decisions that may not be accurate.

For example, in 1967, Chapman and Chapman presented college students with drawings of people that had supposedly been drawn by psychiatric patients, some of whom were paranoid. The students were asked to report how the drawings of the paranoid patients differed from the rest. The students tended to report that paranoid patients drew people with exaggerated eyes, even though there was no correlation between eye size and symptoms of paranoia in the materials, nor had previous research revealed one in actual psychiatric cases. One can see how students could spin a simple explanatory link between paranoia and the salience of other people's eyes, but the ease of generating that story seemed to trump what was actually in the materials. Importantly, the link the students had reported between eye size and paranoia was quite similar to what experienced clinicians reported seeing in their own practice, despite the fact that rigorous scientific observation failed to support the link.

Other work also shows that people rely on pseudorelevant information to their detriment as well as the detriment of those around them. In follow-up work, Chapman and Chapman (1969) showed that reliance on pseudorelevant indicators of psychiatric conditions tended to crowd out indicators that were actually valid. When pseudorelevant indicators were deliberately omitted from diagnostic materials, participants were actually more likely to spot relevant indicators than they would otherwise.

But perhaps the most worrisome use of pseudorelevant information comes from studies of HIV and AIDS. In a number of interviews with college students, researchers discovered that students used information about their sex partner's personality to assess whether those partners carried the HIV virus. They asked whether the person was likeable and trustworthy, whether that person dressed provocatively, whether they had met the person in a bar, whether the person was older, and whether the person used oral contraceptives. All these criteria have little, if any, actual relevance to the partner's likelihood of infection (Williams, Kimble, Covell, Weiss, Newton, Fisher et al., 1992).

Making judgments in the presence of pseudorelevant information has many consequences. One is that as people gain more information they become more confident in their decisions even if accuracy does not follow. Oskamp (1965) demonstrated this problem in an experiment in which he asked clinical psychologists, psychology graduate students, and advanced undergraduates to make 25 different predictions about an actual patient for whom he had real case materials. All participants read a little of the case materials, made their predictions, read some more of the case materials, and then were given a chance to revise their predictions. All told, participants were given four chances to make revisions. Their revised predictions were no more accurate than their initial ones, although participants in each group were much more confident in those predictions the more they read.

Swann and Gill (1997) replicated this dissociation between confidence and accuracy in real-world settings. Dating couples and roommates were asked to predict the other person's sexual history, preferences of activities, or self-views, depending on the experiment. The longer couples or roommates had known each other, as well as the more involved they were with each other, the more they expressed confidence in their predictions, even though relationship length and involvement had nothing to do with accuracy. A follow-up study revealed that longstanding and involved couples were more confident because they had more extensive and coherent information about each other, and that it was this richer, more elaborate, better integrated "representation" of the person that led to greater confidence that was not matched by increases in accuracy.

Other research has shown that experience with a task, at times, conveys more the illusion of competence than the reality. Marteau, Wynne, Kaye, and Evans (1990) asked young doctors about their ability to resuscitate patients after a cardiac arrest. Their confidence was related to the number of arrests they had witnessed, but not to their actual ability. Harvey, Garwood, and Palencia (1987) asked participants to sing pairs of musical notes. Confidence in singing was related to the number of times participants practiced the notes, but not to actual performance.

The inexperienced can often have information that produces confidence in judgment even though that information directly produces error. People rarely approach a novel task with absolutely no information to which they can turn. They can import experience and knowledge from other experiences that have the appearance of helpfulness, even though they may be misleading.

For example, consider the high school student learning factorization in her math class and confronting the term $2^0$. That term equals 1, but a student not knowing that could reasonably conclude that $2^0 = 0$, because doing nothing with a 2 would have to equal nothing. After all, as previous math classes had shown, anything multiplied by 0 is 0 (Duffin & Simpson, 1993).

Other work focusing on mathematics shows that inexperienced or poor-performing students often have some information that they have imported from elsewhere that supports their erroneous answers (for a review, see Ben-Zeev, 1998). For example, lacking a deep understanding of the math problems they face, students can turn to superficial features of the problem to assist them in their valiant quest for some sort of answer (Chi, 1978; Chi, Glaser, & Rees, 1982). For example, students given a nonsense word problem will desperately start to do subtraction if they see the word *left*, because that word has superficially been linked to subtraction in the past (e.g., if you subtract 3 from 8, how much do you have *left*?) (Schoenfeld, 1988).

Other misleading but seemingly helpful glitches can be procedural in nature. For example, elementary school students subtracting a three-digit number from another three-digit for the first time commonly make the following mistake (VanLehn, 1986):

$$492 - 135 = 267 \tag{3.2}$$

The mistake students make is to carry the "1" they need to begin from the "4" instead of the "9." Apparently, as students deal with two-digit numbers, they mistakenly learn the lesson that they should carry the one from the left-most digit all the way to the right, instead of carrying the digit from the column just to the left. Dealing with two-digit numbers, this mistaken conclusion can be construed as reasonable.

Other mistakes of the inexperienced or unknowledgeable come from importing superficially appropriate, but misleading, analogies from one domain to another. Consider the following physics question. Suppose I begin to twirl a ball on a string, and then let it go. Look at Figure 3.1. What is the most likely trajectory the ball will travel once I let go? The correct answer is depicted in Panel D, although many people get it

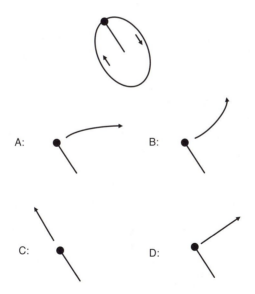

**FIGURE 3.1.** Four possible paths that a ball being twirled on a string might take after letting go. Which is correct?

wrong, either thinking that the ball will initially continue to rotate but gradually lose that motion (Panel A), or that the ball will be flung outward by centrifugal force (Panels B or C). Only 10% of students with some college-level physics get the question wrong, but a full 40% of those without physics make an error (McCloskey & Kohl, 1983).

Such errors by inexperienced students are understandable, however, once one realizes that there are analogies people can take from everyday experience that suggest one of the wrong answers, particularly the one depicted in Panel B. In everyday life, people see that rotation continues after the initial force starting an object in motion ceases to exert its force. Wheels keep turning after someone stops pushing them, and the earth keeps rotating around the sun even though there is no physical attachment to it. These analogies are mistaken, but to someone who does not know "better," they can seem perfectly appropriate.

## The Problem of Confirmatory Bias

In short, if people do not have accurate factual or procedural information in hand, they can still rely on a surfeit of world knowledge that *might* lead them to the correct answer, but might instead steer them toward an incorrect one confidently believed. People's tendency to rely on seemingly helpful but ultimately deceptive information is exacerbated by an enviable competence people seem to possess: They can argue anything. If asked to argue that some assertion "A" is true, people can do that. If next asked to argue that the opposite of "A" is true, they can do that, too, often with the exact same ease and effectiveness. For example, Anderson and Sechler (1986) asked college students to explain why firefighters who took risks tended to achieve more success in their profession. The students could do so and were significantly convinced by their arguments. However, when asked next to explain why cautious firefighters achieved more success, they were just as able to explain this relationship and were equally convinced by these new arguments.

A more remarkable demonstration of people's ability to argue anything comes from work on logical reasoning. Evans and Wason (1976) presented participants with a difficult type of logical reasoning problem to solve. They then told separate groups of participants that a different solution to the problem was correct and asked participants to explain why that particular solution was the right one. Regardless of the solution specified, and regardless of its actual appropriateness, participants were quite able to provide rationales for the solution, endorsing those rationales with great confidence.

This ability to argue anything can cause trouble when combined with another tendency. When testing a hypothesis, people tend to emphasize evidence that confirms the hypothesis over information that disconfirms it. For example, if I asked someone whether he or she was an outgoing individual, that someone will likely sit back to think about times he or she had been an extroverted, sociable person (e.g., I always say "hello" to my office mates; I like to throw dinner parties). The person would not think of examples that indicate the opposite of outgoing, although those examples can be relevant. However, if I asked the same person whether he or she is the shy type, he or she would likely think of exactly those opposing examples because they confirm the new hypothesis suggested by my question (e.g., I really do not like to go to cocktail parties where I don't know anyone; I'm nervous if I have to speak in front of a large group). Needless to say, the impression people have of themselves after answering the first question can be quite different from the impression held after replying to the second (Kunda, Fong, Sanitioso, & Reber, 1993; Snyder & Cantor, 1979).

In short, once a question has been asked or a hypothesis advanced, people assess their answers by looking for positive evidence that the hypothesis is true and neglect searching for evidence that the hypothesis is false. The initial hypotheses that people consider can come from many sources. They may come from the way a question is posed (e.g., Dunning & Parpal, 1989; Kunda, Fong, Sanitioso, & Reber, 1993). They can come from some initial hunch. They may come from what people expect to happen. They can come from what people *wish* to happen (Pyszczynski & Greenberg, 1987). For example, negotiators reading over the same materials can come to divergent—and usually self-serving—conclusions about which settlement an impartial third party will see as most reasonable (Babcock & Loewenstein, 1997).

More importantly, once a hypothesis or some tentative hunch is in place, people begin to look for and distort information in a confirmatory manner (Brownstein, 2003). For example, Carlson and Russo (2001) asked college students in one study and prospective jurors in another to go over case materials related to a jury trial. They were asked to playact being a member of the jury and to scrutinize a number of affidavits that either favored the plaintiff or the defendant. As they finished each affidavit, they were asked which side they believed was ahead on the evidence, although they were told to suspend their final judgment until after they had read all the evidence.

If participants expressed a tentative belief toward the beginning of the evidence concerning who was ahead, they tended to distort their evaluations of subsequent evidence toward that belief. Participants who felt the plaintiff was ahead in the beginning tended to think that the final bits of evidence favored the plaintiff; those who initially thought the defense was ahead tended to believe that the final evidence was more favorable to the defense. Russo and colleagues found similar confirmatory tendencies in other situations. Whether auditors find a company's books to be in order depends on their initial hunches about the quality of the company's accounting (Russo, Meloy, & Wilks, 2000). Whether consumers choose to have dinner at *Chez Moi* or *Cuisine Deluxe* depends on which restaurant they initially favored (Russo, Medvec, & Meloy, 1996; Russo, Meloy, & Medvec, 1998).

The confirmatory bias poses two problems for human judgment. First, it can make people too confident in their choices. For example, Koriat, Lichtenstein, and Fischhoff (1980) asked college students to answer a number of general knowledge questions and then to estimate the chance that their responses were the right ones. Participants were also asked to write down explicit reasons why their answers might be right or wrong. As is typical, people overestimated the chances that their answers were correct, and the basis for this misjudgment could be found in the reasons they wrote down. Participants tended to write more reasons supporting their choices than they did reasons questioning those choices. Indeed, participants seemed to pay attention only to supportive reasons when arriving at a confidence estimate.

Further evidence demonstrates that people tend to base their confidence on confirmatory reasoning. Explicitly asking people to write down reasons affirming their answers tends not to influence their confidence, presumably because these are reasons people are thinking of anyway (Koriat, Lichtenstein, & Fischhoff, 1980). However, asking people explicitly to write down why they might be wrong tends to influence their confidence and align it more appropriately with actual rates of accuracy. The corrective effect of considering how one might be wrong has been found in experiments with answers to general knowledge questions (Koriat et al., 1980). It has also been found in real predictions about actual prospects of business school students hitting the job market. When business school students are asked to write down reasons why they might not get a job with a high starting salary, they make more accurate predictions of what starting salary they would receive. Asking them, instead, to write down reasons why they would get a high salary had no effect on the accuracy of their predictions (Hoch, 1985).

A confirmatory approach also may prevent people from realizing when they are reaching wrong conclusions. This was most elegantly shown by Wason (1960) when he asked students to determine the rule he was using to generate a three-number series, such as 2, 4, 6. Students could generate their own three-number series and ask the experimenter if the series fit. When they were done generating as many series as they wanted, they could then announce what they thought the rule was. Students generated many elegant rules (e.g., first double, then triple the first number in the series) that they were quite confident about. However, they tended to be wrong. The rule that Wason brought to the lab was a simple one—each number had to be more than the one that preceded it—but many students recognized this rule only with great difficulty.

Why the difficulty? Students tended to test their hypotheses with a confirmatory strategy. If a student thought the rule was a *doubling then tripling* rule, he or she might generate *4, 8, 12*, and *3, 6, 9*, and ask the experimenter if these numbers fit the rule. Of course they did, but that fit was misleading. What students failed to do (except those who got the rule right the first time they announced it) was to test their hypotheses by explicitly trying to disconfirm it, that is, by generating a three-number series they thought contradicted the rule they believed in (e.g., *3, 6, 7*). Students who generated contradictory series soon realized their more complicated hypotheses were wrong and inevitably groped their way to the simple rule that Wason had in mind.

## ☐ Basing Confidence on Fluency

People also use "nonanalytical" cues to arrive at a level of confidence in their answers. In particular, when answering a question, they take note of the *fluency* of their response. By fluency, I refer in general to the familiarity of the terms contained in the question as well as the ease and speed with which someone comes to a response. People tend to be more confident to the extent that they feel fluent, and hesitant to the extent that they are not (Bjork, 1999; Metcalfe, 1998).

One obvious indicator of fluency is the speed with which people come to a response. The quicker a person says, for example, that Sydney is the capital of Australia, the more confident she tends to be in her answer (Benjamin & Bjork, 1996; Costermans, Lories, & Ansay, 1992; Kelley & Lindsay, 1993). At first blush, speed would seem to be a terrific cue to assess the accuracy of an answer. When we know the answer, we should be quick about it. When we do not, we should experience a slower and fumbling advance toward our response. And there is, indeed, enviable experimental evidence that shows that decision speed is associated with accuracy. For example, when eyewitnesses identify someone out of a police lineup, those who announce their decisions more quickly tend to be more accurate than those who take their time (Dunning & Perretta, 2002; Dunning & Stern, 1994; Sporer, 1992, 1993).

Furthermore, in many other domains in life, inducing people to laboriously analyze their judgments, rather than going with whatever comes naturally and easily to mind, often causes them to reach more inaccurate conclusions. After analyzing the reasons for their judgments, people less accurately judge which courses they should take (Wilson & Schooler, 1991), whether they will behave in a friendly way toward others (Wilson & LaFleur, 1995), how long their romantic relationships will last (Wilson, Dunn, Bybee, Hyman, & Rotondo, 1984), and which piece of artwork they would like to have in their dorm room (Wilson, Lisle, Schooler, Hodges, Klaaren, & LaFleur, 1993).

# Problems

But there are limits to the usefulness of decision speed as an indicator of accuracy. Although there are many types of decisions in which fast conclusions are likely to be more valid than slow ones, there are also types of decisions in which the reverse must be true. Complicated decisions that depend on a good deal of analysis are more likely to be correct when made deliberately than when made quickly. For example, I would trust that a person has correctly proved the Riemann hypothesis, done my taxes right, and come up with a workable plan for Mideast peace when I hear they have spent a good deal of time on the project rather than a few seconds.

Decision speed is also only an imperfect indicator of accuracy (Benjamin, Bjork, & Schwartz, 1998). Although it is true that people are more confident when they reach an answer quickly, they do so regardless of whether the answer they come up with is correct or incorrect (Kelley & Lindsay, 1993). Other factors having nothing to do with accuracy can have an impact on fluency—and thus give an air of validity whether that air is deserved or not.

## *Recent Exposure Can Mislead*

For instance, fluency is influenced by any recent exposure to any target answer. For example, if I ask you what is the capital of Australia, you are likely to be more confident in your answer of Sydney given the fact that I have just mentioned that city in the last paragraph (as did 65% of respondents in the informal poll of 20 individuals mentioned elsewhere in this chapter).

But fluency can be a double-edged sword. Recent exposure to a right answer can make a person confident in his or her response; recent exposure to a close but wrong answer can also make people confident in an erroneous response. Kelley and Lindsay (1993) asked participants to answer a number of general knowledge questions, such as *What was the last name of Buffalo Bill*? Those who had been briefly exposed to the right answer (*Cody*) on some list they had read a few minutes before gave that answer more quickly and confidently. However, those who had been exposed to a wrong but plausible answer (*Hickock*) gave *that* answer more frequently, confidently, and speedily on a subsequent test.

Fluency can also be influenced by recent exposure to terms in the question being posed, even though such exposure does nothing to increase the chances that participants provide the correct answer. For example, Schwartz and Metcalfe (1992) asked participants how confident they were that they could answer such questions as *Who was the first prime minister of Canada?* (MacDonald, by the way.) Participants were more confident if they had just recently seen the words *prime* and *minister* on some irrelevant task (see Metcalfe, Schwartz, & Joaquim, 1993; Reder, 1987, for comparable findings). In a similar way, Reder and Ritter (1992) found that participants thought they knew the answers to multiplication problems such as $45 \times 56 = ?$ if they had been exposed previously to the numbers contained in the question (e.g., $45 + 56 = ?$). Arkes, Boehm, & Xu (1991) found that asking students questions about China made them more confident about any statement about China they subsequently read.

## Repetition Can Mislead

But perhaps the biggest influence on fluency that has nothing to do with accuracy is repetition. The more a person has heard some statement in the past, the more that statement evokes some sense of recognition or familiarity, and the more that person will consider the statement to be true. Because of this, I should confess. Despite my repetitions of the fact, Sydney is not the capital of Australia. Australia's capital is Canberra. But several studies have shown that repeating statements to people—even false ones—makes them come to believe in them (Arkes, 1993; Arkes, Boehm, & Xu, 1991; Bacon, 1979; Boehm, 1994; Hasher, Goldstein, & Toppino, 1977; Hertwig, Gigerenzer, & Hoffrage, 1997).

Two studies have directly shown that exposure to statements in real-world situations enhances the credibility of those statements in people's eyes, regardless of whether those statements are true. Gigerenzer (1984) surveyed people in their homes every week for three weeks over the phone. He read 60 statements to them and asked whether they thought those statements were true (such as *There are more Roman Catholics in the world than there are Muslims*). Imbedded in those surveys were 20 statements that were repeated each week. Respondents tended to endorse repeated statements as more credible over the course of the surveys, although they did not do so for statements not repeated. Importantly, this enhanced believability was roughly the same for statements that were false as it was for statements that were true.

A study by Toppino and Luipersbeck (1993) demonstrated how this repetition effect could complicate what students learn from their courses. They asked college students to read biographical materials about 12 U.S. presidents and then to take a true-false quiz on the material. A week later, the researchers gave students the statements that had been used on the quiz, as well as some new ones, and asked them to rate the validity of each. Students rated the statements they had seen before as truer—even if those items were false according to the materials they had read before. Merely putting false statements on the test caused students to believe those statements to a greater degree a week later.

Other research shows that self-generated repetition can cause people to believe that which they should not. Eyewitnesses to crimes are often asked to repeat their testimony again and again after they have seen a crime. That repetition causes them to inflate confidence in their testimony (Shaw, 1996; Wells, Ferguson, & Lindsay, 1981), even though such repetition does nothing to enhance accuracy.

Repetition can also damage eyewitness accuracy in another way. As research over the last 30 years has shown, eyewitness memories can be altered by misleading questions on the part of interrogators (Loftus, 1979). If the interrogator's questions contain some false fact or detail, witnesses quite often begin to incorporate that detail into their memories. The incorporation of misleading information, however, often depends on repetition. Witnesses recall the detail with confidence and swear that they actually saw it with their own eyes much more frequently if the misleading detail is suggested to them repeatedly (Zaragoza & Mitchell, 1996).

## Implications for Learning

Thus, although fluency might on many occasions be an indicator of well-placed confidence, it is hardly infallible. Fluency can lead people to attribute inappropriate certainty to their knowledge and choices. Indeed, the experience of fluency can often cause inexperienced people to harbor unwarranted confidence in their skill. Let me provide one illustration. For years, I was puzzled by a chronic complaint students kept making about one of the courses I taught. Before each exam, I posted a practice test on the course website that students could take to assess their knowledge. Students frequently complained that the practice test was too easy and that it misled them about how difficult the actual test was going to be. This complaint puzzled me because the questions placed on the practice test were chosen exactly because they were a little bit too tricky, specific, nuanced, and difficult for the actual test. Why did students see these more difficult questions as easier?

One day, the answer (or, at least, one answer) came to me. Students typically studied for the test by "cramming" for a day or so, and then immediately turned to the practice test and took it—of course, when all the facts and figures of the course were still fresh in their heads. Finding that test easy because at that moment they were fluent in course material, they put the books away and waited for the actual exam. All the while, their memory of course material decayed, the information became less fluent, and they were left in much worse shape to tackle the test they faced during exam time.

To be sure, I do not know whether this analysis is right, but I do have two pieces of data suggesting it is true. First, the year I began announcing to my class that they should put the book away for a few hours before taking the practice test, the complaints stopped. Second, rigorous research on memory shows that people provide significantly more accurate guesses about how much material they can remember if they put the material away for a while before guessing, compared with guessing just after they have finished reading the material (Dunlosky & Nelson, 1992; Nelson & Dunlosky, 1991).

There is also a good deal of research suggesting that the way students study, and the way instructors typically teach, often leads to illusions of competence like the one I have just described. There are two ways that people can study. First, they can study a little bit at a time, distributing their study efforts over a number of days. Second, they can cram, studying course materials in a few intense and concentrated sessions. As cognitive and educational researchers all know, the former approach produces better retention, comprehension, and performance over the long run (Dempster, 1990, 1996; Glenberg, 1992). If you want a medical student to know how to handle a chest complaint, an amateur aviator to fly planes successfully, or your child to play defense on the soccer field correctly, the best type of training is to distribute the training in little chunks over several sessions.

The problem with this approach, however, is that people tend to feel more satisfied and more competent after "mass training" than they do after more training that is distributed over time (Baddeley & Longman, 1978; Bjork, 1999; Simon & Bjork, 2001). Mass training gives the illusion of rapid improvement. At the end of mass training, correct responses are much more fluent than they are after more spaced training. As a consequence, people feel very competent. What they fail to recognize is that mass training is often followed by rapid decay in knowledge and skill. If you do not "use it," you do, indeed, lose it. More spaced training, because it contains several "reminders" along the way, prevents this rapid decay from occurring.

The fact that mass training leads people to have undue overconfidence in their ability to handle future events also potentially explains one puzzling—and deadly—paradox in education. People who take formal courses in driver education tend not to have lower accident rates. Indeed, when driver education makes a difference, the difference tends to one toward *higher* accident rates rather than lower ones (Brown, Groeger, & Biehl, 1988; Christie, 2001; Christensen & Glad, 1996; Mayhew & Simpson, 1996). Indeed, after Quebec in 1983 mandated formal driver education, the accident rate among 16- and 17-year-olds went up, not down—causing the mandate to be repealed (Wilde, 1998).

One key contributor to this paradox may be that training young drivers in emergency maneuvers gives them a false sense of security. On the day of their training, they, indeed, may know how to control a skid, but their skill atrophies over the time where they might have to use that skill in the future. However, left with the impression that they can handle most if not all emergency situations, they take chances they should not take (Christie, 2001; Schneider, 1985; Wilde, 1994). This has led some scholars to suggest that driver education should not focus on teaching people how to handle emergency situations, but should emphasize to students how limited their skills are to handle these situations (Gregerson, 1996).

## ☐ Top-Down Confidence: The Use of Pre-Existing Self-Views

So far, I have treated performance evaluation as a *bottom-up* process. By bottom-up, I mean that people look toward their specific experiences completing a particular task (e.g., are the answers coming quickly, do I have solid reasons for my answers) and then infer from this experience whether they are doing well. Performance evaluation, however, can also involve a heavy dose of *top-down* analysis. That is, people often approach a task with some theory or expectation about how well they will do, and that theory can influence their performance evaluations even before they get to the data of their experience.

A top-down perspective suggests that a hefty portion of a person's performance evaluation is formed well before a person walks into the room to confront the task. People clearly have views about their abilities. They know, or at least *think* they know, whether they are smart or dumb when it comes to scientific reasoning, telling a joke, selling someone something, or keeping track of their finances. A top-down perspective suggests that people simply read off these preexisting impressions when asked about how well they did on any specific performance. For example, if we gave people a pop quiz on geography and asked them how well they did, their answer would be influenced heavily by what they thought about their acumen on geographic matters before we ever pulled out the paper containing the quiz. If they thought they knew their geography, they would estimate that they did well on the quiz. If they thought more negatively of their geographic knowledge, they would estimate that they did more poorly.

In short, people's perceptions about the quality of their performances are based, at least in part, on preconceived notions they have about their skill. A good preconceived impression of skill would lead to confident performance estimates; a negative self-conception would lead to more pessimistic assessments. Perhaps more important, a reliance on preconceived notions of self could lead to erroneous performance estimates, causing people to give worse performance estimates than they would if they completely ignored the views they held of themselves as they approached the task.

Now, that last statement calls for a full stop. How can I argue that preconceived notions of skill lead to error over accuracy? These preconceived notions have to be based on something, and the most likely candidate is that they are based on a person's *past* performance, which in turn would likely be a pretty good predictor of current performance. For example, if a person harbors the notion that she is good singer, then that impression must be based on a lifetime of feedback and experience. And if she has been a good singer in the past, she is likely to be a good singer in the future. Thus, preexisting views of self must be the golden key to accuracy, and not error, in performance estimation.

This logic would be compelling if it were not for two facts. The first is that the views people hold of themselves need not be tied very closely to past performance (more on that in the next chapter). The second important fact is that the views people hold of themselves are not guaranteed to predict current performance. As reviewed in chapter 1, people's self-views are typically correlated only modestly with their objective performance, with the usual correlation hovering a shade under .30 (e.g., Mabe & West, 1982). People also tend to hold inflated views of their abilities that cannot be objectively possible (e.g., Dunning, Meyerowitz, & Holzberg, 1989; Weinstein, 1980). Thus, if people rely on preexisting self-views when evaluating a performance, they are not necessarily going to be led to the truth. Instead, they are quite likely to be led by their overly rosy self-views to overestimate how well they did.

But is the top-down perspective correct? Do people rely on preconceived notions of self when estimating how well they actually did on some task? To address this question, Joyce Ehrlinger and I (2003) conducted a research program to see if people relied on preconceived self-notions, and also to gauge just how strong this reliance was. In our initial study, we brought people into the laboratory and gave them a quick questionnaire asking them to rate their abilities along several different dimensions, including the dimension of "abstract reasoning." We then gave them a pop quiz on reasoning and afterward asked them how well they had done. Participants' estimates turned out to be quite top-down. Across our various measures, their performance estimates were more closely correlated with their previously provided self-ratings than they were with actual performance.

## Altering Performance Estimates by Playing with Self-Views

Follow-up work more closely revealed just how top-down people's performance estimates were. In one study, we switched what self-views participants thought were relevant to a task, to see if doing so would cause them to provide different performance estimates, despite the fact that the switch had no impact on actual performance. We brought participants into the laboratory and gave them all a quiz. However, we told half of them that the quiz focused on abstract reasoning skills, a skill we knew our students thought they possessed in abundance. The other half was told that the quiz focused on the type of logic used in computer programming, a skill our students typically denied having. Despite completing the same test and achieving on average the same score, participants in the computer-programming group thought that they had done much worse than those in the abstract reasoning group.

Raising and lowering participants' self-views had a similar impact in a third study, one in which we focused on geographical knowledge. In this study, participants were given a short questionnaire that asked about their geographical knowledge. For half the participants, the questionnaire posed questions intended to flatter their knowledge. They were asked, for example, whether they had ever visited New York City, California, and Massachusetts—places most of our students had indeed visited. They were further asked if they could name one, two to three, or more than three Canadian provinces. The other half of participants confronted a questionnaire designed to shake any positive views they might have about their knowledge of geography. They were asked whether they had ever visited Mississippi, Wyoming, or North Dakota—locations to which Cornell students very seldom venture. They were asked whether they could name 1 to 5, 6 to 10, or more than 10 Canadian provinces. Not surprisingly, after confronting this more formidable version of questionnaire, participants reported more negative self-views than those receiving the less challenging version.

We then gave all participants a test of their knowledge of North American geography. We handed them a map of North America that was blank, save for depictions of major lakes and rivers. We also handed participants a list of cities (e.g., Boston, Chicago, San Francisco) and asked them to indicate where on the map these cities lay. Answers were considered correct if students placed these cities within 150 map-miles of their true location. Students receiving the challenging presurvey of their knowledge thought they did worse on this quiz than did participants who confronted the more comforting presurvey, a difference that had nothing to do with actual performance.

## Problems with Self-Perceived Expertise

Results from other labs confirm the top-down nature of performance estimates, in that people think they have performed better if they have a preexisting reason to believe they will perform well. Shrauger and Terbovic (1976) asked high and low self-esteem students to perform a concept-learning task. Although both groups performed equally well, the high-esteem group thought they had done much better than the low-esteem group thought they had.

Indeed, people with positive preconceived notions of self often express a sizable degree of confidence in their judgments even when they are simply not in a position to provide any reasonable judgment whatsoever. Two research findings suggest this. In the first, Gill, Swann, and Silvera (1998) asked college students to describe the sexual history and personality of a female college student, with a catch: They provided no information about that female student. Half the participants went ahead and made their estimates. The other half were asked to put on headphones and to listen to someone reading a passage from *The Prophet* by Kahlil Gibran. They were told that, in the background, they would hear someone "subliminally" providing relevant information about the woman they were being asked to describe. And, indeed, as the tape was played, students could hear male and female voices in the background, only the voices provided no real information and actually had been recorded to be completely incomprehensible. But no matter, students hearing the passage, and thus told that they had expert information about the woman, were significantly more confident in their descriptions than were students given nothing. Of course, there was no difference in accuracy.

People with positive self-views also are relatively reluctant to admit when they are ignorant. Bradley (1981), in a clever study, gave students a general knowledge test that contained some questions that were impossible to answer, such as whether the boiling point of mercury (Hg) is 357 degrees Celsius. Students who claimed some expertise in areas related to these questions (e.g., science in the case of the question about mercury) were willing to give an answer and then to stick with it, even when they were wrong. When given a chance to admit that they might not know, self-proclaimed experts were more likely to persevere in their answers and less likely to display uncertainty or admit ignorance, relative to students who claimed no expertise in the area. This occurred even though students, whether self-proclaimed experts or novices, accurately answered these questions only at chance levels.

## Societal Consequences

The top-down nature of performance estimates also reveals itself in ways that have personal, as well as societal, consequences. It has been long observed among the scientific community that a gender gap persists in choices to pursue careers in the physical sciences as well as engineering (National Research Council, 1991). Along the educational ladder, more men tend to stick in a path toward science and more women tend to leave. Women, in general, make up 46% of the labor force in the United States, but their presence among physical scientists and engineers decreases along each step of the educational and career ladder. Only 22% of the bachelors degrees awarded in the physical sciences and engineering go to women; only 13% of the PhDs go to women, with only 10% of the jobs in these fields held by women (Seymour, 1992). Relative to their presence in the labor force in general, women make up a distinct minority of those receiving degrees in computer science, chemistry, chemical engineering, physics, and mechanical engineering (National Science Foundation, 2000).

Many reasons can be cited for this underrepresentation of women in these scientific fields. For example, cultural norms, coupled with a lack of encouragement by friends, family, and educators, might lead girls and women to wander away from science as a career path, as well as to prod men back onto that path (Fox, Benbow, & Perkins, 1983). Because women still continue to hold primary responsibility for taking care of families, whether it be children or their parents, they may decide that they do not have the time for the maniacal obsessiveness required for bench science (Tittle, 1986).

Joyce Ehrlinger and I, however, began to wonder if the top-down nature of performance estimates might contribute to this gender gap in science. Suppose that women, for whatever reason, thought less of their scientific talent than men did. That pessimism might lead to a cascade, depicted in Figure 3.2, of perceptions and decisions that would steer women disproportionately away from science. When performing some task with scientific overtones, women might think less of their performance than men think of theirs, even though there is no actual difference in performance. And because women might think they are doing less well, they might become less enthusiastic about doing more science in the future, opting out of scientific pursuits when given the opportunity. There is evidence for the first part of this proposed cascade. Adolescent girls do rate their scientific and math skills more negatively than boys do,

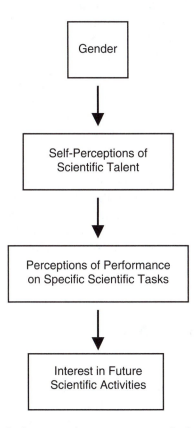

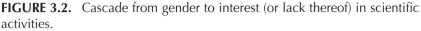

**FIGURE 3.2.**   Cascade from gender to interest (or lack thereof) in scientific activities.

even though there is little, if any, difference in objective performance, and even though girls tend to outperform boys in math and science at the elementary school level (Eccles, 1987).

We decided to see if this gender-perception link would cascade into differential perceptions of performance and finally into disparate decisions about taking part in scientific activities (Ehrlinger & Dunning, 2003, Study 4). We brought male and female college students into the lab and gave them a short test on scientific reasoning. We knew from a survey that had been handed out weeks before that our female participants viewed their scientific aptitude more negatively than our male participants did. Not surprisingly, this more negative perception led women to provide more downbeat performance estimates on our test. Female participants thought they had gotten fewer items right and did less well relative to others than did male participants, even though on either measure the women did just as well as the men (see Beyer, 1990; Beyer & Bowdon, 1997, for similar results in the domain of math).

And those more glum assessments mattered. After finishing the test, participants were asked whether they wanted to take part in a "science jeopardy" game show sponsored by the college later in the semester. Over 70% of the men in the study displayed some interest in taking part, but just less than half the women did, mimicking the gender differences that researchers (as well as educators, parents, and scientists) have seen, and continue to see, in real-life settings. Importantly, the one and only thing that explained this difference was the perceptions of male and female participants about how well they had done on the test. Those who *thought* they did well were more likely to sign up; those who believed they did poorly were not as likely. And even more important, participants' *actual* performance on the test failed to influence their desire to take part whatsoever. In essence, it was the perception and not the reality of performance that influenced whether participants wanted to take part in an "optional" scientific activity.

## ☐ Concluding Remarks

The agenda of this chapter has been to fill in what people are doing when they decide that they have done well or poorly at a task. What clues to competence do they pay attention to, and how well do those clues point them toward accurate self-assessments? The bottom line is that people have a wealth of cues that seem reasonable indicators of accuracy. To the extent that people have explicit reasons for their judgment, they should be confident. To the extent that they reach their judgments with fluency, they again should imbue their judgments with certainty. And to the extent that they hold preconceived notions that they possess expertise in the domain in question, they again should be confident in their responses.

However, although these bases of confidence are all clearly reasonable, they are only reasonable in part. These bases can lead people along the right path toward accuracy, but they do so only to some finite probability. A simple wrong turn in reasoning, fluency, or self-perception can lead people self-assuredly toward a destination fraught with error. Thus, when all is said and done, the problem with our metacognitive maps is that they often clearly mark the route toward an answer, but never divulge whether that destination is the one where we truly want to be. This is a cruel trick awaiting any person interested in accurate self-assessment, but one that each person faces every day. We have the map, but is it leading us the right way?

# The Dearest Teacher

*Why Experience and Feedback Do Not Necessarily
Confer Insight*

At this point, a reader may rebel from the disquieting picture of human insight painted in the first three chapters. To be sure, at times people must be quite ignorant of their true level of ability, but is this ignorance ubiquitous? Perhaps overinflated and misguided views of self are prevalent, even pandemic, among the young and inexperienced, but surely those misconceptions are drummed out as people live their lives, grow older, gain experience, make mistakes, and see what works and what does not. Taking a lifetime of classes in the school of hard-knocks can only serve to reduce naivete and ignorance. As Benjamin Franklin put it, experience is the dearest teacher, in that she gives us hard lessons about our follies and limitations. These are expensive lessons, and so they are lessons we should, and do, take to heart.

To some extent, the idea that experience makes people wiser about themselves must contain some truth. People have a lifetime of experience about their personal triumphs and failures, and this experience must drive, or at least politely nudge, people toward more accurate views of self. But is this always the case? As people encounter the delights and tribulations of life, do they become more insightful about their strengths and weaknesses?

It is safe to say, with perhaps some notable exceptions, that people are wiser in their forties than they are when they are 4. And as the novelist Salman Rushdie put it, our lives do, indeed, teach us who we are. But, that said, many social commentators through the decades have noted that experience is hardly an efficient teacher and may not be an effective one at all. F. P. Jones, for example, asserted that, "experience is that marvelous thing that enables you to recognize a mistake when you make it again." George Bernard Shaw proclaimed that, "what we learn from experience is that men never learn from experience."

Even the systematic experience people gain through education has had its critics. As Ambrose Bierce once noted in his *Devil's Dictionary*, "Education is that which discloses to the wise and disguises from the foolish their lack of understanding." Bertrand Russell was even more cynical, stating that "Men are not born ignorant, not stupid; they are made stupid by education."

But which is it? Does experience move people closer to self-insight or does it pull them away? Undoubtedly, the answer to this question is complex, depending on the task, the experience, and the quantity of that experience, as well as its quality. Whether practice, familiarity, or repetition leaves us wiser about our skills and shortcomings depends on a host of factors.

That said, what I can say with confidence is that experience is not a fail-safe teacher of who we are. I can base that assertion on data. I can also base it on several psychological observations that reveal the ways that the lessons one could glean from experience tend to be incomplete or misleading. I can also base it on several "bad habits" that psychologists have exposed about the way we confront feedback from the world.

## ☐ Learning from Experience: Some Data

First, examine the data. A good deal of research over the past 30 years in social and cognitive psychology suggests that experience is not a very effective teacher. People can gain a good deal of experience, but there are a bevy of reasons why all this information informs them of themselves to only a modest and inconsistent degree.

For example, take situations in which people receive regular and well-defined feedback about their performance: students engaged in their studies in the classroom. Some students are set up to gain more insight from feedback than others. In a class with repeated exams, good students become more aware of just how well they perform over repeated experiences with tests, but the poorest students gain no insight into their plight

(Hacker, Bol, Horgan, & Rakow, 2000), basing predictions of future performance on preconceived notions of their competence.

As one approaches the more chaotic and haphazard structure of the real world, the impact of experience on self-insight becomes even more difficult to detect. Medical school serves as a good halfway house between the structured classroom and the muddled environment of the real world, and in this setting the experience medical students gain fails to align their self-perceptions with reality. In one telling study, at the end of their first rotation in internal medicine, the self-ratings of medical students correlated .25 with the ratings provided by their supervisors. That correlation rose to .29 the next year, but then dropped to .22 the year after that, and then to .10 in their final year (Arnold, Willoughby, & Calkins, 1985; see also Sclabassi & Woelfel, 1984, for similar findings). As these medical students prepared to leave their school, their self-ratings correlated $-.01$ with their board exams, but .54 with the opinions they had held of their skills three years earlier (Arnold et al.,1985).

# ☐ Why Feedback Fails to Inform

To begin to understand why people fail to learn from experience, one has to start with a particular set of pigeons put through their paces by B. F. Skinner in 1948. Skinner placed the pigeons in one of his famous boxes and then deprived them of food. He then presented each pigeon with a speck of food every 15 seconds on the dot. Hungry, the pigeons noticed the food, and hungrier still, they began to repeat whatever behavior they had been engaged in when the food appeared. One pigeon started to toss its head up and down; another began to twirl counterclockwise, even though these behaviors had nothing to do with when the next bit of food would appear. Their experience had taught them something; it just happened to be a something that was utterly spurious.

Such superstitions are not constrained to birds. Nearly 40 years after B. F. Skinner's (1948) experiment, Ono (1987) repeated something like it with humans. College students were brought into a laboratory and placed in front of an apparatus with three levers, three lights, and a counter. They were told to try to get as many points on the counter as they could. They did try, even though their efforts had no impact on how many points rang up on the counter. Despite this, one student began pulling levers in a specific sequence, followed by keeping a hand on one lever. Another student began laying her hands on the levers, the apparatus containing them, a nail in the wall, as well as other objects in the room, in a vain attempt to conjure forth more points.

These experiments, although extreme, illustrate one basic fact of life. The lessons people draw from observing how the world responds to their actions need not be correct ones. People can fall prey to superstitions and wrong-headed ideas. Indeed, the way feedback works in the hectic and unruly real world makes gaining accurate beliefs and exorcising erroneous ones a challenging and sometimes impossible task. Feedback in everyday life possesses four characteristics that make learning from experience a tricky business.

## Feedback Is Probabilistic

Reward and punishment in real-world contexts are probabilistic, in that there is no certain, one-to-one correspondence between choosing the right action and getting rewarded for it. Every parent, teacher, or poker player knows this. Good choices do not automatically produce good outcomes. And bad or irrelevant choices, just through sheer dumb luck or odd circumstance, sometimes produce rewards. A salesperson's warm smile and friendly touch may frequently lead to a sale, but sometimes customers are churlishly put off by this manner. A pushy and condescending salesperson may occasionally find a customer who responds positively to this attitude, even though many turn and walk away, if not answer with a dose of hostility and aggression. Thus, each salesman can claim some level of success, such as that pigeon in Skinner's box that believed that twirling counterclockwise would bring another snack. The fog produced by this uncertain link between behavior and reward often means that it is difficult to determine what the right choice is and how to distinguish it from the wrong one.

## Feedback Is Incomplete

Experience also provides feedback that is incomplete. We can know the outcomes of actions we have taken but often do not know, and cannot know, the outcomes of alternative actions we could have taken (Cohen & March, 1974; May, 1973). Did I, for example, make the right career choice to become an academic social psychologist? It is impossible to tell unless I could borrow the Wayback Machine from Mr. Peabody and travel back to my undergraduate years to follow another career path to compare the results. But such a chance to do so is precluded given contemporary technology and my finances; I cannot gain the comparison I need to know whether I made the right career choice.

The fact that feedback from experience is incomplete, in that people do not know what would happened if they chose another course of action, is a fundamental problem that prevents people from seeing the imperfection of their ways. We do not act like George Costanza, the character from the classic television series *Seinfeld*, who one day decides to do the opposite of everything he normally does—and gets his dream job and even the girl.

Without knowing the outcomes of alternative actions, we can often be left with apparent evidence that we are doing just fine even when we are not. Consider two sets of parents dealing with a child who is going through a particularly cranky and disobedient day. One set decides to sit their son down and reason with him, explaining to him why he should behave, and then sending him off to bed to get a good sleep. The other severely disciplines the child with sharp words and a spanking. The next day, both children are likely to behave better, in that after a particularly good or bad day kids are more likely to revert back to their typical behavior. However, both sets of parents will be left with the impression that their diametrically opposed disciplinary styles worked, even though the evidence they have is logically insufficient.

## Feedback Is Hidden

Feedback can often be hidden. People do suffer consequences for mistaken actions, but those consequences never make themselves visible. One office worker, after misbehaving in a drunken stupor at an office party, may never know how many people decided against inviting him to their dinner parties. Feedback from good behaviors can also be hidden. A person may be promoted at work but not know the exact behavior that earned her the promotion in the first place.

Feedback is often hidden because it comes after errors of omission. People miss an opportunity to act, and because they have missed it, they do not realize the rewards they could have earned. For example, a person shopping for a car may not realize one last wrinkle in a discount he could have asked for. Because he did not ask for it, he fails to see the price he got is higher than what it could have been. The error he has made remains hidden (Caputo & Dunning, in press).

## Feedback Is Ambiguous

Feedback is ambiguous, in that it is difficult to pin down what exactly led an action to be a beneficial or costly one. Imagine that Harry asks Sally for a date, and she turns him down. Why did she do so? What lesson should Harry learn? Was it his hair? Was it his breath? Were his jokes not funny? Is he too short? Is he too poor? Is he not confident enough? Or, instead, could it be something about her? Perhaps she is just too choosy, having a bad day, or recovering from a bad relationship? My, my, what lesson is to be learned here? Unfortunately, feedback is often this ambiguous, and with so many plausible reasons to explain a failure or a success it is difficult to ascertain which is the right one to learn.

The ambiguous nature of real-world feedback is exacerbated by the fact that people tend to obtain feedback one action at a time, and each action presents a situation with so many idiosyncratic features upon which one can hang a theory of success. Harry can ask women out, with some saying yes and some saying no. But each time he asks, there are many different reasons for why he might have succeeded or failed with that particular woman. In all this ambiguity, it is difficult to extract the real reasons that suggest success or failure in Harry's social life.

## Feedback Is Absent

Feedback can also be surprisingly absent. For example, over the past few years, I have given innumerable talks about my research and have rarely received clear, detailed, or unambiguous feedback about how those talks have gone. Indeed, I have only once received one formal and detailed two-page handwritten critique of a talk that I have given.

Without this feedback, I am forced to pay attention to whatever small tea leaves people might reveal in their behaviors when my talk is finished. I have to see whether people excitedly ask questions at the end of the talk, whether they smile, or whether those smiles look forced. Regrettably, this lack of formal feedback is the usual state of social life. For instance, a survey conducted in 1984 by the American Management Association discovered that 75% of organizations provided formal performance evaluations of their employees only once a year, if that (Ashford, 1989). Thus, employees must often resort to searching for *informal* feedback about their skill and place in the organization. They monitor whether the boss looks them in the eye, stops to talk to them in the hall, or invites them over to a weekend barbeque. No matter how good people are at correctly reading these small social signs, these signs are no substitute to formal, explicit, and clear feedback.

There is every reason that without this formal feedback, people are often out to sea when it comes to understanding the signs people flash at them. For example, people who think negatively about their social competence tend to elicit negative reactions from others (Swann, Wenzlaff, Krull, & Pelham, 1992). Such individuals, however, may miss that others react negatively to them, even when those others subtly signal their dislike. Swann, Stein-Seroussi, and McNulty (1992) brought individuals with high and low self-views of their social competence in the laboratory and just asked them to chat for seven minutes with another person. Those conversation partners tended to like the low self-view participants significantly less than they liked confident and animated high self-concept individuals. However, low self-view participants missed this fact, overestimating how much their conversation partners had liked them. Their conversation partners, however, had signaled their relative dislike through the tone and energy of their voice—and observers could catch these differences—even though the words they said were just as pleasant and harmonious as those chosen for high self-view individuals.

## Feedback Is Biased

Perhaps most important, feedback is biased. People tend to tell us things that match the preconceived notions, usually positive, that we hold about ourselves. People do not like to give unpleasant news to others. For example, Tesser, Rosen, and Conlee (1972) asked participants to relay a message to another student. The student's roommate had called to say that the student should call home because of some good news. Participants quite dutifully passed along that message. However, when the message stated that there was bad news waiting at home, participants were much more likely to edit that important detail out, even when probed about what the entire message had been. However, they were very likely to mention that the message contained bad news when asked by a bystander.

Other experiments reveal a similar disinclination to pass along bad news in real-world settings (see Tesser & Rosen, 1975, for a review). Social workers are more reluctant to inform physically disabled clients that they have been denied aid than when they have been granted it, even when the news is routinely sent via a form letter (Tesser, Rosen, & Tesser, 1971).

Such reluctance to transmit bad news, quite naturally, arises in formal feedback sessions. College students playing a supervisor gave much more positive ratings to low-performing subordinates when they thought those subordinates would see the feedback than when they thought the ratings would remain private (Fisher, 1979; see also Ilgen & Knowlton, 1980; and Larson, 1986, for experimental evidence). A good deal of anecdotal evidence from business managers shows that they avoid and delay giving negative feedback to performers. And when they can no longer delay, they distort the feedback to make it more agreeable (Longenecker, Sims, & Gioia, 1987; Veiga, 1988).

Anyone who has lived any portion of adult life has experienced this dissembling of feedback, probably on both sides of the ledger. People try to put the most positive gloss they can on the feedback they give to others. The technical term for the most extreme form of this activity is called "lying." People, however, do not like to lie, and so when they are faced with giving another person unpleasant news, they try to cleverly negotiate a truthful way to avoid conveying their genuine opinion. If an artist shows them a painting they dislike, they may dwell on specific features of the painting that they do like but fail to mention all the features they abhor. They may talk about how much they dislike art of this type but then imply, but not explicitly say, that they like this artist's painting better (DePaulo & Bell, 1996). In this way, people can claim to be truthful yet succeed in their goal of not hurting another person's feelings.

I have seen this strategy in action. I once witnessed a speech by a colleague that caused everyone in the audience to hunch down in their seats to hide their constant wincing, embarrassed giggling, or outright expressions of horror. Once the speech was over, my colleague asked a number of people what they had thought of his speech. A few told him that the speech had been remarkable (true, but misleading). One told him that people would be talking about that speech for years (also very true, but even more misleading).

# ☐ Flawed Habits in Monitoring Feedback

Even when our experience provides clear and unambiguous feedback about our knowledge and ability, we possess "bad habits" of thought and deed that prevent us from hearing what the world wants to tell us.

## People Focus on Positive Co-occurrences

When I was in graduate school, I fell prey to a superstition just as strong as any held by Skinner's pigeons. The elevators in our building were slow: Passengers would punch the button to their floor and then wait for what seemed to be an eternity before the door finally closed and the elevator started to move. Frustrated one day, I hopped up and down softly, to announce the presence of a passenger, and the elevator doors immediately obeyed and shut. Each time after that, I would hop a little hop in the elevator if I felt it was taking a long time for the elevator doors to close. If the doors failed to close after my initial hop, I would hop again more emphatically until the doors closed.

At some level, I knew this was nuts. But at another level, it seemed so convincing that my hopping was causing the elevator doors to close.

How could it seem so convincing? Like all of us (and Skinner's pigeons, too) I was paying attention only to positive co-occurrences of action and outcome—episodes in which my hopping was soon followed by the doors closing. I had experienced a large number of those episodes (Smedlund, 1963; Ward & Jenkins, 1965), and so felt confident in the link between my action and the elevator's reaction.

However, any statistician (and advanced graduate student in psychology) knows that keeping count of these positive co-occurrences is simply insufficient to establish a link between my hopping and elevator response. Every statistician knows that I have to pay attention to not one but *four* different types of occurrences to establish any connection between my actions and the responses of the outside world. First, I have to pay attention to times I hopped and the elevator obeyed. Second, I have to pay attention to occasions in which I hopped, but the elevator did not close (which certainly took place, usually causing me to hop more vigorously). Third and fourth, I had to pay attention to times in which I did not hop, perhaps distracted by my own thoughts or conversation with someone else. When I failed to hop, how many times did the elevator door close promptly and how many times did it just take its time?

To establish a connection between action and outcome, one needs all four pieces of data, not just data from positive co-occurrences. My belief about hopping directly implies that the odds that the door would close after I hopped would be greater than when I failed to hop, and all four pieces are essential to calculate these odds. The odds of closing after I hop consists of the number of times the door closes after hopping divided by the number of times it failed to close after hopping. The odds of closing when I do not hop consists of times the door closed early with no hop divided by the times it fails to close with no hop. If I pay attention only to positive co-occurrences, I am in no position to compute and compare these two crucial odds ratios.

## People Create Self-Fulfilling Prophecies

People have an unfortunate tendency to act on their theories in ways that tend to confirm those theories, no matter how accurate or fallacious those theories are. Consider a police officer who claims that she can spot a lying guilty suspect simply by looking for shifty eyes and a snarly voice. (An example that was not picked at random: Police investigators are no better than laypeople at picking out liars; both groups do just a tad better than chance. See Ekman & O'Sullivan, 1991.) If that officer in the interrogation room decides the suspect's eyes are shifty, she is likely to press harder and longer in her interrogation, breaking down the story of the suspect to find whether that suspect is guilty or innocent. If the officer decides the suspect is telling the truth, she is likely to back off in her interrogation, even if she does not realize it, leaving the suspect looking more innocent, regardless of the truth.

In this way, people can confirm their judgments and decisions even if the theory responsible for those judgments is irrelevant or just flat-out wrong. Many studies in psychology have revealed the power of self-fulfilling prophecies to spin seemingly confirmatory evidence when none is warranted. Although controversial, Rosenthal and Jacobsen (1968) found that telling teachers that some of their students were late bloomers caused those students to perform better as the academic year wore on. The students had been chosen at random; any improvement on their part was presumably due to how teachers treated them. In another telling example, Rosenthal and Fode (1963) gave lab rats to college students and told them to train the rats to run to the correct end of a maze. Half the students were told that their rats came from a "bright" litter; half were told that their rats came from a "dull" one. In reality, rats were labeled as bright or dull completely at random. However, even though the rats did not differ in their inherent intelligence, the rats labeled as bright made over 50% more correct responses than those labeled as dull at the end of five days' training. Again, the actions of their student handlers must have been responsible for this difference between putatively bright and dull rodents.

## People Fail to Recognize Their Mistakes in Hindsight

People may fail to learn about their mistakes because, in hindsight, they fail to recognize that they made any mistake at all. Much psychological research has confirmed that hindsight is 20–20, in that events in retrospect look more inevitable than they did before they took place. Across many experiments, once people know an event took place, they overestimate the likelihood that they would have correctly anticipated it, that they "knew it all along" (Fischoff, 1975, 1977; Hawkins & Hastie, 1990).

This hindsight bias can cause people to miss the fact that they have made a judgmental mistake in the past. Suppose a store manager hires a new salesclerk. The decision is a little risky—the manager has a few doubts—but in the end he confidently decides that the new hire will be a good one. However, suppose after a few months the sales clerk has proved to be so incompetent that he must be fired. Hindsight bias could lead the store manager to miss how wrong his original hiring decision was. In retrospect, the flaws of the new hire will look inevitable, leading the store manager to state that he really knew deep down all along that the new hire was a risk—that he had his doubts and was not very confident the new hire would work out at all. Indeed, he might even state that he knew the hire was probably going to have to be fired down the road.

People do misremember their judgments in this way. In 1978, Wood asked a number of college students to predict some events that could take place in the future. After these events had a chance to take place, Wood came back to the same students and asked them to recall what their predictions had been. Students tended to overstate how many events they had correctly anticipated.

Thus, in hindsight, people's memory tends to erase just how inaccurate their predictions and judgments were. Unable to recognize those errors, people are not in a position to learn from them.

## People Disproportionately Seek Feedback Consistent with Their Self-Image

People do not gather feedback in a fair-minded, even-handed way. Given a choice between feedback that is likely to be consistent versus inconsistent with their self-views, people tend to opt for the consistent feedback. Bill Swann and colleagues have demonstrated across a number of studies in the lab and in real-world settings that people tend to strive for feedback that would verify their self-beliefs over information that would challenge those beliefs (for a review, see Swann, Rentfrow, & Guinn, 2002).

For example, Swann, Stein-Seroussi, and Giesler (1992) asked college students with either positive or negative self-impressions whom they would rather interact with: a person who had a generally positive view of them or the one who had a negative opinion. Participants tended to opt for the person who had a view compatible to their preexisting self-impression. Participants with high opinions of themselves tended to choose the person who shared that positive view; participants with low self-opinions opted for the opposite individual.

Other work has shown a similar preference for information that would only confirm ideas people have about themselves. People prefer to view information that would corroborate preconceived notions of self over feedback that would contradict it. Indeed, they actually would pay more money to see it, and when they get it, they spend significantly more time looking it over (Swann & Read, 1981a, 1981b). It is difficult to see how erroneous impressions of self can be corrected if people tend to opt for data that would not confront those self-impressions.

## People Accept Positive Feedback, Scrutinize Negative

People do not treat positive and negative feedback equally. When they receive positive feedback, they accept it at face value without much protest. However, when people receive negative feedback, they pull out their psychic magnifying glass and give it a good stare, looking for ways they can discount or dismiss it (Dawson, Gilovich, & Regan, 2002; Gilovich, 1991). For example, suppose you are a blonde-haired, left-handed fellow, and that CNN reports a new study showing that such individuals live longer than most other people. My own reaction, if I fit those characteristics, would be *bully!* and I would go on about my life without a second's thought about the validity of the study. However, suppose the study had concluded that blonde lefties were more likely to die at an early age. My reaction would probably be to look up the CNN story, or even seek out the original scientific report on the Web to scrutinize it for any flaws in methodology, limits in its logic, or any bias on the part of the researchers.

In the most direct example of this asymmetric treatment of positive and negative information, Ditto and colleagues (Ditto & Lopez, 1992) brought students in the laboratory and gave them a test for thioamine acetylase (TAA) enzyme deficiency, a condition they were told was linked to worrisome pancreatic disorders in later life. (The reader should know TAA enzyme deficiency is a common malady, but only in the psychological laboratory. It does not exist in the real world.) To take the test, subjects swabbed the inside of their cheeks and then dipped the swab into a laboratory liquid, and then waited to see whether the swab changed color. Compared with those whose test showed no deficiency, participants whose test suggested a deficiency took longer to decide that the test was complete. They were also more likely to redo the test (52% versus 18% in the no-deficiency group).

In a different experiment, participants were told that the TAA test could be invalidated if the participant's blood sugar was unusually high or low that day. Participants whose tests indicated health did not take this information into account when deciding whether to believe the results of the test. Indeed, they just took the test result at face value. Participants whose tests indicated otherwise were much more thoughtful. If the chance that their blood sugar had thrown off the test was high, they were quite eager to dismiss the validity of the test (Ditto, Scepansky, Munro, Apanovitch, & Lockhart, 1998).

# People Code Positive Actions Broadly, Negative Ones Narrowly

People tend to perceive their positive actions as broad and enduring, reflecting central and stable aspects of the self, whereas they perceive their negative actions as narrow, isolated, and fleeting.

This pattern is encapsulated in the very language people use to describe actions that reflect positively and negatively on them. Taris (1999) asked college students to describe some "good" behaviors they had done. They were also asked to describe "good" behaviors that they knew other people had done. When describing their own behavior, respondents used abstract language such as *I was charitable* or *I was helpful* much more than when they described the behaviors of others (e.g., *He donated money to the Girl Scouts; he gave the man some directions to the restaurant*). Taris argued that people used such abstract language to ensure that their good deeds reflected well on the self, that those good deeds revealed an important facet of their character. Not surprisingly, Taris also found that people used more circumscribed language to describe "bad" things that they had done. People compartmentalized and distanced their bad behavior by describing them in concrete language. Whereas a respondent might describe himself as *slapping another person's face*, the same action on the part of another individual would be described as *being hostile* (see Maass, Milesi, Zabbini, & Stahlberg, 1995; and Maass, Salvi, Arcuri, & Semin, 1989, for similar results).

I myself have seen this use of language, and the perception associated with it, in the lab. In pilot work for a series of studies about success and failure, an undergraduate and I put Cornell University students through success and failure experiences. Students would be given a list of three words (such as *post, time,* and *garden*) and be asked to find a fourth word associated with all three (e.g., *bed*). Students in the success experience were given easy items to solve; those in the failure conditions were given extremely difficult ones. After students were done, I asked students "what the test was about." Success participants described it in broad, all-encompassing language. The test was about intelligence, creativity, or smart thinking. Failure participants were more likely to stay with the concrete, such as the test measured a person's ability to find a fourth word associated with three other ones. Many failure participants could not be coaxed to describe the test in any broader terms.

Baumeister, Stillwell, and Wotman (1990) found a similar pattern in respondents' accounts of anger. When respondents were asked to describe an episode in which someone had made them angry, they described a long series of provocations that had long-lasting consequences well after those provocations were over. However, when asked to write about an instance in which they had made someone else angry, they tended to treat the incident as a one-time annoyance that had no enduring aftereffects once the incident was taken care of.

The tendency people have to characterize their mistakes as one-time incidents interacts with another tendency of the outside world. Recall that people do not like to give others negative feedback. Even if they are annoyed—or even enraged—they swallow their irritation and delay giving another person corrective news. Nowhere is this truer than in the workplace. A boss might deal with many, many complaints about the slowness of one of her workers, but she may very well avoid telling the worker that he has to speed up. But, unfortunately, without corrective feedback, the complaints continue and continue until the boss is forced to summon the worker to her office. Regrettably, often the boss calls the worker in because she just cannot take it anymore and is beside herself.

Now imagine the scene from the viewpoint of the worker. He will be motivated to see his slowness as a one-time incident, and his boss might abet this perception by politely emphasizing the latest occurrence. However, if the meeting is about only one incident, the worker will wonder why his boss is so inappropriately mad at him for one simple mistake, making him more likely to reject whatever message the boss is trying to send. Past research has provided evidence for this pattern of delay and escalation, anger, and rejection (Baumeister, Stillwell, & Wotman,1990; Larson, 1986).

People find other ways to perceive their successes as broad and their failures as narrow. They tend to see their proficiencies as reflective of broad traits, their weaknesses as reflective of nothing (Dunning, Perie, & Story, 1991). Thus, when given negative feedback about one of their weaknesses, instead of questioning their overall ability, they compartmentalize that weakness as peripheral to their overall ability.

For example, Greve and Wentura (2003) asked college students to rate their "general knowledge" about the world. He then quizzed them, along with another person who was actually a confederate, on their specific knowledge of history, politics, the fine arts, and the natural sciences. The experiment was rigged so that the participant outperformed the confederate in two topic areas, but was outperformed by the confederate on the remaining two. Afterward, participants were asked how diagnostic each domain was for assessing a person's general knowledge. Participants rated the domains in which they had beat the confederate to be more diagnostic than the domains in which they had lost out to the confederate.

People also compartmentalize their failures by sometimes construing them instead as near successes. They believe that they would have made the right choice, except for some fluke circumstance that no one could have anticipated. For example, Gilovich (1983) asked college students to bet on the outcome of an NCAA basketball final. Some students, naturally, lost their bet and swore that they would bet less in the future. However, if reminded of a fluke play during the last minute of the game that had prevented their team from winning, their confidence in their betting acumen was restored. Interestingly, reminding bettors of the fluke play after they won did not lead them to question their betting expertise. Only losing bettors took the opportunity to view the outcome as a fleeting, accidental, and isolated.

## People Attribute Positive Outcomes to Self, Negative Ones to Anyone or Anything Else

People credit their successes to something about themselves, such as their ability or effort, and lay blame for failure elsewhere. For example, Lau and Russell (1980) scoured the sports pages for how baseball teams explained their wins and losses. Wins tended to be attributed to the self and to superior ability, strategy, or effort. Losses tended to be attributed to external factors, such as bad luck or happenstance.

People tend to have many options to explain away negative outcomes that they do not invoke after positive ones. In the Ditto and Lopez (1992) experiments described earlier, participants cited many more temporary irregularities that might have thrown off test results after those results revealed that bothersome TAA enzyme deficiency than when it suggested perfect health. They also criticized the validity of the test, echoing a result in lots of research (and professors' offices) that good performance on a test reveals the truth, but bad performance reveals how truly bad the test really was.

## People Misremember Feedback

The final bad habit people apply to feedback is their inability to remember it accurately. People's memory of the feedback they receive tends to migrate back toward general preconceptions they hold about themselves. For example, Story (1998) brought participants with high and low self-esteem into the laboratory. She asked them to fill out a long battery of personality tests, and then went into the next room to score them. When she returned, she handed to participants what she described as a comprehensive set of results describing their overall personality. Participants were then allowed to pour over the personality report.

What participants did not know is that the personality profile they were given was based on a self-description they had given a few weeks earlier. Most of the entries on the profile just parroted back to participants what they had said earlier. But, for some of the entries, the feedback had been pushed up in a positive direction; for some others, the feedback had been bumped in a negative direction.

Participants gave the personality profiles back to the experimenter, filled out a few filler questionnaires, and then were given an unexpected memory test. They were given a blank version of the profile and asked to reconstruct the one that they had been given. For the most part, participants did a good job of remembering the feedback, but their errors were instructive. High self-esteem individuals rather correctly remembered the entries that had been distorted in a positive direction but misremembered the negative items, recalling them as more positive than they really were. Low self-esteem individuals did the exact reverse. They faithfully remembered the items that had been pushed in a negative direction but misremembered the positive items as being more negative.

Other research resonates with this pattern. Swann and Read (1981b) found that people with high opinions of themselves remembered more good things another person has said about them than did people with low self-views. Low self-view participants remembered more negative statements than did their high self-view counterparts. Because most people hold high views of themselves, it is perhaps not a surprise that people remember more positive aspects of the feedback they receive over the negative features (Feather, 1968; Ilgen, 1971; Ilgen & Hamstra, 1972; Shrauger & Rosenberg, 1970).

# ☐ Concluding Remarks

Experience is a cruel teacher. As Vernon Law, the venerable Pittsburgh Pirates pitcher from the 1950s, once observed, she gives the test first before presenting the lesson. The material in this chapter suggests that beyond being cruel, experience at times may be an inscrutable teacher, hiding valuable feedback behind a veil of probabilistic, incomplete, hidden, ambiguous, biased, and even absent information. Obscuring the lessons we could learn from our lives are the bad habits we use when we look back upon what our experiences might be trying to tell us. As such, it might be the case that as people get older, they do get wiser, but there are many reasons why that wisdom, although hard-earned, is far from perfect.

# False Uniqueness

*Characteristics That Lead People to Think
They Are Special*

I think I should have known that I was headed for a career in scientific research on that cold winter night when I was 6 years old and someone mentioned that every snowflake was unique. I decided to put this assertion to a test later that night as the snow started to fall in the chilly Michigan air. I ran out with a piece of cardboard to catch snowflakes, taking along a flashlight and a magnifying glass, to see if I could spot any two that looked alike. I knew that this procedure would fail to completely test the idea that there had never been two snowflakes in the history of Earth that were identical, but I felt that if I surveyed a few hundred and found two that pretty much resembled each other, that this would be a major scientific discovery that was within the grasp of a 6-year-old. Alas, after about an hour, I abandoned my quest without any prominent scientific news to report. Cold, hungry, and a little bored, I returned indoors after finding that, indeed, simple six-pointed snowflakes could come in a wide variety of aesthetics.

I am still skeptical about snowflakes, but I do have to concede that people are probably even more likely to be unique packages of skills, traits, quirks, attitudes, physical characteristics, mannerisms, appearances, likes, dislikes, experiences, and areas of expertise that provide no exact resemblance to anyone else on Earth. The terrain of each of our characters must present a unique geography never duplicated elsewhere. After all, my combination of skepticism, inquisitiveness, and ambition at age 6 had sent me out running to catch snowflakes in the driveway. And this unique concatenation of attributes had predisposed me toward a career in scientific inquiry.

However, one can overplay these perceptions of personal uniqueness. Although each of us is, indeed, special, in systematic ways, we may not be as exceptional as we perceive (Shepherd, Carroll, Grace, & Terry, 2002). In this chapter and the next, I review specific circumstances that lead us to believe that we are peculiar or distinctive when we, in fact, might be just like everyone else.

In particular, I examine the characteristics of characteristics that promote beliefs of personal uniqueness that tend to be false. I focus on personal qualities that too many people, ironically, tend to believe that they possess to an exclusive degree. Of course, these personal qualities usually tend to be desirable ones, leading people to believe that they possess exceptionally attractive and enviable personalities, although this is not always the case.

Along the way, the material in this chapter will also demonstrate when and where people do *not* see themselves as exceptional. For example, although it is true that people might feel that they are more likely than their peers to live until age 55, they may not feel the same about reaching 105 (Weinstein, 1980). Although they might believe they are hardly likely to rear-end some other car while driving, they might be more likely to worry about being rear-ended (McKenna, 1993). Despite their belief that they can control their diet to maintain a healthy weight, they may not hold such optimistic beliefs about avoiding bacterial infections (Sparks & Shepherd, 1994). They may believe themselves to be especially idealistic, disciplined, or intelligent—but not necessarily thrifty, neat, or mathematically gifted (Dunning, Meyerowitz, & Holzberg, 1989). People may feel that they are uniquely self-sacrificing or self-critical among their acquaintances, but not necessarily more poised or daring (Miller & McFarland, 1987).

In total, I examine characteristics and related events that fall along three separate dimensions. The first dimension is *control*. When people believe that they can apply effort to obtain the characteristics or event in question, does that lead them to believe they are uniquely positioned to apply that effort? The second dimension is the *observability* of the characteristic. Does the characteristic refer to behaviors that everyone can see, or only to private reactions known only to the person harboring them? The final dimension, to be discussed in the next chapter, is *ambiguity*. Some characteristics are rather obvious in their meaning, whereas others are more indistinct. Does this indistinctness lead to self-inflation?

# □ Controllability

To the extent that people feel a trait is controllable, they are more likely to see themselves as superior on that trait relative to their peers. They see themselves as much more *cooperative, polite,* and *self-disciplined* than their peers—all traits whose expression can be controlled—but do not tout their superiority as much when it comes to relatively uncontrollable attributes such as *intelligent, creative,* and *lively* (Alicke, 1985).

People also see themselves as more likely to achieve favorable outcomes than their peers when those outcomes involve control. People see themselves as less likely than others to experience an auto accident when they are the driver of the car, but not when they are the passenger (McKenna, 1993). They believe they are less likely than their peers to avoid accidents when they are changing lanes, turning sharply, or driving fast—all situations under the driver's control. They do not, however, believe they have any special ability to avoid uncontrollable accidents that involve black ice, a tire puncture, or brake failure (McKenna).

More generally, people display unrealistic optimism about their ability to attain positive outcomes and avoid negative ones when those outcomes are conceivably controllable (Klein & Helweg-Larsen, 2002). For example, people say they are more likely than their peers to avoid getting fired on their first job, have their marriage end in divorce, and contract a sexually transmitted disease. However, they are not more likely to say that they will avoid outcomes largely dictated by the fates. For example, they are much less likely to claim that they can avoid being a victim of a burglary, having their car stolen, or catching a one- to two-day virus (Weinstein, 1980, 1987, 1989). In a similar vein, people believe themselves to be much less vulnerable, relative to their contemporaries, to the risks associated with high-fat diets, alcohol, and caffeine. However, they do not consider themselves especially invulnerable to risks associated with pesticide residues, environmental contamination, and genetic manipulation (Sparks & Shepherd, 1994).

Why do people show this controllability bias? More importantly, why do people show little or no bias when considering events not under one's control? There are many potential answers to these questions, and the psychology behind the impact of perceived control on unrealistic self-assessments has, as of yet, not been fully worked out (Harris, 1996; Budescu & Bruderman, 1995). However, one can spin at least two simple and plausible stories about why people exhibit the most unrealistic self-views when considering conceivably controllable events. One story is based on wishful thinking. The second suggests that the bias could be quite rational.

First, the story based on wishful thinking. It is safe to stipulate, because there is ample evidence, that people covet positive images of themselves. They want to possess positive traits and to attain favorable life outcomes (Alicke, 1985; Weinstein, 1980). Thus, if considering whether one will attain a positive trait or life event, and if that event could conceivably be attained by effort, then it serves the individual's psychic needs to assume that he or she will supply the relevant effort. After all, if an individual desires an outcome, it is quite easy to assume that this individual will apply the effort when the relevant moment comes. As a consequence, people see themselves as uniquely likely to acquire positive traits and meet favorable fates, relative to their peers. If there is no effort or tactic that the individual can identify to bring about a positive outcome, this route of wishful thinking is foreclosed.

Now, the story based on rationality. Once again, let us presume that people wish to bring about agreeable fates and acquire positive characteristics. If they perceive that a little effort and diligence will help them achieve these ends, there is one thing they know about themselves that they do not know about others: that they will *want* to apply that effort to achieve those ends. Because they know (or, to be completely accurate, *think* they know) they possess the desire to expend the effort necessary to achieve favorable fates, but do not necessarily know this fact about others, they can conclude that they are in a unique position to attain congenial outcomes.

Whichever of the above stories is correct, or whether some other story explains the link between controllability and unrealistic self-views, the belief that one can control one's fate drives people's preferences for the situations in which they choose to place themselves. People choose to take risks they think they can control over those they believe they cannot, even if those controllable risks are greater than the uncontrollable ones. Klein and Kunda (1994) asked college students which of the following drugs they would prefer if they faced a life-threatening illness. Drug A was very effective, but produced fatal side effects in 1 out of every 100,000 cases that neither patients nor doctors could do anything about. Drug B produced similar side effects in 2 out of every 1,000 cases, but these side effects could be negated if detected early enough by the patient. Regrettably, roughly 1% of patients failed to detect these side effects, leaving a fatality rate of 2 out of every 100,000. Nearly three times as many students preferred Drug B, the one offering some control, over Drug A even though the overall chance of fatality was greater.

The preference for controllable risks extends to choices with real consequences. In a follow-up study, Klein & Kunda (1994) asked participants which of the following two games they would prefer to play. Game A offered little control. The experimenter would generate two random numbers between 10 and 19. If the two numbers failed to match, the participant would win $1. This procedure could continue for as long as 10 trials, but if the experimenter on any trial generated matching numbers, the game would end. Obviously, on each trial, the chance that the game could end was 1 in 10, but the participant had no control over that outcome. In contrast, Game B provided participants with some control over their fate. In this game, the chance that the game could end on any given trial was 1 in 3. However, the participant could then complete a task to resume the game, but the game would continue only if the participant completed the task better than the average student. When that task looked easy (i.e., checking for spelling errors), and thus well under the participants' control, participants chose Game B 66% of the time, even though Game A presented a better chance at winning good money.

## Missing Insights

People's overly optimistic beliefs about control can be construed as a by-product of two possible errors. One error centers on beliefs about others. The second centers on beliefs about one's ability to *really* control events.

### Beliefs About Others

As mentioned previously, people's beliefs about control can flow from either wishful thinking or rational calculation. A person can know that he or she will, at the very least, *want* to expend effort to bring about positive events and to avoid negative ones; thus, that person can conclude (either through wishful thinking or logical deduction) that he or she is particularly likely to attain favorable outcomes in life.

However, in reaching that conclusion, the individual is not considering one fact that is obviously relevant. Everyone else considering controllable events is thinking the same thing. Other individuals are likely to conclude that they will also desire to apply the effort necessary to bring about happy outcomes. In essence, everyone is willing to make the same commitment to a positive outcome, so why should any of them presume that they will be among the few most likely to achieve those outcomes?

In essence, if people believe that they are more likely than others to achieve controllable outcomes, they must be making mistakes about the circumstances of other people. They might be assuming too quickly that other people are just lazy bums who are not as willing to exert the needed effort. Or, people might be the lazy bums themselves and fail to consider that other people, on average, have just as much right to claim that they have a special desire and ability to bring about advantageous events. Supporting this latter idea is the finding that, when asked, people do admit that others have just as much capacity to control events as they do themselves (Harris & Middleton, 1994).

In essence, the controllability bias might be a result of people's inattention to the desires and skills of others. People are not considering how much other people will react in the same way to the events and circumstances confronting them. But there will be more on this later. When it comes to how much people think of others in their self-assessments, I am getting ahead of the story.

### Beliefs About the Self

People believe they can control events. How much of that belief is a rational one, and how much of it is contradicted by reality? Although the answer to this question is undoubtedly a complicated one, depending on both an individual's unique set of skills and capabilities, as well as the specific circumstances he or she faces, recent research suggests that people extend their beliefs about control to circumstances in which they clearly have none.

For example, people who frequent casinos know that gamblers often make a distinction between three different sources of success: skill, chance, and luck (Keren, 1994; Keren & Wagenaar, 1985). The definition of skill is rather straightforward. Blackjack players need to know the odds associated with taking a hit when they have a hard 13 versus a soft 18.

But chance and luck? At first blush, these two concepts would seem to refer to the same obvious random element in any casino game, but gamblers make a clear distinction between the two. Only chance refers to the randomness of any event. Chance refers to the uncontrollable and unpredictable component of the outside world that turns a losing poker hand to a winning one, or vice versa. Luck, in contrast, refers to some property of the gambler. Like some people are tall or short, fair-haired or dark, some people are lucky and some are not. And luck, according to gamblers, matters. Blackjack players assign 45% of the responsibility for their peers' success to luck, 37% to skill, and only 18% to chance (Keren & Wagenaar, 1985).

In short, people do not necessarily recognize purely random events for the haphazard, chaotic, unpredictable, and uncontrollable happenings that they are. In assigning a gambler's fate to luck, people imbue random events with some sort of regularity, and thus some sort of predictability. But people go further than that. Even when events are produced via purely random means, people often believe they possess some control over the outcome. This misperception is not evident in every random circumstance, but it commonly crops up depending on the situation and the person involved.

People see control in situations in which no control actually exists. People are more likely to bet on a roll of a die if it has yet to be thrown rather than after it has been thrown (Rothbart & Snyder, 1970). Clearly, the odds of winning are the same in both instances, but people tend to feel some modicum of influence if the event has yet to take place. Similarly, they are more likely to hold onto a lottery ticket if they pick them out of a box rather than having one handed to them by the experimenter (Langer, 1975)—again, a situation that confers the illusion of control but that does not alter the chance of winning. As well, people are more willing to bet on the toss of a coin if they get to toss it (Langer & Roth, 1975). If people need a high number on a pair of dice, they throw the dice harder (Henslin, 1967), an action that increases how much the dice will bounce around but not what number the dice show at rest. Casino owners and state gaming agencies all know of the importance of this illusion of control. There is a reason why state lottery games often feature letting players pick their own lotto numbers or allowing them to scratch to reveal the numbers on instant tickets (Clotfelter & Cook, 1989; Langenderfer, 1996).

People also imbue chance events with some level of control if they tend to harbor an internal locus of control (Rotter, 1966). People with an internal locus of control tend to believe that they are the masters of their own fate, in contrast to people with an external locus who believe their outcomes are largely shaped by outside influences. People with an internal locus of control tend to believe they are particularly invulnerable to health problems (Hoorens & Buunk, 1993) and exceptionally skilled drivers in difficult situations (DeJoy, 1989).

Perhaps these perceptions are not irrational, for people with an internal locus do show behaviors that work to their benefit. They do, after all, redouble their efforts after failure, whereas people with an external locus tend to give up more (Weiss & Sherman, 1973). The problem with high internals, however, is that they tend to believe they have control over patently chance events. People who desire and believe they have control tend to be more frequent players in state lotteries (Miyazaki, Brumbaugh, & Sprott, 2001; Sprott, Brumbaugh, & Miyazaki, 2001), a game that is clearly ruled by chance. In addition, problem gamblers tend to emphasize their skill in gambling behavior over chance (Carroll & Huxley, 1994; Toneatto, 1999).

## Overcoming the Controllability Bias

All the previous research suggests that a hefty portion of unrealistic optimism is prompted by overly sanguine perceptions of control. In doing so, it also suggests an indirect remedy for these biased perceptions. If people could be convinced that events are, at times, out of their control, they may form more cautious and appropriate self-assessments. At times, life presents these types of lessons (Helweg-Larsen & Shepperd, 2001).

In the risk perception literature, it has often been observed that people provide much less optimistic assessments about negative events in their future if they have encountered those events in the past (Weinstein, 1980). People who have been victims of crime in the past are much more skittish about their ability to avoid crimes in the future (Frieze, Hymer, & Greenberg, 1987). People who contracted a sexually transmitted disease are much more cautious in their optimism about avoiding these diseases in the future (van der Velde, Hooykaas, & van der Pligt, 1992). Importantly, these aversive events need not happen directly to the person for them to have their effects. People are more cautious about their future health when a friend or family member is undergoing cancer treatment (Blalock, DeVellis, & Afifi, 1990). They are more wary of their future financial situation if they have recently watched an acquaintance lose a substantial amount of money (Helweg-Larsen, 1999).

Given these results, it is easy to propose interventions that would rid people of undue optimism about their ability to control events. These interventions, although conceptually elegant, would unfortunately not be very practical to implement. I doubt many people would favor mugging people to diminish their sense of invulnerability to crime. One would not want to introduce a virus to convince people that they can easily be infected.

However, at times, one can introduce the event without introducing its unfortunate consequence. This, I think, is the principle behind one of the most ingenious health interventions I have ever heard about. In the National Basketball Association (NBA), rookies are called to attend preseason seminars on their new life. They are taught how to handle their finances, talk to reporters, and to cool out unruly fans, among other topics. Often, in the hotel lobby before these sessions begin, attractive and flirtatious women will approach these rookies to arrange a time a few days later to rendezvous. Rookies are then surprised when the women show up at the seminar the next day to explain that they are part of the program and that they are also HIV-positive (Kaufman, 2003).

One note is necessary about this type of intervention. Research suggests that the intervention must be aimed at the specific person's sense of control. Either his or her personal control must be challenged, or that of a loved one. It does no good to present an intervention focusing on the ability of people in general to avoid negative events. In 1984, Tyler and Cook presented Chicago residents with films depicting just how vulnerable people were in their city to crime. People took these films to heart, somewhat. The films caused them to raise their perceptions of how prevalent crime was in society in general, but did not influence at all perceptions of risk for their own personal lives.

## ☐ A Digression About Comparative Judgment

I know that you, gentle reader, possess an inquisitive mind. Indeed, I bet that this is why you have diligently read this book up to this point. Such dedication deserves a reward, and I have one for you. As a psychologist, I am in tune with the type of intellectually curious individual who is likely to read a book on self-insight and, indeed, I knew that you—yes, you—were specifically going to pick up this book and give it a careful read.

Because I knew you were going to acquire this book, I decided to do a little background checking on you. I have searched public records and asked some probing questions of your friends and family. I have even "Googled" everything there is to find out about you on the Internet. From this, I have created a psychological profile designed especially for you, so that you can get some feedback and garner a little personally tailored self-insight.

From my investigations, I have found out the following about you: You pride yourself on being an independent thinker and do not accept others' statements without satisfactory proof. You have found it unwise to be too frank in revealing yourself to others. Even so, you have a great need for other people to like and admire you. At times you are extroverted, affable, and sociable, while at other times you are introverted, wary, or reserved. Disciplined and self-controlled outside, you tend to be worrisome and insecure inside. You have a tendency to be critical of yourself. Some of your aspirations tend to be unrealistic. At times you have serious doubts as to whether you have made the right decision or done the right thing. However, although you have some personality weaknesses, you are generally able to compensate for them. You prefer a certain amount of change and variety, and become dissatisfied when hemmed in by restrictions and limitations. You have a great deal of unused capacity that you have not turned to your advantage.

How could I have such remarkable insight into your psyche? How could I have such detailed, concrete, and specific knowledge of your psychological life? The answer is, of course, that I have none of these things.

The descriptions above were not tailored to you, gentle reader; they were tailored to be true of *anybody*. The traits, feelings, conflicts, and hopes enumerated here are merely those that people tend to believe of themselves. In fact, the meat of my description of you came from a study conducted by Forer in 1949 that I reproduced above with little alteration.

In his study, Forer asked college students to take a battery of psychological tests and then, without looking at them, gave students versions of the previous descriptions, which he claimed were derived directly from the tests. Students evaluated the descriptions for their accuracy and tended to rate them somewhere between *good* and *excellent*. In follow-up studies, researchers have found that people find nonspecific descriptions like the previous ones to be more true of them than they were of people in general (Baillargeon & Danis, 1984; Hampson, Gilmour, & Harris, 1978; Snyder, Shenkel, & Lowery, 1977, although see Greene, 1977; and Harris & Greene, 1984, for contrary evidence). Furthermore, they rate these descriptions as just as insightful about themselves as descriptions actually tailored to the individual based on his or her real responses to real psychological tests (Dies, 1972; Hampson, Gilmour, & Harris, 1978; Harris & Greene, 1984; Merrens & Richards, 1973; O'Dell, 1972).

The fact that such descriptions seem tailored specifically to the individual is a demonstration of the *Barnum effect* (Dickson & Kelly, 1985), named after the famous circus producer who observed that there is a sucker born every minute. Phineas T. Barnum exploited this namesake phenomenon in his own "psychic mind reading" act, in which he would delight his audience by describing audience members to a degree that would astonish them. Barnum was probably not the first person to take advantage of this phenomenon, and he certainly was not the last. So-called psychics, palm readers, handwriting "graphologists," and astrologers still exploit the underlying psychology of the Barnum effect to this day.

Many underlying processes produce generic descriptions that seem molded to fit the individual in a direct and comprehensive manner. First, such descriptions take advantage of ambiguity. They are stuffed full of indistinct phrases that can be defined to fit any individual, such as *unused capacity, self-disciplined, independent thinker*, and so on. As such, all the processes I discussed about ambiguity (e.g., Dunning, Meyerowitz, & Holzberg, 1989) apply to such descriptions.

## ☐ Egocentric Thought

However, I should highlight two other processes that produce unwarranted credence in Barnum descriptions. The first problem is not that such descriptions are applicable to the person reading them. (Indeed, they are designed to be applicable to the reader.) The problem is that readers do not recognize that such descriptions could just as easily describe any other reader. But more than that, the problem is that readers do not think of other people at all.

This chapter focuses on why people tend to believe that they are idiosyncratic, special, or unusual creatures. They often believe this because they fail to recognize that other people often possess the same strengths, suffer the same weaknesses, experience the same feelings, hold the same doubts, and confront the same contradictions as they themselves. They fail to recognize these facts because they simply do not think of other people, even in situations that logically call people to consider other individuals.

For example, let us return to the demonstrations of unrealistic optimism discussed so much at length in this chapter. Recall that people tend to believe that they are more likely to have long-lasting marriages and good-paying jobs than their peers, while being uniquely able to avoid serious illness and injury (e.g., Weinstein, 1980). Although participants in these studies are making comparative judgments of self to peers, they appear to do so thinking exclusively about themselves and not about other people (Klar & Giladi, 1999). In a word, they are being *egocentric*: Their comparisons contain a heavy dose of thinking about themselves but very little, if any, consideration of others. Tellingly, forcing people to consider information about the strengths, plans, and weaknesses of others causes them to curb their unrealistic optimism, albeit only a little (Weinstein, 1980; Weinstein & Lachendro, 1982).

The egocentric nature of supposedly comparative judgments carries many implications. It explains, for example, when people will consider themselves *worse* than their peers. For example, college students tend to think that they are inferior to their peers when it comes to juggling, playing chess, and computer programming. They hold these beliefs because they think egocentrically. They know they are awful at these skills in some absolute sense, but when they compare themselves to their peers they fail to consider that the vast majority of their peers are just as awful. Their comparisons give heavy weight to their own skills and virtually no thought to the likely skill of others (Kruger, 1999).

Such egocentrism holds consequences for behavior. Much of life is a competition with other people—for grades, for jobs, or for promotion. As such, successfully navigating life means being able to anticipate when one is likely to win or when one is at risk for losing. The egocentrism hypothesis suggests that people often make incomplete assessments about competitions, focusing exclusively on their own strengths and weaknesses and neglecting to consider the strengths and weaknesses of others.

Indeed, the egocentrism hypothesis anticipates many of the beliefs people hold about their chances in competitions that, after a little reflection, seem curious. For example, consider a college class in which grades are "curved" (i.e., a student's grade depends solely on how his or her performance compares against everyone else's in the class). Tell students that the final exam will be easy, and students tend to shout for joy, believing that they will achieve a higher grade—neglecting, of course, that the exam is going to be just as easy for everyone else. Tell students instead that the instructor is going to deduct 10 points from everyone's grades, and students glower, thinking their own grade will suffer—forgetting the fact that everyone else is suffering equally (and thus doing nothing to a student's standing and grade in the class) (Windshitl, Kruger, & Simms, 2003).

Egocentrism leads people to reach other curious notions in competition. Ask college students whether they would rather compete with another student on a trivia quiz involving Adam Sandler movies or the history of Mesopotamia, and they overwhelmingly prefer the former. Obviously, they know that questions about Adam Sandler movies are a much easier category for them. What they miss is that the category will also be easier for their opponent, and so their chances of winning are not necessarily any greater. Similarly, students bet more on poker games that contain a lot of wild cards. Such wild cards obviously help the students achieve terrific hands. Of course, those cards have an equal chance of boosting the hands of their opponents, meaning that the presence of wild cards really does nothing to raise comparative odds of their winning (Windshitl, Kruger, & Simms, 2003).

Perhaps the most stunning demonstration of egocentric thinking in competition comes from another trivia contest in which students could compete with either a set of easy questions (e.g., *How many inches in a foot?*) or difficult ones (e.g., *How many verses are there in the Greek national anthem?*), with actual money involved. Students bet more when competing with the easy set of questions than they did with the difficult set, even though their chances of winning were the same in each situation. Of key note, however, was another variation in the trivia contest. Participants all knew that they would be competing against five other students. Roughly half were told that they merely had to beat only one of those five students to win, whereas the other half were told they would have to beat all five other students. Clearly, the odds of winning were higher when students had to beat out only one other individual—indeed, the chance of beating one opponent was 84%, but beating all five was only 16%—but the number of others that the students had to beat had no effect on the size of their bets. Apparently, students were so egocentric that they focused exclusively on the ease of the trivia questions for themselves and ignored any information relevant to other people, such as the number of people that had to be beaten (Moore & Kim, 2003).

# ☐ Observability

Perceptions of uniqueness, however, are fueled even more when this tendency toward egocentrism is coupled with another circumstance. Often information about other people is not readily available. We may be able to see characteristics of others that happen on the "outside" of the person. For example, we can tell when other people are tall or heavy, short or thin, pale or dark. But often the most telling characteristics of the person happen on the "inside," privately and internally. For example, go back to the Barnum description a few pages ago that I purportedly crafted for you. The bulk of that description focuses on the interior life of the individual, the internal attitudes and ideas that we experience within ourselves and that are not really observable on the outside, events such as being reserved, worrisome, having serious doubts, preferring a certain amount of change, priding oneself on being an independent thinker, and having aspirations that are unrealistic.

In essence, the observability, or rather lack thereof, of a characteristic goes a long way toward producing undue beliefs of personal uniqueness. One key to the Barnum effect, for example, is that it focuses on the internal psychic life of the individual, a life that one is well aware of within oneself but never really gets to see so vividly in other people. Just imagine how effective the Barnum effect would be if it concentrated on characteristics that were generally true of everybody but that were also clearly observable, such as *you have two feet with ten toes; you like to eat generally three times a day, but have been known to snack; you prefer to change the clothes you wear more than once a week.*

## Pluralistic Ignorance

The relative accessibility of our own private internal life, coupled with a lack of access to the internal lives of other people, leads to many consequences. Most important, it leads to a state of *pluralistic ignorance*, in that we can come to believe that we hold attitudes and beliefs that differ from other people when those beliefs differ not at all (Allport, 1924; O'Gorman & Garry, 1977). People tend to believe, for example, that they are more *self-critical, hesitant, bashful, choosy,* and *self-conscious* than other people—all characteristics with primarily internal referents. They do not tend to believe that they are more *poised, orderly, aggressive, wordy,* or *sarcastic* than others—traits that have more external referents (Miller & McFarland, 1987).

Most important, the unique access we have to our interior lives leads to beliefs that we are more emotional, prone to doubt, fraught with ambivalence, and governed by inhibitions than are other people. We may think that we uniquely possess a complicated and vexing internal life, but we miss that the interior lives of others are just as intense and profound.

## Emotion

People overestimate the relative force of their interior lives—or rather underestimate its force in others—in many ways. First, they tend to believe that they experience more frequent and deeper emotions than do others. Sabini and colleagues presented college students with hypothetical scenarios and asked how they and others would emotionally respond to them. Students tended to say that they would feel more embarrassment than others if they slipped and fell, covering themselves with their lunchtime salad. They would experience more sadness if they found out they had missed a deadline to apply to a summer internship, anger if their employer fired them after suddenly changing the job description, guilt if they forgot an appointment to meet a friend, jealousy if an attractive person preferred their roommate, and more shame if they had too little money to go out on the town with their friends (Sabini, Cosmas, Siepmann, & Stein, 1999; but see Suls & Wan, 1987, for contradictory results in the realm of fear).

People also think they suffer more discomfort than others. McFarland and Miller (1991) asked college students whether they would prefer to avoid taking part in a study in which they would have to panhandle strangers in a shopping mall or one in which they would view film clips of doctors operating on serious wounds. Students split roughly equally on which study they would like to avoid. When quizzed about their preferences, students stated that they would feel more uncomfortable than the average student if they had to actually take part in the study they preferred to avoid, regardless of which of the two experiments they designated as their least preferred options.

## Uncertainty and Ambivalence

People also believe they feel more uncertainty, doubt, and ambivalence than other people. Quiz college students on campus and one finds that they believe they are more uncomfortable about the drinking habits of their peers than other students tend to be (Prentice & Miller, 1993). They think that they harbor more misgivings about sex without commitment than other students do, including students of the opposite sex (Lambert, Kahn, & Apple, 2003). They believe they have more qualms about smoking and illegal drug abuse than their classmates (Hines, Saris, & Throckmorton-Belzer, 2002). They also state they have more reservations about politically correct attitudes than their peers (Van Boven, 2000). College women assert that they have more objections to the pressure to be thin than their contemporaries do (Sanderson, Darley, & Messinger, 2002).

The feeling that one uniquely holds reservations and doubts shows up in many ways. Ask partisans on either side of the abortion issue, and they tend to have extreme and simplified impressions of what the other side favors. People who are prochoice tend to overestimate how unsympathetic prolife supporters are to women considering an abortion, whereas prolife supporters overestimate how much sympathy prochoice partisans express toward the same individual. Of key importance, abortion partisans also tend to hold overly extreme and simplified impressions about what other people *on their own side* believe. (By the way, in doing so they grossly overestimate the degree to which prolifers and prochoicers disagree with each other.) In effect, people state that others are more extreme and ideologically driven than they themselves are. The net effect of these beliefs is that people tend to believe that they are "lone moderates," individuals who uniquely see the nuanced and complicated middle of the issue (Keltner & Robinson, 1996; Robinson, Keltner, Ward, & Ross, 1995; see Sherman, Nelson, & Ross, 2003, in the realm of affirmative action).

## Inhibition

People also believe they suffer from more inhibitions than others. For example, college students were asked to imagine a scenario in which they met someone who was really attractive, yet failed to ask the person out on a date. When asked to describe why they would fail, respondents stated that they were restrained by a fear of rejection. However, when asked why another person in the same situation would not ask, they stated that the other person probably was not interested in pursuing a romantic relationship. In essence, the same behavior in the self reflected inhibition; for another person it reflected lack of interest (Vorauer & Ratner, 1996).

This study about making the first move—or, rather, failing to make the first move—illustrates a central component of pluralistic ignorance. Because people think they are unique in their feelings and inhibitions, they often draw different lessons about the behavior of others than when they themselves perform the same behavior. Usually, the behavior involved is one of inaction. Our own inaction reveals our inhibitions; the inaction of others just reveals a lack of motivation (Miller & Nelson,

2002). People fail to make the connection that the inhibitions they are feeling—the fears, confusion, or ambivalence—might be just as powerful a determinant of others' behavior as they are for themselves.

Consider one telling example. Miller and McFarland (1987) brought groups of college students into the laboratory and told them they were about to take part in a group discussion about the "self-concept." Before the discussion, however, students were asked to prepare by reading an article on theories of the self. The experimenter explained that she would be in her office while they read the article, and if they had questions they could see her there. Students then turned to the article, which had been deliberately fashioned to be as dense and impenetrable as possible. Although the article defied rational human understanding, no student got up to ask the experimenter about it.

Upon the experimenter's return, she asked students a few questions about the article and the experiment. Students reported that they understood the article less than others in the room, had less knowledge about the self-concept, and anticipated doing worse in the group discussion. Apparently, students had attributed their lack of seeking out the experimenter to fear of embarrassment. For other people, this *exact same inaction* was attributed to an adequate understanding of the article (Miller & McFarland, 1987).

## Consequences

In sum, this asymmetric knowledge of our own interior lives versus the lives of others leads people to believe that they are different, exceptional, or a misfit when such beliefs could not be further from the truth. Thus, it is not surprising that pluralistic ignorance about the internal lives of others can carry some substantial consequences, not all good.

First, pluralistic ignorance can lead people to conform to norms that, in some real sense, do not exist. Prentice and Miller (1993), for example, found that male students tended to shift their drinking attitudes over time to where they thought other students stood. Female students, however, resisted conforming in this way. That said, female students who felt they were discrepant from other women on thinness norms tended to be the ones most likely to show evidence of eating disorders (Sanderson, Darley, & Messinger, 2002).

Pluralistic ignorance can also cause alienation. To the extent that people feel they are "different" from others in their group, they may disengage and withdraw. Evidence for this was found in a survey about a ban on keg beer that Princeton University imposed on its students. For the most part, students were not as upset with this ban as they thought their peers were.

Importantly, those who thought their attitude toward the ban was discrepant from other Princeton students indicated less allegiance to the university, indicating that they would attend a fewer number of class reunions after they graduated from the university (Prentice & Miller, 1993).

## Interventions

How does one prevent these consequences of, on the one hand, conformity to illusory norms and, on the other hand, alienation from people one erroneously believes are different? More importantly, how does one stop some of the costly implications that pluralistic ignorance carries for teenagers or college students, who might decide to smoke, drink, or use drugs because that is what they think everyone else wants to do?

One recent intervention strategy is a simple one and aims at dispelling the effects of pluralistic ignorance by simply informing teenagers or college students about their peers' true attitudes. This *social norm approach* has been applied to alleviating alcohol abuse on college campuses and can be done through newspaper advertising, radio programs, lectures, or by placing posters around the campus. This education can be furthered by bringing students together in workshops or group discussions. Several interventions of this type have been aimed at moderating college drinking, and with some success.

Results, of course, vary across studies and interventions, but some programs of this type have reduced high-risk drinking by as much as 20% (Berkowitz, 1997; DeJong & Langford, 2002; DeJong & Linkenbach, 1999; Haines, 1996, 1998; Haines & Spear, 1996; Perkins, 2002; although this approach is not without its controversial critics, see Wechsler, Nelson, Lee, Seibring, Lewis, & Keeling, 2003). In short, by making students realize that their misgivings about drinking are not out of the ordinary, the worst type of drinking episodes—with attendant costs—are more likely to be avoided. These types of interventions are now being applied to other problem behaviors, such as tobacco use, drug abuse, sexual aggression on the part of men, and eating disorders on the part of women (Berkowitz, 2003; Linkenbach & Perkins, 2003).

## ☐ Concluding Remarks

At age 6, I displayed a unique set of dispositions that predicted what my career would be. Or did I? At age 6, was I really more skeptical than my peers? Was I really more inquisitive? After all, I have known many disbelieving and curious children in my lifetime with a bent for informal scientific investigation. I am reminded of the one who wished to see if foam rubber burns (the answer is *yes*, spectacularly, in a way that will stop the heart of any parent), as well as the one who wanted to see what happens when you poke a water balloon with a needle (it bursts, spectacularly, in your face). Many of these children have as adults gone into non-scientific careers such as investment banking, real estate, construction, bus driving, and the law.

Perhaps I was too quick to believe in my own uniqueness to claim that any special characteristics predisposed me toward science. People are special, to be sure, but at times are just not as special as they might believe. We share more with our peers than we may have insight into.

# In a Word

*The Self-Serving Resolution of Ambiguity*

One problem with the world, and with the task of self-evaluation, is that so much of it is uncertain and ambiguous. We rarely deal with concrete and exact data, but must infer the exact meaning from information that is more vague and indistinct in meaning. Someone tells us we are "pretty good" at public speaking, and we must deconstruct what that person means by "pretty." Does pretty good mean we are more than adequate in all phases of public speaking? Does it mean we should not consider ourselves all that "good" because "pretty" means we have some areas where we need to improve? What exactly does the "pretty" in "pretty good" mean?

In this chapter, I want to make two points about the ambiguity we face in the task of self-evaluation. The first is that vagueness and ambiguity are much more prevalent than we might believe. There is much more that is ambiguous about self-evaluation than just the fuzziness of the feedback we get from the world. Second, people tend to resolve any ambiguity they confront in their own favor. If "pretty good" can mean "just less than outstanding" versus "a tad better than middling," they will more likely conclude that the speaker means the former than the latter.

Recent work illustrates how people tend to resolve uncertainty and ambiguity in their favor. Indeed, one of the royal roads to constructing a pleasant and congenial self-image is the constant exploitation of ambiguity and uncertainty. For example, Hsee (1996) asked college students to take a multiple-choice test on "intuition," with their score determining how much money they could win in a lottery. On the test, students looked at 20 different Chinese characters and, for each, had to guess what its meaning was. Afterward, they were asked to score how well they had done, after being told that the correct answer on the multiple-choice quiz was always "A."

There were, however, two twists. One group, before scoring their exams, was told that only odd-number items would count toward their quiz score. This left little ambiguity about how well they had scored. These students dutifully counted how many times they had answered "A" on odd-numbered items and reported that result. The other group, however, was told that the only 10 items to be scored were those that looked more like the Chinese character *yang* than *yin*. Now, there is some ambiguity here: Different characters can look more yang-like and less yin-like depending on how you look at it. Given this ambiguity, participants took advantage of it and reported significantly higher scores than the first group (see also Hsee, 1995, for similar results).

## ☐ The Vagueness of Traits

The issue of ambiguity, however, becomes even more important and consequential when one turns to the words, concepts, and dimensions by which we judge ourselves and other people. For many traits, such as *intelligence*, *maturity*, and *idealism*, it is difficult to pin down which habits, characteristics, actions, and achievements best reflect them. To be intelligent, is it crucial to be mathematically skilled? Verbally proficient? People savvy? To be a good parent, is it essential to be a strict disciplinarian or to give one's children permission to control their own behavior? To be a good driver, is it more important to drive fast or to cling to caution?

The yin and yang of many such traits are open to interpretation and people do interpret such traits differently. People tend to define traits in self-flattering ways. For example, consider the personality trait of *dominance*. People who consider themselves dominant, once the trait is broken down into its concrete specifics, tend to have a different image in mind than those who do not consider themselves dominant. Self-perceived dominant individuals tend to imagine a person who takes command of the situation after an accident, is committed to many community activities, and settles disputes among group members. In short, self-described dominants tend to have a rather beneficent definition of the trait in mind. People who do not consider themselves dominant have a much more off-putting definition in mind. They tend to think about an individual who monopolizes conversations, orders other people off the phone, and is unwilling to listen to other people's points of view (Dunning & McElwee, 1995).

The self-serving nature of people's definitions of personality traits reveals itself in other ways. For desirable traits, such as *intelligence*, people tend to adopt definitions that flatter themselves, in that they emphasize those habits and achievements that they themselves possess. If people consider themselves good at math, they hold that skill to be more central to intelligence than if they are not mathematically skilled. If people are more intuitive than logical, then they are less likely to consider logical proficiency to be a central component of intelligence (Dunning, Perie, & Story, 1991; see also Beauregard & Dunning, 2001; Greve & Wentura, 2003; and Kunda, 1987).

Of course, people do the reverse when it comes to undesirable traits; they deemphasize whatever habits and attributes they themselves possess. People who do not complain when overcharged in a store, or at times agree that they are wrong even if they believe inside that they are right, tend not to think of these behaviors as *submissive*, although people who would refuse to perform such behaviors think these behaviors indicate the trait. People who visit museums alone, or who would socialize little at a family function, tend not to think of these actions as *aloof*, although people who would never perform these behaviors think that they do reflect aloofness (Beauregard & Dunning, 2001; Dunning, Perie, & Story, 1991).

## Judging Others

If you ask people explicitly to provide concrete definitions of traits, the definitions you are likely to hear are ones that flatter the person you are asking (Beauregard & Dunning, 2001; Dunning & McElwee, 1995; Dunning, Perie, & Story, 1991). But people reveal the self-serving nature of their trait definitions in other ways. Ask them to evaluate another person, and the evaluations they provide tend to show evidence of self-serving trait definitions.

For example, in one study, we asked socially oriented students—those who considered themselves particularly *approachable, persuasive*, and *tactful*—to describe the leadership skills of classic leaders from history, such as George Washington and Mahatma Ghandi. We also asked task-oriented students—who tended to describe themselves as *persistent, competitive*, and *independent*—to do the same. Both groups tended to paint portraits of these leadership heroes that looked a good deal like themselves. Socially oriented students, relative to their task-oriented peers, highlighted people skills in their descriptions of these leaders. Their task-oriented contemporaries, however, were more likely to stress task skills in their portraits of these same heroes (McElwee, Dunning, Tan, & Hollmann, 2001).

Other work affirms that people operate from self-serving definitions when they judge others. People judge other people as *intelligent, outgoing,* and *socially skilled* to the extent that those other people share the same concrete talents and habits as themselves. They judge others as *neurotic, lazy,* and *indecisive* to the extent that those others look different from themselves in the concrete behaviors and features potentially relevant to those traits (Beauregard & Dunning, 2001; Dunning & McElwee, 1995; Dunning, Perie, & Story, 1991).

## Self-Bias

The use of self-serving trait definitions has one central implication. If people judge themselves and others on a specific trait definition tailored to make themselves look good, it is no wonder people on average think of themselves as anything but. If I am an approachable guy, and if I think leaders should possess a healthy measure of this characteristic, then I truly can be above average in my leadership ability relative to other people. If, instead, I am a persistent and competitive individual, and believe that leaders should possess a surfeit of those traits, then I can be truly above average relative to others. (At the very least, I am certainly superior to that approachable guy over there.)

In many studies, we have shown that self-serving refinements of what it means to be *intelligent, idealistic,* or *disciplined* are at the heart of the above-average effect by comparing two classes of traits. One class was broad in nature, in that any of the traits within this class could refer to a large and varied set of behaviors and attributes. One example of such a trait is *sophisticated*, which could refer, for example, to knowing all about foreign films, or the best in wines, or all the classic books, among many, many possible markers. (And if you think these are strange criteria to judge your level of sophistication, just take that as evidence of how ambiguous these traits are.) The other class of traits was narrow in nature, in that each trait in this class referred to a circumscribed number of behaviors. For example, to be punctual means to show up on time, and it is hard (although not impossible—more on that later) to come up with a different definition more in keeping with one's self-esteem.

We asked college students to rate how they compared against their peers along traits that were broad and narrow in nature, as well as desirable and undesirable. For the broad traits, people on average tended to see themselves as anything but average. For desirable traits (e.g., *sophisticated, disciplined, sensible*), people on average saw themselves in the 64th percentile. When the traits were undesirable (e.g., *neurotic, impractical, submissive*), they saw themselves as falling in only the 38th percentile, on average. However, when the traits were narrow, students showed little, if any, distortion in their self-ratings. With positive traits (e.g., *neat, studious, punctual*), students saw themselves as barely above average. With negative traits (e.g., *gossipy, clumsy, wordy*), students on average saw themselves as almost exactly average (Dunning, Meyerowitz, & Holzberg, 1989; for similar findings, see Suls, Lemos, & Stewart, 2002).

In a sense, that last finding—that students did not see themselves as above average on narrow traits—was the key finding of the study. Above-average effects, as chapter 1 attests, are easy to find and simple to document. What is more difficult is finding trait dimensions along which people do not aggrandize themselves, no matter how desirable those traits are to possess. However, we found that when traits were sufficiently narrow in terms of the behaviors they referred to, people's self-ratings showed little or no hint of bias.

Follow-up work affirmed the important role of trait breadth or ambiguity in biased self-judgment. In one such study, we asked people to judge themselves but constrained the habits and accomplishments to which they could refer. For example, we asked college students how *talented* they were but gave some of them only two criteria they could judge themselves on (e.g., *paints, is a good storyteller*). For others, we loosened up the criteria a little bit and gave them two additional criteria they could use (e.g., adding *writes stories, acts*). For yet another group, we gave them two more criteria to consider, for a total of six (e.g., adding *sings, does a craft like pottery*). A fourth group, facing the most ambiguous circumstance of all, were just asked to rate how talented they were without any mention of explicit criteria. As breadth of the trait loosened up, so did people's favorable views of themselves. For desirable traits, people's average self-ratings rose from the 48th percentile in the two-criteria condition to the 52nd percentile in the four-criteria group to the 58th percentile in the six-criteria group to the 59th percentile for the group not constrained by any specific criteria (Dunning, Meyerowitz, & Holzberg, 1989, Study 3).

Most telling was another study in which we constrained students' definitions in a different way. In this study, we asked one group to describe the criteria they used to judge themselves along a certain trait (e.g., *talented*) before they gave self-ratings. We then took the criteria that each student had written down and gave them to a different student and asked this new student to provide self-judgments using only the first student's criteria. In essence, for this second group, we forced them to judge themselves using *another person's* definition of the trait. Not surprisingly, having to use someone else's definition, their own self-ratings plunged by some 12 percentile points and were no longer self-aggrandizing (Dunning, Meyerowitz, & Holzberg, 1989, Study 4).

As an aside: Although we never reported this in the original research report, we were struck by how strenuously students resisted using someone else's trait definitions. We would show students the criteria we were asking them to use, and they would start to complain, often passionately, that the criteria made no sense, did not capture the meaning of the trait at all, or were irrelevant to their own lives. These complaints arose, even though someone else much like them, a college student at an elite institution, had proposed these criteria in good faith. In any event, to quell the complaints, we finally had to ask participants to use the criteria offered no matter how irrelevant or harebrained they thought the criteria were. I took this experience as a lesson on how zealously people adhere to their personal, self-flattering trait definitions.

## ☐ The Genesis of Self-Serving Trait Definitions

Why do people construct idiosyncratic, self-serving definitions of traits? A good deal of evidence suggests they do so exactly because these definitions are self-serving. People build these definitions out of a need to maintain their sense of self-worth. Indeed, there is no more efficient shortcut to thinking of yourself as *smart*, *moral*, and *socially adept* than deciding that you already have the characteristics that define these traits.

A good deal of work shows that people craft their trait definitions in order to put their skills and talents in a good light (Dunning, 1999). In my own lab, we have seen students reevaluate the meaning they assign to traits when it is in their immediate psychic interest to do so. In one such study, we brought groups of students into the lab and told them that we were interested in the psychology of being a therapist. We had already asked professional therapists to play-act how they would handle certain situations in their office and now wanted to see how college students without any professional training would manage in the same situations. As such, one person in the group would be chosen at random to play the role of a therapist mediating a conflict between two other group members, also randomly chosen. Others in the group would just watch and record their impressions of the role-play (Dunning, Leuenberger, & Sherman, 1995). Students were taken to individual cubicles and drew an index card to see what their role would be. Roughly half of the students were assigned to play the therapist; the rest were assigned to be observers.

We presumed that students assigned to play the therapist would feel some psychic pressure to think they could handle the situation. Consequently, they would decide they had what it took to be a successful therapist. Students assigned to be observers would feel no such pressure. To see if this pressure prompted soon-to-be therapists to decide they had what it took, we left students for a few minutes with a questionnaire to fill out. The questionnaire described a successful therapist named Beth and asked students to look over a few characteristics (e.g., *tall*, *did well on the verbal SAT*, *held a college group leadership position*) and rate each one as to how helpful it was to be a competent therapist. Looking at participants' ratings afterward, we found that students assigned to play the therapist rated the characteristics they shared with Beth to be significantly more important than characteristics they did not share with Beth. Students assigned to be observers showed no such tendency.

One follow-up study showed more conclusively that people construct self-serving trait definitions out of a need to maintain their self-esteem. Failure is not a pleasant experience, and it often can cause people to strive to bolster themselves. Thus, we decided to put some college students through a failure experience to see if it would cause them to manufacture a congenial trait definition in an area that had nothing to do with the failure. We confronted college students with a quiz on which virtually no one could do well. Each question on the quiz presented students with a set of three words (e.g., *red*, *kings*, *skunk*) and asked them to identify a fourth word that was related to all three (any guesses?). In all, there were 10 such items, and students were lucky to get one right if any (the answer to the triad above is *cabbage*). Another group of students encountered a much easier version of the quiz that provided no pressure on their self-esteem.

After completing the quiz, students in both the hard and easy conditions were given a filler questionnaire that presented them with an individual who had achieved a long and rewarding marriage. Students were asked to rate which of several characteristics (e.g., *having parents who divorced, being religious, being the oldest child*) were most likely responsible for the long-lasting marriage. In the failure condition, students emphasized those characteristics they themselves had over the ones they did not. In the success condition, no such pattern arose.

However, despite the evidence, I should hasten to add that people may not always construct self-serving trait definitions out of a need to maintain their self-esteem. People can come by their self-serving trait definitions "honestly," without any desire to distort their views to think of themselves as lovable and capable people.

For the most part, as people wander through life they encounter mostly positive feedback about themselves (as was discussed in chapter 4). Because of this, people can reasonably conclude that they have exactly what it takes to succeed. For example, a student who meticulously combs over her lecture notes and course readings five times before an exam, rewriting and reorganizing her note cards on every pass, might conclude that diligence, organization, and hard work are essential to be a good student if she gets a passing grade. Another student, not so inclined to put in the long hours, might approach an exam thinking about what is the one brilliant, "out of the box" idea he can describe in an essay to get full credit. To him, creativity and brashness might seem the qualities vital for academic success.

Each student has ample evidence that he or she has what it takes to succeed in the classroom. What they fail to recognize is that there is more than one way to pass a class. Their own qualities are useful but not the essential ones for achieving success. Other people can achieve similar success by a variety of other routes. However, there is no way we can expect our two students, or any of us, to recognize this fact unless we have a chance to live in another person's skin, follow their strategies, and witness their successes.

In our laboratory, we have found that success prompts people to believe that their own idiosyncratic skills are the ones necessary for achievement. In one such study, we gave students a test that supposedly evaluated their "clinical diagnosis" skills. They were given 20 pairs of suicide notes. In each pair, one note was real and the other fake. Students were asked to pick the real note in each pair. We then told roughly half the students that they had done quite well on the task. Others were told that their performance fell just barely above chance. This feedback had the predicted effect. When later asked to describe their image of the competent clinical diagnostician, successful participants were more likely to describe someone who shared their skills and personal characteristics. Participants experiencing failure were significantly less likely to do so (Story & Dunning, 1998).

A follow-up study demonstrated the same process in an actual classroom. Students in an introductory psychology class were asked at the beginning of the semester to rate the importance of 40 different habits (e.g., reading each textbook chapter twice) for getting a good grade in the class. They also described whether they followed these habits in their other classes. After their first exam, students were again approached and asked to rate this series of habits. Students getting an A or a B in the class became more self-serving in their portrait of the good student, finding their own habits to be increasingly more crucial toward achieving academic success, relative to those who got a D or an F.

# ☐ Vertical Versus Horizontal Ambiguity

So far, I have been describing ambiguity in a way that can be construed as "horizontal" in nature. All the criteria relevant to *leadership*, for example, can be laid out in front of the individual, and that individual can pick and choose which criteria he or she will highlight in his or her definition of the trait. However, once those criteria are selected, one could imagine that the issue of ambiguity is over. The trait has been concretely specified and there is no more wiggle room for people to redefine what they mean.

One might think that, but even after concrete criteria for judgment are selected there is still is a good deal of ambiguity left for people to exploit in self-serving ways. In particular, they can exploit what I would term *vertical ambiguity*. Let me illustrate vertical ambiguity by focusing on a trait that, for a college student, has only a little horizontal ambiguity: studiousness. Studiousness really has only one concrete criterion to judge it: the number of hours per week that the student typically hits the books. But this is where vertical ambiguity comes in. Although it is true that hours per week is an obviously relevant indicator of studiousness, just how many hours every week does a student have to study to qualify as a studious scholar? Five hours? Twenty? Sixty? Just how far up this performance criterion does a student have to go?

In our lab, we have found a good deal of evidence that people take advantage of vertical ambiguity in their social judgments. When asked how much a student must study to meet the requirements of "studiousness," those who hit the books only a few hours a day cite a much lower number than their counterparts who spend several hours a day at their desks. The same holds true in a number of trait domains (Dunning, 2000; Dunning & Cohen, 1992; Dunning & Hayes, 1996). In essence, people low on the performance criterion cite a low standard so that they can claim to have the trait. Those high up on the performance criterion name a much more stringent standard so that they can be in a more exclusive club.

The exploitation of vertical ambiguity also reveals itself in judgments of other people. Low performers, adopting a lax standard, tend to judge everyone else rather positively, regardless of the performance of those other people. In one study, low performers in athletics judged a person engaged in athletics only an hour a week just a tad less athletic than one who spent five hours a week in fitness activities, or in turn was just a tad less athletic than someone who devoted 15 hours to athletic pursuits. Regardless of their performance level, all three individuals were judged to be quite athletic. High performers were much harsher in their judgments. The 15-hour devotee was seen as athletic, but the 5-hour person was judged to be neither athletic nor nonathletic. The 1-hour person was judged quite unfit (Dunning & Cohen, 1992).

Other work shows that people raise and lower their performance standards to maintain positive images of themselves. Alicke and colleagues asked college students to take a quiz. Although the students did okay on the quiz, there was always another student in the room (actually, a plant by the experimenters) who outperformed them. Students handled this uncomplimentary situation by describing the other student as quite intelligent. Indeed, they were more likely to describe this other student as more of a *genius* than did other college students who merely observed this other student take the quiz. Apparently, by extolling the genius of this other individual, these outperformed college students could leave with their self-perceptions of intelligence intact. Consistent with this view, college students who were given a chance to rate the other student's intelligence walked away from the experiment viewing themselves as more intelligent than did students not given such a chance (Alicke, LoShiavo, Zerbst, & Zhang, 1997).

Work in our lab shows more conclusively that people take advantage of vertical ambiguity out of a need to maintain self-esteem. In one such experiment, we had college students succeed or fail on the "integrative orientation" test described previously. Then we asked participants to rate the intelligence of Chris, another student who had achieved a score of 1320 on his combined SATs, while they waited to take another version of the integrative orientation test. After failure, students were quite self-serving in their judgments of intelligence. Students with low SATs rated Chris as rather intelligent, presumably as a way to claim intelligence for their own. Students with high SAT scores rated Chris rather unintelligent, thus denying him entrance into their exclusive intellectual club. After success, with the need for self-esteem under little pressure, no such pattern emerged. All students, high and low SAT scores alike, rated Chris as rather intelligent (Beauregard & Dunning, 1998; see also Dunning & Beauregard, 2000).

# ☐ Consequences

The existence of trait ambiguity suggests two major issues that are fundamental to accuracy and error in self-evaluation. The first issue is that trait ambiguity might imply that people are really not all that biased when too many of them say they are above average. After all, if Jerry bases his definition of *intelligence* mostly on the specific and distinct skills that he possesses, then he very well is above average relative to other people. If George bases his definition of *intelligence* on a different set of intellectual gifts, one he just happens to possess, then he, too, can be above average. In short, people's claims of competence may be accurate under their own individual definition of the trait.

However, there is a major caveat to this argument. People might be correct in their self-evaluation under their own definition, but they are not right under all plausible and relevant definitions of a trait. And for people to be completely accurate in their self-judgments, they would have to be aware of that fact. They would have to know that their self-evaluation is relevant only under their own peculiar characterization of the trait, but that all bets are off once one steps outside that specific definition.

However, in our work, we have not found that people are necessarily aware of alternative definitions of traits. If they are aware of those alternatives, they do not consider them legitimate. Remember our troubles, described earlier, when we asked students to judge themselves using someone else's trait definition (Dunning, Meyerowitz, & Holzberg, 1989, Study 4)? If people could easily see that their perspective on a trait is only one of many possible, those objections to our instructions should not have taken place.

In any event, the issue of accuracy is not the important one when considering trait ambiguity. Even if one concedes that people provide accurate judgments under their own unique definitions of traits, the existence of trait ambiguity still sets in motion the potential for much social mischief. Specifically, trait ambiguity can lead to much disagreement and social disharmony.

People tend to disagree in their judgments of each other to the extent that they are dealing with ambiguous traits. In Hayes and Dunning (1997), we asked college roommates to describe themselves and each other, looking to see how much people's impressions of themselves would match what their roommate thought of them. The degree of agreement we found depended on the breadth or ambiguity of the trait under discussion. When the trait was quite broad in potential meaning (e.g., *eccentric*) agreement was much lower than when it was narrow (e.g, *religious*).

More to the point, in a follow-up study we asked roommates to specify their definitions of traits before providing judgments (Hayes & Dunning, 1997, Study 2). When roommates were forced to use the same definition (e.g., Bud and Lou were both forced to use Bud's definition of *generous*), their judgments agreed more with each other than when each person used his or her own personal definition. A more recent study has replicated this finding, showing that two people judging a common acquaintance agree more in their assessments if forced to use the same definition rather than their own private one (Story, 2003).

This disagreement can lead to overconfidence and interpersonal rancor. Imagine a business office where four middle managers know that there is a promotion coming down the pike. Paul, using definition *leadership*$_{Paul}$, may think that he's the most qualified for the promotion. John, using definition *leadership*$_{John}$, may think he's the most logical candidate. George, under *leadership*$_{George}$, may in his head have already spent the raise. Even Ringo, consulting *leadership*$_{Ringo}$, might think he has an outside chance. Because only one person can be promoted, three others are going to be surprised, disappointed, and perhaps even angry. Those three may not know why the fourth received the promotion or, worse yet, may think they know why (e.g., *I am a victim of office politics—again!*), which may damage group cohesion, allegiance to the firm, and office productivity. In essence, because we live in a world in which we are not sealed off from other people's trait definitions, using only our definition of the trait in the prediction of future outcomes may lead to overconfidence, disillusionment, and interpersonal acrimony.

# ☐ Concluding Remarks

But an even larger issue lurks behind the existence of trait ambiguity in self-evaluation. People have firm views of themselves. They may think they are intellectually gifted or perhaps intellectually challenged. They may think of themselves as charismatic leaders or perhaps as submissive chumps. They may think they have what it takes to succeed as a novelist or professional musician. And people hold these beliefs so firmly that they tend to act on them (e.g., Ehrlinger & Dunning, 2003).

But here's the rub: How can people have such confident views of themselves in the face of trait ambiguity? Trait ambiguity suggests that there is no sure way to assess who is competent and who is not. There is no set of sure-fire behavioral criteria that one can point to that would perfectly and precisely measure how much leadership ability, social skill, or morality a person possesses. To be sure, this is not an issue in all trait domains. I believe I could get a handle on a person's mathematical ability by constructing a test that started with questions on addition and ended with problems on structured, finitely generated abelian groups. But other trait domains defy such easy measurement. How am I to measure a person's charisma in a way that satisfies everybody? Or whether he or she is sensible, creative, or idealistic? Because these qualities are so ambiguous, it is difficult to construct a test that would measure them in a Platonically pure fashion.

This issue has been noted before. It is easy, for example, to measure a medical student's technical knowledge on such matters as diabetes or asthma. But how does one come up with a cheap, efficient, and accurate measure of a medical student's communication skills or professionalism (Ward, Gruppen, & Regehr, 2002)? These are important qualities, but they are intrinsically difficult to assess. One could presume that one could measure professionalism by asking experts, such as the medical students' supervisors, but there are some problems with this. First, supervisors are not in a position to watch their charges every minute of the day, and so their evaluations can be error-prone and unreliable (Ward et al.). Second, if supervisors use their own idiosyncratic definition of professionalism to judge their students, they may provide judgments that miss the student's strengths. Indeed, it has been shown that supervisors tend to emphasize technical skill over social skills in their evaluations of students, relative to what students give weight to (Ward et al.).

In any event, the key issue that trait ambiguity opens up is how people come to hold such certain views of themselves when those skills turn out to be intrinsically difficult to evaluate. In a sense, the most normative answer people can give when asked to judge themselves along an ambiguous dimension is to refuse to answer, citing the trouble with coming up with a concrete and well-defined set of measures that most, if not all, people would accept as valid.

But people tend not to refuse. Instead, they are inclined to have a firm idea of themselves even in circumstances in which, upon reflection, no confident view of the self is really possible, at least to the usually precise, observable, and quantifiable standards associated with science. In some sense, this is the real mystery of self-evaluation. How can people believe they know themselves when trait ambiguity suggests that traits themselves are not knowable?

# The Merest Decency

*False Impressions of Moral Superiority*

On September 11, 2001, two jets slammed into the twin towers of New York City's World Trade Center, bringing down the fifth and sixth tallest buildings in the world, extinguishing nearly three thousand lives, and introducing the United States to the new dynamic of the twenty-first century.

On this day of unprecedented horror, the world witnessed the extremes, for better or worse, of human character. The world saw countless acts of individual selflessness—of off-duty firefighters rushing to the scene of unimaginable tragedy, of office workers helping others out of the crippled buildings only to die themselves as those buildings collapsed, of construction workers digging for days through precarious piles of rubble in a frantic search for survivors (Gibbs, 2001). But the world also witnessed reprehensible acts of moral depravity. On the day of the attack, 92 people phoned in bomb threats to the police in New York City (Time.com, 2001). When police rushed back to the scene after the collapse, they arrested a looter with fire department boots on his feet (Gibbs). In a district where four burglaries had been committed the year before, 76 were reported within 2 months (WNBC.com, 2001).

Few people had the ill fortune of being in lower Manhattan on that fateful day, and thus most of us do not know how we would have reacted to these extraordinary events. Would we have acted with bravery and heroism, or would our actions been shaped by selfishness and insensitivity? On this day in which there was no script to follow, no role models to guide, how would we have reacted? If we were completely free to write whatever tale of our moral character we wished to, what story would we have written?

This chapter focuses on the tales people believe they would write about their moral character. When a choice can be made between a selfless and a selfish act, what choice do people believe they would make and how does that choice match up against their actual behavior? Do people have an accurate understanding of their moral character, knowing when they will act in altruistic, ethical, or generous ways? Can they accurately pinpoint their moral failings, knowing when they will succumb to the temptations of greed, pleasure, convenience, and self-interest?

## ☐ The Moral Pedestal

The basic theme of this chapter is that people tend to place themselves on a pedestal of moral superiority, thinking their moral character is far superior to that of other people. For example, when Williams College students were surveyed about their ethics, a full 80% said they would refuse to copy answers from someone else's exam, but that only 56% of other Williams College students would similarly refuse. A full 74% said they would give back extra change mistakenly given to them by a store clerk, but that only 46% of their peers would do likewise. Such vaulted views of superiority also extended to impressions of generosity and sacrifice. Of respondents, 51% said they would share their pizza with a hungry student, but that only 36% of their contemporaries would. Almost all, 90%, said they would help someone else change a flat tire, but that a mere 34% of other Williams students would do the same (Goethals, 1986; see Goethals, Messick, & Allison, 1991; Liebrand, Messick, & Wolters, 1986; and Messick, Bloom, Boldizar, & Samuelson, 1985, for similar results).

Indeed, of all of the ways that people tend to hold themselves as superior to others, moral superiority seems to be one of the strongest and most pervasive forms of the effect. People are more willing to claim moral superiority, for example, than they are intellectual advantage. Allison, Messick, and Goethals (1989) asked college students to write down some "good" and "bad" behaviors they had done as well as some intelligent and unintelligent ones. They were also asked to write down similar actions that they had seen other people do. Not surprisingly, participants reported more good behaviors for themselves than they did for other people, as well as fewer bad behaviors for themselves than others. This air of moral superiority did not extend to the intellectual. Participants wrote down equal numbers of intelligent and unintelligent behaviors for oneself and others.

Van Lange (1991) replicated this basic finding in an experiment in which he asked participants to write a story about an episode in which they had influenced another person, as well as one in which another person had influenced them. Participants afterward tended to rate their own influential behavior as more "fair" than the behavior that someone else had done, although they were not more likely to claim that their behavior was particularly intelligent.

Why is an air of moral superiority more prevalent than one of intellectual supremacy? There are three separate answers.

## Moral Behavior Is Desirable

First, morality is just more desirable and salient in our social worlds than intelligence is—and people do like to claim personality traits to the extent that they are desirable. In 1968, Anderson took 555 personality traits and asked participants to rate them on their desirability. Morality-related traits elicited the strongest reactions, certainly more than traits related to intellectual competence. Of the traits rated the most positive, five of the first 10 unambiguously refer to moral behaviors (*sincere* at #1, with *honest, loyal, truthful, trustworthy,* and *dependable* all on the list). Only *intelligence*, on the intellectual side, sneaks into the top 10. On the bottom, a full nine of the bottom 10 involve morality-related issues (*liar, phony, mean, cruel, dishonest, untruthful, malicious, dishonorable,* and *deceitful* making the list; *obnoxious* is the only interloper). The first unambiguously intellectual term, *incompetent,* does not appear until 54 more places up the list. There is some evidence that people claim to be more moral (or more specifically, honest) exactly because they view that characteristic to be more desirable than intelligence (Van Lange & Sedikides, 1998).

Other work affirms the central and salient place that moral assessments play in social judgment. When learning about others, people are more interested in information about morality than about competence. Moral information predicts a person's overall impression of another individual, and whether that impression will be a favorable one (Wojciszke, Bazinska & Jaworski, 1998). People are quicker to make moral judgments than competence-related judgments when receiving negative information about another person (Bazinska & Wojciszke, 1996). When judging political figures, questions of morality dominate over those of competence (Wojciszke & Klusek, 1996).

## Moral Behavior Is Controllable

Second, morality is more an issue of choice and control than intelligence is, and people tend to possess an illusory sense of control over their behavior (Alicke, 1985). Not telling a lie is not a matter of competence, but rather one of choosing to resist the temptation. In contrast, solving a set of simultaneous equations does not really involve choice and control (well, actually, it does; one can choose instead to pick up the remote to see what is on television) as much as it does mathematical competence than one either has or does not have. Because moral behaviors center exactly on choice and control, people are much more likely to inflate their sense that they would do the right thing.

## Moral Behavior Is Ambiguous

Third, what constitutes moral behavior is more ambiguous than what constitutes sound intellectual performance. Because of this ambiguity, people are freer to define morality in terms of what they do (Dunning, Meyerowitz, & Holzberg, 1989). For example, getting a 90 on a trigonometry test unambiguously reflects more math skill than getting a 0 (although see chapter 6 for some qualifications of this assertion concerning vertical ambiguity). But is giving a $20 bill to a homeless person on the street more moral than giving nothing? One can argue, as has been done on many a street corner as well as the houses of Congress, that it is wiser and more compassionate to give nothing, to force the homeless person or the government to do something about the person's plight. Similarly, should a doctor tell a patient about a terrible terminal illness? What is the moral choice? Telling certainly satisfies the tenets of honesty, but does it serve the principle of compassion? Whichever choice a physician makes, he or she can claim a moral higher ground.

# ☐ A Vexing Ambiguity

All this material, however, disguises a vexing ambiguity for any scholar trying to understand why people possess such airs of moral superiority. As the Goethals (1986) data directly suggest, the typical person tends to think that he or she is more likely to adhere to the just and honorable path than other people are, a statistical impossibility. But this discrepancy might be caused by two very different errors that suggest very different psychologies.

The first potential error is that people might have an accurate grasp of their moral fiber but might underestimate the moral character of their peers. Their mistake is to be overly cynical about other people, and systematically underrate how often other people will act in a kind, generous, and ethical manner. This would suggest that biases toward moral superiority are not a problem in self-insight, but rather of social insight. People somehow acquire erroneous intuitions about how their peers would behave, and the research psychologist needs to discover where and why those intuitions err.

The second potential error is that people actually have their peers right but misjudge themselves, overrating their own moral tendencies and the kindness of their heart. This would suggest that undue perceptions of moral superiority are a problem in self-insight, and the research psychologist would have to examine how potential problems in self-judgment come into play.

## Which Error Is It?

In 2000, Nick Epley and I published a series of studies to try to gain some understanding of this theoretical and empirical Necker cube about self-perceptions of moral superiority. We knew from past research (e.g., Goethals, 1986) that people predicted that they would perform altruistic and ethical behaviors more frequently than their peers—but which set of predictions, self or peer, were the right ones and which the wrong? Thus, across several studies, we presented participants with a number of hypothetical situations with moral or altruistic overtones and asked them how they would behave, as well as how their peers would act.

Of course, we expected that people would predict their behavior would be more honorable and benevolent than that of their peers. That would not be news. What would be news would be the results of a second step, in which we later confronted participants with the actual situation to observe their real behavior or, alternatively, confronted an equivalent group of participants with that real situation. Would self-predictions better predict what people actually did, with predictions of others proving too skeptical? Or would peer predictions prove to be accurate, locating the moral superiority error in overly charitable views of self? Of course, we were prepared for the possibility that perceptions of moral superiority might arise from both types of error, in whatever proportion.

## Basic Findings

After the studies were conducted, we discovered that we had a clear and simple bottom line. Only one error was responsible for undue views of moral superiority. For example, in one study we asked Cornell University students to consider an annual charity drive that took place on campus just as the usually cold winter of Ithaca, New York, grudgingly gave way to a slightly warmer spring. Fraternity brothers would go out to the street corners on campus and hawk daffodils, one for a dollar, with the proceeds going to the American Cancer Society.

Five weeks before one annual edition of "Daffodils Days," we surveyed the students in a 250-person course about how many daffodils they would buy. We also asked them to predict how many daffodils the typical student in the course would buy (Epley & Dunning, 2000, Study 1). Not surprisingly, respondents made more complimentary predictions about themselves than they did about their peers. A full 83% said they would buy at least one daffodil, but that only 56% of the students in the room would do likewise. On average, respondents said they would buy two flowers, but that their peers would buy only 1.5.

But which set of predictions, self or social ones, were accurate? We waited 5 weeks (making sure to buy daffodils ourselves) and surveyed the class again. Only 43% of the students had actually bought a daffodil, and the average purchase was 1.2 flowers—figures that were closer to what respondents had predicted for their classmates than what they had expected of themselves.

In another study, we brought students into the lab and paid them $5 to spend about 20 minutes filling out questionnaires (Epley & Dunning, 2000, Study 3). For roughly half the participants, we asked them to make a prediction about how they and others would respond to a hypothetical opportunity to donate any or all of their fee to any one of three charities: the Salvation Army, the American Red Cross, or the Society for the Prevention of Cruelty to Animals. Informational brochures about each charity were given to participants just in case they were not familiar with the organizations. Participants were asked if they would donate anything, how much they would donate, and to whom they would donate. They were also asked what percentage of other students would donate, as well as how much (factoring in those who donated nothing).

Students, again, provided morally superior predictions. Every single student said that he or she would donate at least some of their fee, and that their typical donation would be $2.44. They expected only 51% of their peers to donate, and that the typical donation would only be $1.83.

But, again, what set of predictions was right? To assess this, the other half of participants were asked to donate for real. They were left with the same brochures, as well as an envelope in which they could leave their donation privately and indicate where it should go. As in the Daffodil Days study, these actual donations reflected more what participants had predicted about their peers than what they had claimed for themselves. Roughly 61% of participants left a donation, and the average amount donated was $1.53—close to the rate predicted for peers but far below that predicted for self.

## Sensitivity to Moral Principles Versus Self-Interest

One additional follow-up study was more complicated and was aimed at examining whether people had an accurate view of the situational influences that shape their behavior versus that of their peers. We reasoned that if people place themselves on a high moral pedestal, then they should believe that their behavior would be influenced more by situational changes that feature moral principles rather than those involving self-interest. In contrast, they would believe that others, compared with themselves, would be more sensitive to self-interest rather than the moral nature of the situation.

We brought one set of participants into the lab and presented them with four hypothetical situations. All four scenarios shared the same basic setup: Participants had been paired with an experimental partner who was in another room. Participants had seen a photograph of their experimental partner, who for some participants was a typical looking college-age guy wearing a sweatshirt, baseball cap, and a sullen, bored air.

Halfway through the experiment, participants were asked to make a decision about which of two tasks they would like to do next, thereby assigning the experimental partner to do the task that was rejected. In one scenario, the two tasks were similar, but one took 5 minutes longer to complete. Of key interest was whether participants predicted that they would be selfless (taking the slightly longer experiment for themselves) or selfish (choosing the shorter experiment) in their choice, as well as what they thought other students would typically do.

From this basic setup, we influenced the degree to which the situation invoked moral concerns or self-interest. To manipulate self-interest, we described the longer experiment as difficult and more time-consuming in a second hypothetical scenario. Indeed, it was 25 minutes longer than the shorter task. Participants again predicted which experiment they and their peers would choose.

The last two variations involved the arousal of moral concerns. In one, participants considered a choice between two experimental tasks that differed only 5 minutes in their length, with their partner again completing the task that they rejected. Who that partner was, however, changed. Instead of a typical college-aged man, their partner was a 10-year-old girl with an angelic face and a smile informed only by innocence. In the fourth variation, the little girl again served as the experimental partner, but the choice of tasks was between a short one and the more arduous one that would take 25 minutes longer to complete.

With these four variations, we could see how much participants thought they would be influenced by self-interest (whether the longer experiment meant a small sacrifice of 5 minutes versus a larger one of 25) and by moral concerns (whether the partner was a sullen guy or a 10-year-old girl). We could also see how much participants thought their peers would be influenced by the same situational variations.

As seen in Figure 7.1, participants described themselves as more sensitive, moral creatures than they did for their fellow students. When asked how the specified situational variations would influence their behavior, participants said they would not be influenced by self-interest. Whether the altruistic change involved a sacrifice of 5 or 25 minutes would not matter. Instead, they stated they would only be influenced by moral concerns, as denoted by the fact that they would be roughly 35% more likely to choose the longer experiment when their partner was a little girl rather than when the partner was a college student. Their peers, however, would not be so saintly, being only 15% more likely to choose selflessly when the partner was a little girl rather than a college student. Instead, their peers would be influenced by self-interest, being 15% less likely to choose altruistically when the sacrifice was represented as 25 minutes rather than 5.

But which of these predictions better mirrored reality? To assess this, we had an additional group of participants face a real choice, with each confronting one of the four scenarios described previously. As seen in Figure 7.1, when the choice was real, the only factor that influenced behavior was self-interest. When participants faced a potential 25-minute sacrifice, they were almost 40% less likely to choose the longer experiment than when the sacrifice was only 5 minutes. Whether their experimental partner was a college student or a girl had no impact whatsoever on their decisions.

## ☐ Why Wrong About the Self?

Taken together, these findings suggest that people harbor a mistaken sense of moral superiority because of a deficit in self-insight. The rather favorable views they hold about their moral fiber are not justified by the concrete actions they take. What is behind this error? Why is it that people hold these flawed views of their moral temperament?

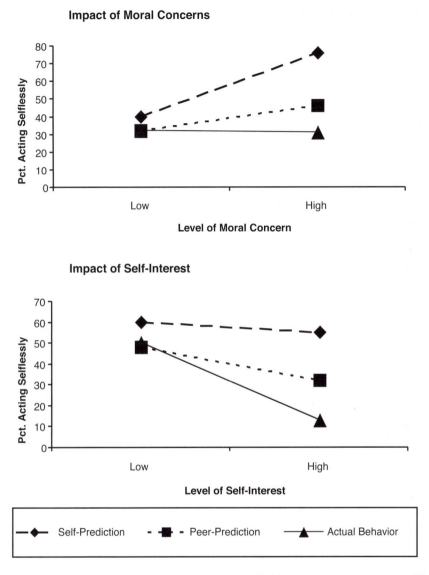

**FIGURE 7.1.**  Predicted impact of moral and self-interest concerns on self- and peer-behavior compared against actual impact (from Epley & Dunning, 2000, Study 4).

# A Surprising Competence

To understand why people hold these erroneous self-impressions, one must first explain an equally surprising competence. Across our studies, participants did a decent job of predicting how their peers on average would react. Their predictions were not perfect, but they did anticipate how often their peers would choose the altruistic option over the self-centered one to a roughly accurate degree.

Past research indirectly provides an answer for this competence. People appear to automatically encode the frequency of events, even when there is no reason to do so. In one demonstration, Hasher and Chromiak (1977) presented participants with a long list of words, with some of the words appearing up to five times on the list. Half the participants were explicitly told beforehand to take note of the frequency of words; half were not. After reading the list, participants were asked to report how many times each word had appeared. Participants' estimates were remarkably accurate, even among those not instructed to pay attention to frequency (see Hasher & Zacks, 1984; Hasher, Zacks, Rose, & Sanft, 1987; and Zacks, Hasher, & Sanft, 1982, for similar findings and discussion).

If people automatically encode the frequency of a variety of events, this leads them to be rather accurate about the prevalence of events in the social realm, including rather important ones involving moral behavior. Nisbett and Kunda (1985) asked a number of University of Michigan undergraduates to estimate the frequency of a number of attitudes, preferences, and behaviors among their peers. Respondents were asked to estimate, for example, what percentage of their peers attended religious services, went to concerts, and played tennis. They were also asked, for example, to report the general shape of their peers' attitudes toward abortion, increased defense spending, and MacDonald's hamburgers. Although there were some biases, respondents' estimates in the main were remarkably accurate.

In short, people seem to have imperfect but rather useful information that they bring to bear in their predictions of others. Given this, the most informative question about self-prediction is not why people are so wrong about themselves but why people fail to apply the wisdom they use in social prediction to self-prediction. What is missing in self-prediction that produces greater accuracy in the prediction of others?

# Internal Versus External Approaches to Prediction

To identify what is missing, one first must consider two very different strategies people might adopt as they try to predict the deeds of a particular individual. The usual strategy people tend to adopt is an *internal* strategy (Kahneman & Tverksy, 1979a). That is, they try to gather "case-based" information about the specific individual and situation in question. For example, let's say I was trying to predict whether Benjamin, a 19-year-old who just proposed to his girlfriend Margaret, is likely to make it to the marriage altar. The internal approach would be to try to gather information about Ben (e.g., does he look google-eyed at Marge, does he fight often with her, is he impulsive) as well as the situation he is in (e.g., do his parents approve, is Marge impulsive). From this information, I would then spin narratives to see which outcome, a happy wedding or an unfortunate breakup, seemed most probable.

This strategy seems so natural that it is difficult to imagine an alternative, but there is one. The *external* approach to prediction (Kahneman & Tversky, 1979) involves looking away from internal workings of the person at hand to gather data about how similar people in comparable circumstances tend to act. In Ben's case, it would involve asking how often do engagements between 19-year-olds make it to the wedding altar? Is it a rare occurrence or a common one? This approach to prediction relies heavily on *distributional* information, data about the raw prevalence of an event without knowing the first scrap of case-based information about the person at hand. For example, if you asked me if 16-year-old Eddie is going to pass his first driver's test, I would predict that he would, even before knowing anything about Eddie's driving skills. Passing the driving test is a frequent event, and so I can be fairly confident that Eddie will do adequately. However, I would not predict that Eddie would make it on the U.S. Olympic bobsledding team. This is a rare event, particularly for a 16-year-old.

Successful prediction depends on properly combining an internal approach with an external one, blending case-based and distributional information in a proper mixture. That said, a bevy of research suggests that people do not blend these two types of information well. People show a strong preference, and often an exclusive one, for basing their predictions on case-based information, thus underweighting or even ignoring useful and diagnostic distributional information (Dawes, 1988; Dunning, Griffin, Milojkovic, & Ross, 1990; Kahneman & Lovallo, 1991; Kahneman & Tversky, 1973, 1979a, 1982; Klayman & Schoemaker, 1993; Nisbett & Ross, 1980; Read, 1987; Zukier, 1986). Often, this preference for case-based information arises even though it demonstrably degrades the accuracy of people's predictions (Dunning, Griffin, Milojkovic, & Ross, 1990; Vallone, Griffin, Lin, & Ross, 1990).

## The Neglect of Distributional Information

In our experiments, we affirmed the observation that people tend to have pretty good distributional intuitions about the prevalence of altruistic and selfish behavior in their peer group. They could guess, within reason, the percentage of their peers who would act in a generous and ethical way. And if we asked about a random person for whom they had no specific (or case-based) information, they could fall back on these rather accurate distributional intuitions and give a good guess about how the person would behave.

The problem began when we asked them about a person—namely, themselves—for whom they had truckloads of case-based information. As soon as they were asked about themselves, thoughts (both valid and diagnostic) about the distribution of these behaviors disappeared from their minds and they began to make their predictions based on inflated case-specific beliefs they had about their own moral urges.

Other research, not in the moral domain, has shown how people ignore useful distributional information to make self-predictions that later turn out to be wrong. When faced with projects that they need to complete, people consistently underestimate how much time they will take to complete it, a phenomenon known as the *planning fallacy*. Students misjudge how long they will take to finish their term papers. Taxpayers underestimate how much time it will take them to finish their tax returns. Apartment dwellers fail to anticipate how long it will take to finish cleaning up their place (Buehler, Griffin, & MacDonald, 1997; Buehler, Griffin, & Ross, 1994; Newby-Clark, Ross, Buehler, Koehler, & Griffin, 2000). People consistently commit this planning fallacy even though they have firm knowledge of distributional information indicating that people tend to take much longer to complete a project than they anticipate. They commit this fallacy even though they have distributional knowledge from *their own lives* that they typically fail to complete projects as soon as they hope or expect to (Buehler et al., 1994).

Buehler and colleagues (Buehler et al., 1994) connected the emergence of the planning fallacy to a near-total preference for case-specific information over distributional information when making predictions. In one of their experiments, participants were asked to predict when they would finish a school project that was due within the next 2 weeks. They were then asked to describe how they had made their predictions. Students mostly dwelled on case-based information: 71% discussed their plans for getting this specific project done, and 15% mentioned the deadline they were under. They did not regularly mention anything approaching distributional information, drawn either from their observations of other people in similar circumstances (only 1% mentioned the experiences of other people) or of themselves (6% mentioned past successes and only 1% mentioned past failures in getting projects done). In a later study, forcing participants to pay attention to distributional information coming from their own lives prompted them to make predictions that largely avoided the planning fallacy.

## Application to Moral Prediction

In our own work on moral behavior, we discovered that the same neglect of distributional information led to the inflated predictions people make about their own moral behavior. In one study, we asked participants to consider the donation study I described earlier. We presented them with the same hypothetical scenario we had used and asked them how much of their $5 fee they would have donated if they had been in the experiment, as well as how much they thought the typical student would have donated. Again, participants on average tended to see that they would have given significantly more (something north of $2.75) than their peers would have ($2.20). But then we revealed how much three randomly selected participants from the original study had donated and asked them to predict again. We then showed them data from another four participants, asked them to predict again, and then finally showed them how much all 13 participants had donated and asked for a final set of predictions.

We found that this distributional information led to more accurate predictions—but only for predictions of other people. As we revealed more information, predictions of how much other students would donate went from $2.20 to $1.66, quite close to the $1.53 our original participants had actually donated. Self-predictions, however, were not influenced in the slightest by this distributional information. Participants thought they would donate more than $2.75 at the beginning, and they still thought the same thing after seeing how other people had responded to the situation.

A final experiment more closely tied overly inflated predictions of moral behavior to the neglect of useful distributional information. Like the study just described, this experiment required participants to predict how much they and a randomly chosen Cornell student, one they knew nothing about, would donate, after finding out how much three, seven, or all 13 individuals had responded in the original experiment. Like before, this distributional information affected predictions of the random person, with those predictions becoming progressively more accurate with greater information. Self-predictions, on the other hand, remained unmoved and inflated.

But, of key interest, participants also predicted the behavior of a person for which they had a little bit of case-based information. Each participant was given a sheet of paper in which some other individual had listed five words that described him or her, as well as a short essay detailing who him or her were. Armed with this rather minimal case-based information, participants tended to predict that this other person would donate just as much as they would themselves. And predictions of this person remained unaffected as participants gained more distributional information about the donations of participants in the original study.

## Accentuating the Positive a Little Too Much

This is not the only tendency that prompts self-predictions to be less accurate than predictions of other people. People do not treat the case-based information they have about themselves in an even-handed way. Instead, they focus on favorable information and disregard the negative. For example, when college students in a study predicted when they would finish a computer assignment, 93% focused on their plans for completing it, but only 10% focused on potential obstacles. As part of the procedure of this experiment, participants had written down their thoughts about completing the assignment, as well as their memories of past successes and failures when facing comparable assignments. When other students were given this information and asked to make a prediction, only 34% dwelled on future plans and a full 37% focused on possible obstacles. Not surprisingly, the predictions of this second set of participants were much more pessimistic than the original participants' self-predictions (Buehler et al., 1994).

In addition, when participants are explicitly asked to write down best-case, worst-case, and most realistic scenarios about completing some project, their most realistic estimates more closely resemble best-case estimates than worst-case ones. Writing down a worst-case scenario has little or no impact on their own task-completion estimates, although looking at someone else's worst-case scenario causes them to be more pessimistic about that person's plans (Newby-Clark et al., 2000).

In short, when predicting their own behavior, people appear to put the best spin they can on the information they have, something they will not do when it comes time to predict other people's actions. We have seen this habit in our own data. We asked college students in romantic relationships to predict whether they would still be involved in the relationship six months later (Epley & Dunning, 2004). Although 73% of participants thought their relationship would last, only 55% did.

Of key interest, however, was that all participants rated their relationship along some relevant traits (e.g., *honest, trusting, compatible*) and reported how much time they spent with their beloved, how many arguments they tended to have, and what activity they enjoyed doing most together. When this information was given to a second set of participants, who were told to look it over objectively, they predicted that 55% of the relationships would last—a figure that almost exactly matched the reality. However, when another group of participants were given this information and told to interpret it in the most optimistic light possible, they predicted that 75% of the relationships would last, a figure that almost exactly matched the undue optimism of the original respondents.

## Long-Term Sources of Error

More long-term processes may also play a role in diminished self-accuracy. Each of us has a long history of interactions with other people, and in that history we have the opportunity to count and catalogue the moral and immoral actions that other people commit. In doing so, we may acquire rather accurate intuitions about how responsive other people are to selfish and selfless influences. Presumably, we could do the same cataloguing for our own behavior, only we have a few problems in doing so.

These problems are best exemplified by the plight of Eduard Wirths, a German doctor known for his successful battles against typhus as well as his research on cervical cancer. Those under his care described him as polite, kind, and honest. Those supervising him described him as conscientious and dutiful. Dr. Wirths's problem, however, was that he was the chief SS medical officer at Auschwitz, responsible in part for selecting Jewish inmates to be executed by Zyklon-B gas. In his spare time, he would further his research by injecting acids and other corrosives into the cervixes of female prisoners. Clearly, Dr. Wirths was party to one of the most brutal atrocities committed in human history, but Dr. Wirths did not see it this way. In several of the letters he wrote during his work, he construed his actions as strengthening Germany's future for his beloved family and children. He considered himself doing "God's work" because he had saved so many Auschwitz inmates from the ravages of typhus (Lifton, 1986).

Dr. Wirtz's predicament was extreme, but it illustrates an issue that all of us face more benignly in our everyday life. Although it is easy for us to "see" others commit immoral acts, to be added to our intuitive account books on human nature, it is difficult for us to see our own immoral acts. Gazing at these acts, our eyes are often wrapped in a gauze of excuses, rationalizations, and self-serving attributions. For example, we may claim that our questionable actions are actually righteous ones, or at least not morally objectionable. We may claim that swerving our car close to a wayward pedestrian is meant to teach him to watch where he is going. Yelling at telemarketers is in their self-interest, in that it saves time so that marketers make calls to people who are really interested.

Even if we are forced to concede the blameworthy nature of our actions, we can still point to how our actions were coerced by outside circumstances. We yelled at a colleague because he had insulted us first. We lied to a coworker because her request was illegitimate. And despite these mitigating circumstances, we may still feel remorse over our actions, clear evidence of our sensitivity to moral issues. When people describe times in which they have transgressed against another, their accounts dwell on these rationalizations more than when they describe occasions in which they suffered transgressions at the hand of another person (Baumeister, Stillwell, & Wotman, 1990; Hansen, 1987; Laumann, Gagnon, Michael, & Michaels, 1994).

Regardless of the goodness or badness of their actions, people also believe that their intentions count more than other people observing them. Kruger and Gilovich (2004) asked college students to hold their hands in ice-chilled water for as long as they could for a charitable cause. Before doing so, they were asked how long they intended to hold their hand in the water. Anyone who has casually tried to do this task knows that it gets horribly painful within seconds. Thus, it was not a surprise that the length of time people held their hand in the water failed to match their intentions. Participants were subsequently asked how "altruistic" their effort had been. Participants gave weight to both their intentions and their actual performance when deciding how altruistic they had been. Even if participants took their hand out quickly, the fact that they *intended* to keep their hand in a long time was evidence of how altruistic they were. People watching participants gave those intentions no weight in their judgments of altruism by that person, leading them to view participants as less altruistic relative to how the participants viewed themselves.

To be sure, these rationalizations may be legitimate and at other times they may not. Their presence, however, can leave us with a self-impression that we are rather responsive creatures when it comes to the moral pressures of a situation. We do the right thing. However, when we fail, it is because of an extreme circumstance. Further yet, if we plan to do a charitable act and fail to meet our expectations, at least our intentions count. And when we commit an unambiguous offense, we take pains to be dismayed and penitent.

If these are the lessons people learn from their lives, it is not surprising that participants in the Epley and Dunning (2000) surveys thought of themselves as morally superior to their peers when they walked into our laboratory. Their "count" of their own moral behavior had been tainted by countless rationalizations taking place over their 18 to 22 years of life before they ever volunteered for our experiment. Naturally, those excuses led to misestimates of how they would act in the future, even though their experience had given them an accurate, untainted account of how other people behave, leading to more correct predictions of peers.

Other long-term processes can leave people with a mistaken impression of moral superiority. At times, we see immoral behavior on the part of others, but there's a catch—the behavior actually is not immoral. Consider teasing. People commonly tease each other, but it appears that people who are teased misunderstand the intentions of the person doing the teasing. Often, teasing is done in a spirit of affection and playfulness (Keltner, Capps, Kring, Young, & Heerey, 2001; Keltner, Young, Heerey, Oemig, & Monarch, 1998; Shapiro, Baumeister, & Kessler, 1991), and teasers attempt to convey these intentions through subtle nonverbal cues (Drew, 1987; Shapiro et al., 1991). However, those who are being teased tend to miss these benign aims. Roommates describing teasing incidents tend to differ in their accounts. When they describe a time they teased their roommate, people tend to describe the action as more humorous and lighthearted than does the person being teased, who instead rates such incidents as more malicious and annoying. The good intentions of teasers are just not as obvious as teasers believe (Kruger, Gordon, & Kuban, in press).

## ☐ What Good Is Self-Knowledge?

At this point, the reader might be tempted to ask the radical question of whether self-knowledge has any worth at all. If the storehouse of knowledge we all have about our little personal triumphs and failures, plans and goals, desires and fears leads us astray in anticipating our future actions, what good is it?

Up to now in this chapter, I have described how self-knowledge is a detriment to anticipating our future actions, but I should now temper that portrait somewhat. It is not that self-knowledge is completely misleading. It does lead to accurate self-prediction at least under one criterion.

In the work described earlier, when I described self-predictions as being in error, I have focused on the *mean level* of those predictions. I compared the average level at which people predicted moral behavior and compared it against the mean level of that actual behavior. Typically, people overestimate the mean level of their altruism and generosity. However, accuracy can also be measured in terms of *discrimination*, that is, the way that one person's behavior differs from another's. In the previous studies, some people bought a daffodil and some did not; some insisted that the little girl complete the short experiment, whereas others claimed that task for themselves. Could participants' self-predictions anticipate these differences, even if they were getting the mean level wrong?

Nick Epley and I decided to see if people's self-predictions did supply some discriminative accuracy. We asked people whether they would perform desirable behaviors, again expecting people to overestimate the likelihood that they would, and examined whether these predictions could discriminate between those who performed the desirable behavior versus those who did not. More specifically, when a person said he or she would perform a desirable action, was he or she, indeed, more likely to perform it than someone who said he or she would do the opposite?

To begin, we asked eligible college students whether they would vote in the 2000 presidential election about 4 weeks before the polls opened (Epley & Dunning, 2004). A full 85% said they would vote, but that only 57% of their peers would. After the polls were closed, we again contacted the students and found that 64% had voted, a result echoing the original Epley and Dunning (2000) studies. Self-predictions, however, showed some discriminative accuracy. A full 69% of participants who said they would vote actually did so, but only 32% who said they would not did the same.

A follow-up study asked students whether their current romantic relationship would last another six months (Epley & Dunning, 2004). Participants as usual tended to be overconfident, with 85% of them saying that their relationship would last when only 64% actually did. In a pattern that should seem familiar, when participants instead predicted whether some random couple would stay together, the predicted rate was 62%. But, again, self-predictions showed some discrimination. Of those predicting romantic stability, 72% still were in the same romantic relationship half a year later. Of those predicting dissolution, only 25% remained in the relationship.

As such, self-predictions do carry some worth, in that they help to discriminate those who do one thing versus those who will do the opposite. That said, it does not take much "self-knowledge" to achieve the levels of discriminative accuracy our respondents demonstrated. In another condition of the romantic prediction study, we gave participants some information about another person's romantic circumstance, namely five words plus a short paragraph that the person felt best "exemplified" the relationship. Participants given this scant information were just as accurate predicting the stability of that person's relationship as was the person actually in the relationship (74% accurate versus 73% accuracy rate for self-predictions). Interestingly, these peer predictions revealed no real hint of optimistic bias (68% predicted the other person to have a stable relationship versus an actual rate of 64%). Follow-up studies affirmed this pattern: Those given just a little information about another person tended to be as accurate as the person's self-predictions—but without the overall optimistic bias so evident in self-predictions (Epley & Dunning, 2004).

# ☐ Consequences of Illusory Perceptions of Moral Superiority

In the eyes of many world religions, it is a problem when people place themselves too high on a moral pedestal. People are to be reminded at all times that they are sinners, and that redemption can be achieved only by painstaking efforts to lead a virtuous life. If people mistakenly believe that a life of virtue comes easily to them, it can only lead to sinful indulgence and transgression, leading to ultimate damnation.

But are unwarranted perceptions of moral superiority a problem? Do these perceptions carry harmful consequences, or are they perhaps beneficial? What are the consequences of moral superiority for the individual believing in it, and for the society he or she lives in? Social psychological research suggests a complicated picture of consequences. There is both bad and good news when it comes to undue beliefs in moral superiority.

## Attributional Consequences

First, the bad news. If people overbelieve that they will act honorably when their character is tested, it may lead them to judge too extremely those whose moral character has actually been tested. People judge others based on what they believe they would have done in a given situation. Alicke (1993), for example, asked respondents how blameworthy they viewed a person who found a good deal of money in an unmarked paper bag and then decided to keep it rather than take it to the police. Those who said that they would return the money blamed the person much more than those who said they would keep it. Similar reactions were found for many different scenarios. Those thinking that they would choose righteously, relative to those saying they would not, judged a person more harshly when that person cheated on their taxes, shot a prowler, cheated on their spouse, and handed over a wallet to a thief.

If people harbor undue impressions of their moral superiority, this might lead them to make overly extreme, and wrong, inferences about other people. In one study, a student of mine decided to examine this possibility (Balcetis, 2003). She asked respondents to predict how they would respond to a situation charged with altruistic overtones and then to report what inferences they would make about people acting selflessly and selfishly in that situation. A few weeks later, we confronted respondents with the actual situation, thinking that their real behavior would fail to match their estimates, and again asked them to report what they thought of those who had acted altruistically or not. We expected that respondents would report more muted, cautious, and accurate inferences about others after experiencing the situation themselves and finding that they failed to act as righteously as they thought they would.

In the study, we again turned to the Daffodil Days event held at Cornell University (Balcetis, 2003). Roughly a month before the event, we asked about 90 Cornell students whether they would buy a flower in the charity event. Roughly 83% said they would, but that only 43% of their peers would do likewise. We next asked them to report what they thought of the typical student who bought a daffodil versus one who did not. Respondents were given a series of vignettes involving charity (e.g., volunteering to help out a roommate with a classroom skit) and asked how likely a person buying a daffodil and one who did not would perform these charitable behaviors. Not surprisingly, respondents thought that daffodil buyers would act much more charitably than those not buying a flower. In a second questionnaire, participants were asked to guess the political attitudes of those buying a daffodil versus those who did not. Respondents thought that daffodil buyers would be much more liberal (e.g. lobbying to increase taxes in a developed country to pay for refugee care) than those not buying a flower.

We then waited for the event to take place and returned to our respondents shortly after. Only 24% had actually bought a daffodil. We again asked respondents to report the likely generous behaviors of people buying daffodils versus those who did not, using the same scenarios as before. This time, respondents were much more muted in their inferences of flower buyers versus nonbuyers. Looking at estimates of political attitudes, they were also more accurate in the inferences they were willing to draw. When participants were asked to estimate the attitudes of daffodil buyers and nonbuyers, respondents refused to perceive any difference—which was exactly right. In our own examination of the political attitudes of those who actually bought a flower versus those who did not, we found no difference whatsoever.

## Behavioral Consequences

Now the good news. People err when they overassert their honorable, ethical, giving, and kind natures. But, then again, would you prefer that people made the opposite error? Would you prefer to live in a world in which people too quickly professed themselves to be dishonest, conniving, self-centered jerks? I know I would not, because I know of one true fact of human nature. Although they do so imperfectly, people do at least strive to live up (or down) to the expectations and labels they apply to themselves. Calling oneself moral impels one to act in a decent and honorable manner.

Examples of this influence are easily found in psychological literature. Once people form an expectation of themselves, they tend to act on that expectation. Sherman (1980) called residents in the Bloomington, Indiana, area and asked them, hypothetically, how they would respond to a request from the American Cancer Society (ACS) to donate three hours of their time helping to raise money. The caller took pains to explain that she was just conducting a survey from the psychology department, that she had no link to the ACS, but that the ACS was, indeed, contacting people in the area. A full 48% of respondents said that, if called, they would donate their time. However, of a comparable group of people called on the phone and given an actual request, only 4% complied. Again, the expectations people held of themselves far outstripped the actual altruism of a comparable group of individuals.

However, three days later, the group that had predicted their behavior was contacted again by a different experimenter who described herself as a representative of the ACS. Given a real request to donate time, 31% volunteered to do so, a rate of altruism far higher than the 4% of the group contacted without making a prediction first. In essence, once articulated, people's rather favorable expectations of themselves become more likely to emerge in reality.

Not an isolated incident, researchers have discovered that asking people whether they would perform a desirable behavior prompts them to perform that behavior with more frequency than they would without a prediction. Asking people whether they will vote increases turnout (Greenwald, Carnot, Beach, & Young, 1987). Asking also increases recycling behavior (Sprott, Spangenberg, & Perkins, 1999), trips to a health club (Spangenberg, 1997), and donations from alumni to their alma mater (Obermiller & Spangengerg, 2000). It also decreases the likelihood that a student will cheat on a classroom test (Spangenberg & Obermiller, 1996). These boosts in desirable behavior occur even when respondents make their predictions in complete anonymity (e.g., Spangenberg, 1997; Spangenberg & Obermiller, 1996). The rise also occurs regardless of whether people remember their prediction at the time they choose to behave in a desirable way (Sprott, Spangenberg, & Fisher, 2003).

People also respond to the labels placed upon them by outside agents. Suppose that you wanted to convince elementary school children not to litter, how best to persuade them? Should you convince them of the importance of tidiness? Or might you just make sure to *label* them as tidy?

Miller, Brickman, and Bolen (1975) produced data suggesting that the latter technique was the most effective. In their study, they compared two classrooms of fifth-graders in the Chicago area. In each classroom, they began their investigation by giving students a specially marked reading assignment that was to be thrown away at the end of class. Despite the instruction to throw away the assignment, very few students did so (around 20% in each classroom).

Next, in one classroom, the researchers attempted to make the students tidier by convincing them of the importance of neatness. The teacher gave a lecture on pollution and the ecology. The teacher, during a lunchtime session, also talked about how garbage drew flies and endangered everyone's health. The school principal visited the classroom and extolled the need for clean classrooms. A poster was placed in the classroom scolding kids not to be litterbugs. All these persuasive efforts worked, to an extent. One day, just before recess, students were given a piece of candy in colored cellophane to eat. More than 40% of the children threw the cellophane away before leaving for recess.

In a second classroom, the researchers took a different approach, labeling the kids as neat and tidy. The teacher commended the children on being ecologically minded. The janitor passed a note to the class thanking them for being the neatest class in the school. The principal made the same point on a brief visit to the class. The teacher lectured the class on the ecology, noting all the ways the class was helping. One day, the teacher noticed paper on the floor and explained that a visiting class had left it, remarking that her class would never litter like that. This intervention produced much more dramatic results on the day that children were given a piece of candy to eat before recess. More than 80% of children threw away the cellophane wrapper before going outside.

Other work affirms the notion that labeling people as kind and generous increases their prosocial behavior. Telling fourth-graders that they were particularly generous in giving another student a piece of gum prompts them to be more likely to repeat the act at a later date (Holte, Jamruszka, Gustafson, Beaman, & Camp, 1984). Giving college undergraduates a personality test, and then telling them that they scored unusually high on kindness and thoughtfulness, increases the likelihood that they will help another student who dropped some index cards, relative to students told instead that they were intelligent or that kindness was important (Strenta & DeJong, 1981).

In sum, this work suggests that when people label themselves as kind and generous people, or when others do the labeling, they are more likely to act in desirable, prosocial ways. In effect, undue self-views of morality can lead to profound benefits—for those believing in their morality as well as for those surrounding them. It is because of this that I am gratified to know that the readers of this book are some of the most open-minded, thoughtful, and considerate individuals one is ever likely to encounter.

Overclaiming moral superiority can prompt socially desirable behavior through a more indirect route. Individuals do not live alone but are surrounded by untold numbers of other people, such as colleagues, family members, acquaintances, authority figures, and underlings. As psychologists, anthropologists, and sociologists have long noted, the presence of these other people constrains our behavior greatly, especially through the establishment of social norms (Cialdini, Reno, & Kallgren, 1990; Hirschi, 1969; Reckless, 1961; Schanck, 1932). Because of the norm against stealing, we do not do it. Because of the norm against aggression, we only rarely punch out the next person who angers us.

Overclaiming moral superiority might add to norms that promote prosocial behavior and diminish antisocial actions. When people claim for themselves a sterling moral character and go out of their way to reproach those who fail to act morally, they strengthen a social norm of desirable behavior that impels others to act in an ethical and altruistic way, despite the private temptations that people would rather act upon. People may privately wish to cheat on their taxes, their spouse, or on the job, but might be put off from doing so because they are aware that other people would deny they would ever do it themselves and would judge harshly anyone who did.

This, in a sense, is the converse of the observations made by Matza (1964) among juvenile delinquents. He found that teenage gang members privately expressed misgivings about their antisocial behavior but would never express these reservations to their peers. They watched other gang members assert their commitment to the antisocial customs that the gang adhered to (when, in fact, those gang members actually had doubts) and decided their own actions had to live up to these norms, thus leading the gang to more ambitious antisocial exploits. One might wonder if, at times, the rest of us are subject to this type of spiral, but one that works, fortunately, in a virtuous direction. On occasion, we may privately wish to morally transgress in any number of ways, but when we look at others we see them enthusiastically proclaiming their commitment to a strong moral code. Because of this, we choose not to act on our less than admirable impulses. Because we choose to act morally, the behavior of others is further constrained in a righteous direction.

# ☐ Concluding Remarks

In early 2000, through strange circumstances I found myself on a radio talk show chatting with a politically conservative host. Finding out about my work, the host began to grill me mercilessly on how Bill Clinton could have succumbed to the charms of White House intern Monica Lewinsky, thus triggering the impeachment proceedings that crippled the second term of his presidency. Along the way, the host shot off into a long disquisition about how he would never, ever have fallen prey to the temptations of infidelity. As he talked, I began to struggle with whether I should bring up the data I had about what people believe about their moral fortitude versus the reality. The data were as yet unpublished, and so I resisted the temptation to explain to the talk show host that, not having been in the situation, he really could not know how he would have acted.

But I presume any words on my part would have been inconsequential. People tend to believe fervently in their moral superiority and, in doing so, fail to learn perhaps the single most important lesson they can learn about themselves. That lesson is that the behavior of other people is a valuable indicator of how we would react in the same situation. If another person fails in a situation, it is a good indication that we run a substantial risk of failing similarly. We should prepare ourselves accordingly.

But, as this chapter has suggested, this is not a lesson that people typically learn. People tend to construe themselves as special, as unique, as more invulnerable to the situational pressures that cause others to act selfishly and unethically. As Goethe, the German poet, observed, "self-knowledge comes from knowing other men," but this is an observation we often do not take advantage of. Perhaps this is not surprising. As the anthropologist Clifton Geertz once observed, one of the most difficult tasks bedeviling self-perception is to see ourselves as no more than "a local example of the forms human life has locally taken, a case among cases."

That all said, as the discussion in this chapter suggests, at least in terms of morality, the stance of seeing ourselves as no better than others could be useful and diagnostic. Indeed, I also could argue that seeing ourselves as no more ethical and altruistic than others is also the morally correct thing to do. As Clifton Geertz also wisely observed, to see others as sharing a nature with ourselves is simply "the merest decency."

# CHAPTER 8

# Beyond One's Self

*Why Accurate Self-Prediction Involves Insight
into Situational Circumstances*

I sometimes wonder what it would be like to be standing just outside the village of Namche in the crisp and arid air of Nepal, staring up at the mountain that the locals refer to as Sagarmatha, the goddess of the sky. Rising over 29,000 feet (or 8,000 meters), the mountain fascinated the British when they first came to the Indian subcontinent. At first, they designated it as Peak XV, later giving it the name Everest, as it is better known today. Today, the fascination with Mt. Everest continues unabated, with hundreds of mountaineers every year attempting to climb its ice and rock to reach the roof of the world, the highest point on Earth.

But one fact remains clear for those attempting the summit. To scale Everest, climbers had better have an accurate idea of what exact situation they are getting themselves into. They have to understand that on the day they try the summit, they will have to awaken early in the morning, if they have had any sleep at all, to walk the last 3,000 vertical feet to the summit. They will be cold; they will be hungry. They have to know that, at that elevation, that the atmosphere contains only a third of the oxygen of sea level, and that even with supplemental oxygen their cognitive functions will be dramatically impaired. They have to know, too, that winds can reach hurricane force, and that the wind chill can drop to −150 degrees Fahrenheit. Not only do they have to know those facts but they have to know how quickly exposed skin freezes at such wind chills (within seconds), and just how cold that wind chill *feels* hour after hour as they walk ever so slowly and carefully for the several hours necessary to reach the summit.

# ☐ The Importance of Getting the Situation Right

Sometimes, knowing yourself and what you are capable of is not about understanding your own character at all. Rather, it is about understanding the relevant situation. Can you stay on that diet? The answer may not depend on some notion of your willpower, but rather on how strong the pangs of hunger escalate and envelop every moment of your consciousness as you forego food. If you underestimate how strongly your body will be screaming to you to eat, you will overestimate your ability to stick to the diet. Can you take on that high-pressured investment banking job? That depends on a number of factors, such as what exactly you'll be doing on a moment-by-moment basis. Will you be working on clear-cut contracts that involve a minimum of cognitive stamina, or will you be dealing with confusing contracts and difficult people coming at you on an hourly basis? And how many hours each day will you have to work, really, and how many hours a week will you be allowed to sleep?

In sum, to the extent that people mistakenly predict or fail to take into account the specific features of the situations they might confront, their expectations about their behavior will fall prey to error. Take, as an example, students from the last chapter who overpredicted the likelihood that they would buy a daffodil on a street corner for charity (Epley & Dunning, 2000). Perhaps when they made their prediction, they imagined a situation conducive to buying a daffodil. They imagined a bright sunny day, with lots of time before their next class, and many free coins jingling in their pockets. And, given these circumstances, they very well might have bought daffodils at the rate they predicted. However, when the day to buy a daffodil arrived, the situation might have been a far different one. They might have found themselves scurrying late for class through bone-chilling rain with only maybe enough money to buy a vending machine KitKat bar for breakfast. To the extent that students failed to anticipate these less-than-optimal circumstances, they would overrate the chance that they would buy a daffodil.

The key point is not that people mistakenly predict situations, although they might on a frequent basis. The key point is that the specifics of situations are just simply unpredictable. One cannot know what the weather will be like when the daffodil day charity drive begins. One cannot know how much money will be in one's pocket. One cannot know how preoccupied with other business one will be. One cannot know if the daffodil sellers will be approachable. What people fail to do is to take all this uncertainty into account when they make predictions. As a consequence, their predictions are overconfident.

## Misconstruing the Situation

Much research shows that people are skilled at filling in presumed details of situations, often without even knowing that they are doing it. They fill in gaps in description, or resolve any ambiguities, to arrive at a plausible and coherent model of the situation they are considering. In a word, they *construe* what they think the event will look like. Indeed, such filling in of the unknown is often essential for understanding the social world (Griffin & Ross, 1991). Almost all descriptions of any event or situation presented to us are incomplete or ambiguous. For example, consider the following headline on a leaflet advertising an event on the Yale University campus a few years ago: *Panel Tonight on Sex with Four Professors*. Although the ambiguity in that announcement is rather obvious, the usual ambiguities we face tend to be more subtle and nuanced.

And those ambiguities tend to be ubiquitous, meaning that people must become quite skilled at filling in unspecified details and resolving uncertainties. Because we acquire so much practice at filling in these details, we become quite quick at it, and filling in details becomes an automatic, reflexive response that we are not aware we are doing. For example, if I mention that *Some thought the politician's statements were untrue*, many will assume without knowing it that I am saying that the politician is lying. Note I did not specifically say that; the politician might simply have been mistaken, which is what people are more likely to assume if the sentence is about a physicist. Similarly, if I mention that *The nun was upset about the amount of liquor being served at the party*, many readers will presume that the nun wants to do away with the liquor, although if you look carefully at the sentence, I did not exactly say that. The nun might be upset because there is too *little* liquor, as some presume when I replace the nun in the sentence with a rock star (Dunning & Sherman, 1997).

In 1990, Dale Griffin, Lee Ross, and I published a paper showing that people make predictions based on these assumptions of situational details. We presented participants with simple and familiar scenarios, such as going up to San Francisco to celebrate the end of the academic term, and asked them for a pointed prediction, such as how many dollars they would spend on dinner during that night on the town. After making this prediction, we asked participants to express their confidence in each prediction by placing a "range" around their prediction. For example, if a person said she would spend $14 on dinner, we asked her to name a range around that figure such that "the correct answer would be as likely to fall in that range as it would outside," with errors equally likely to fall too high or too low. Obviously, small ranges (e.g., $12 to $16) meant that participants felt they had a confident notion of how much they would spend. Broad ranges (e.g., $5 to $50) meant that they harbored more uncertainty about what they would actually spend (Griffin, Dunning, & Ross, 1990).

After making such predictions and providing their "confidence ranges," participants were asked to review their predictions under four different conditions. In the first condition, a control condition, they were simply asked to reconsider their predictions and ranges. This request prompted very few changes in prediction or confidence ranges. Indeed, the range participants placed around their predictions constricted by only 5%. In a second condition, participants were asked to reconsider their predictions after writing down the details of each scenario as they envisioned them. Much like the control condition, this request led to few changes in prediction or confidence (ranges inflated by a mere 3%), presumably because participants had already thought of these details the first time around (Griffin, Dunning, & Ross, 1990).

The third and fourth conditions were the most telling. In the third, participants again were asked to write down the details of each scenario as they had imagined them and were told to make a new set of predictions *assuming that these details were exactly how these scenarios would unfold.* When making a second set of predictions, participants again provided mostly the same prediction at the same level of confidence (their ranges constricted by only 3%), giving evidence that not only had participants the first time around filled in these details but had also assumed that these details were perfectly true.

The fourth condition, however, proved to be the one that changed participants' thoughts. In that condition, participants were asked to report the details of how they had imagined the scenarios, but then were asked to imagine how the scenarios might unfold differently. Next, when asked to reconsider their predictions, they were reminded that the situation might unfold the way they first described it, it might unfold in any of the alternative ways they described, or it might unfold even differently from that. Given this admonition, participants endorsed their predictions with much less confidence, inflating the ranges they placed around their predictions by some 38% (Griffin, Dunning, & Ross, 1990).

# "Underconstruing" the Situation

Other research reveals different ways in which getting a situation wrong can lead to mistaken predictions and overconfidence. At times, people may mistakenly predict because they fill in the details of a situation incorrectly, but sometimes they might mistakenly predict instead because they fill in the details incompletely. They "underconstrue" the event. They base their predictions on a few salient, high-order features of a situation and ignore the fact that their behavior might depend on more lower-level, concrete, or incidental details.

This is especially true when people consider behaviors far in the future (Liberman & Trope, 1998; Trope & Liberman, 2000, 2003). When considering far-off situations, people tend to make predictions based on a cursory consideration of a few abstract and central features of that situation, giving relatively little weight to more concrete details, even if those details are known and influential. As the situation approaches, predictions begin to give more weight to those crucial concrete details. For example, if someone approaches me to ask if I can hold a celebratory dinner for a colleague some six months hence, I focus on the pure joy of holding such a dinner and commit myself to it. Little do I pay attention to the fact, as I will the night before the dinner, of a million nasty little details that I should be able to anticipate: that the house is dirty and must be cleaned, the refrigerator is full and must be emptied, and all this food must be bought, but I forgot to figure out how many vegetarians might be coming. I might have come to a different answer about my ability, and willingness, to hold such a dinner if I had thought about these details originally.

For example, students taking a social psychology course at Tel Aviv University were given a choice between two different assignments, each taking a week to complete. The first assignment centered on an enticing topic, such as the stages of romantic love, but the details of the assignment made it difficult, in that the assignment required reading some papers in English, which was not the students' native language. The second assignment centered on a more mundane topic, such as defining the "attitude" concept, but the concrete details were easier, involving some readings in Hebrew, the students' native language (Liberman & Trope, 1998).

When the assignment was nine weeks off, students based their choices on the more central and abstract feature of what the assignment was about, thus preferring the assignments with more alluring topics, giving little weight to concrete details signaling the difficulty of the assignment. However, when the assignment was only one week off, participants reversed themselves, giving weight to the concrete details of the assignment and preferring the easy ones on more mundane topics (Liberman & Trope, 1998).

People also "underconstrue" situations in other ways. Each year, thousands if not millions of U.S. citizens vow to mail in their tax forms well ahead of the April 15 deadline. They feel confident in this pledge, thinking through the details involved in getting the tax return done. They consider how much time it will take to gather up all the relevant receipts, print out the relevant forms off the Web, find and turn on the calculator, and sharpen all their pencils. These details are central to the goal of completing a tax return, and people appropriately consider all of them when they make predictions.

If these goal-relevant steps were the only details relevant to finishing one's taxes, people would probably fulfill their pledges and file their tax return well ahead of the deadline. However, one does not file a tax return in a vacuum. Life has a sneaky habit of interceding, and many other events take place that have nothing to do with the goal of finishing a tax return but have everything to do with hampering one's ability to do so. Sick kids must be tended to. The leak in the bathroom must be fixed. The report that the boss unexpectedly asked for must be completed, *schnell*! The snow blower needs a new belt. The parents-in-law drop in for a visit. These events have nothing to do with filing a tax return; they can conspire to delay finishing off the return until one, once again, is cursing the IRS Web site on the evening of April 14th in a desperate attempt to download the form requesting a filing extension.

In short, people mistakenly predict their future behaviors because they prove guilty of the *focusing illusion* (Schkade & Kahneman, 1998) or *focalism* (Wilson, Wheatley, Meyers, Gilbert, & Axsom, 2000). When predicting their behavior, they concentrate on the steps or situational details that are central to achieving some goal but fail to take into account the details of life that are irrelevant to the goal but that will inevitably interfere.

Focalism has best been documented in people's affective reactions to events that befall them. When university students are asked about how happy they will be if their football team wins, as well as how miserable they will be if the team loses, they tend to overpredict the intensity and duration of their feelings (Wilson, Wheatley, Meyers, Gilbert, & Axsom, 2000). However, if they are first asked to fill out a diary of their likely activities in the days after the game, they provide less extreme and more accurate predictions of their emotional well-being. In effect, reminding students that after the game they will still have to go to classes, study, meet up with friends, and go out on dates alerts them to the fact that the football game is only one event out of many that will influence their daily mood.

Similarly, in predicting the emotional influences of events, people tend to latch onto and overemphasize salient and unique features that define a situation and underemphasize important features not unique to a situation. Survey Midwesterners and Californians, and they will both tell you that Californians tend to be more satisfied with life than Midwesterners—and why not, given all that sunshine and warm temperatures on the left coast (Schkade & Kahneman, 1998). To be sure, Californians are more satisfied with their weather than Midwesterners, but this difference does not translate into an increased satisfaction with life in general.

Why do people predict a difference in overall satisfaction when none actually exists? The error people make in comparing California with the Midwest is that people give great weight to the features unique to California but fail to consider the impact of features that this location shares with most others. One's satisfaction with life does, in part, depend on the weather, but it is also influenced by traffic jams, irritating coworkers, and the growth rate of one's credit card balance, as well as the warm laugh of one's 5-year-old child and a good martini shared with even better friends. People should give these other features substantial weight when assessing potential life satisfaction—thus recognizing that life in California would not be that much different from life in the Midwest—but people edit these common features out of their unduly focalized omparisons.

# Implications

The mistaken or underconstrual of situations can have many implications for self-insight.

## *Time Course of Confidence*

First, it might explain why people tend to be so overly confident in their skills well before those skills are tested, but much more cautious when the moment of truth arrives. Tom Gilovich and colleagues have shown that people are inappropriately confident when an event lies far in the future, but less confident when the event draws near (Gilovich, Kerr, & Medvec, 1993). On the first day of an introductory psychology course, participants boasted that they would perform at the 82nd percentile on the first class exam, but that confidence shrank to a more appropriate, albeit still overinflated, level on the day of the exam (67th percentile).

This shrinking of confidence could have been produced via construal processes. Well before the exam, participants based their predictions on a few abstract and central features of the situation (i.e., it's important to do well on the exam, so I will!). However, when the exam drew near, students became more informed about important, low-level situational details (*"Gee, there's an awful lot to read in this textbook!"*). They also become informed about outside events that will interfere with their performance (*"What do you mean the organic chemistry test is tomorrow?"*). More informed as the time grows near, people become less inappropriately confident.

## The Relation of Attitudes to Behavior

Construal processes may also underlie a surprising fact that arises from psychological research: People's attitudes tend to bear only a modest relationship to how they actually behave (for classic reviews, see Schuman & Johnson, 1976; Wicker, 1969). In the archetypal demonstration from the 1930s, although over 90% of restaurants and hotels surveyed reported that they would refuse service to people of Chinese descent (these were different times, remember), only one establishment in 128 actually refused service to a Chinese couple the researcher sent out (LaPiere, 1934).

If people base their attitudes on some mistaken or underspecified construal of situations relevant to an attitude, then one reason for this inconsistency becomes evident: People may base their attitude on some representation of the situation they have in their head, but the situations they actually face in real life might differ quite a bit. For example, would you enjoy an evening dinner with someone who works hauling trash for a living? Your attitude would probably be negative, and probably based on some image of what such a trash hauler would look like (and perhaps even smell like). Trash haulers in the flesh, however, may differ from that image. Imagine, because it is plausible, that I know a trash hauler who has read all the books by Jared Diamond and John Updike, who prefers the wines of Australia over all others, and who loves to show people pictures of his daughter attending Bryn Mawr. If this is the trash hauler I introduce to you at dinner, your behavior and enjoyment of the meal might differ from the attitude you held earlier (Lord & Lepper, 1999).

For example, in 1984, Lord, Lepper, and Mackie asked Princeton University students how much they would like to work with members of certain eating clubs on campus. At Princeton, eating clubs are social organizations that function much like fraternities and sororities at other universities. Respondents rated their willingness to interact with members of two particular eating clubs and then also described the personality of the typical person they associated with each club. They were then dismissed.

A few months later, they were brought back to the lab and told that they were to be paired with some other student to complete a joint project (Lord, Lepper, & Mackie, 1984). There were three students who could end up being their partner, two of which came from the eating clubs associated with the first phase of the study. Participants looked over some information about all three potential partners and rated their preferences about whom they would like to work with. In one variation of the study, the information participants received about the personality of the eating club members exactly matched the description they had given in the original phase of the study. Under this circumstance, participants' work preferences strongly matched the attitudes they had expressed earlier ($r = .69$). However, in another variation, the descriptions of the eating club members were altered to make them much less typical by partially morphing the personalities of the two eating club members into each other. Under this circumstance, the correspondence between expressed work preference and original attitude was much lower ($r = .32$).

This construal account of attitude-behavior inconsistency also potentially explains one circumstance in which attitudes and behaviors tend to be more in harmony. If people have previously experienced situations relevant to the attitude, their attitudes do a better job of predicting subsequent behavior (Fazio & Zanna, 1981). For example, students in a laboratory study were shown a variety of brainteasers involving, for example, mazes, word problems, and spatial reasoning tasks, and were asked to rate how interesting each type of teaser was. They were then allowed to play with the puzzles. Ratings of interest failed to strongly predict which puzzles they played with first and longest. However, when participants were allowed to play with a sample problem from each brainteaser before rating their interest, their ratings strongly predicted which puzzles they would do first and do more of. One can presume that interacting with the puzzles provided more accurate interest ratings because experience with each puzzle provided a more detailed and accurate construal of what that puzzle was like. Any error of construal had a chance to be corrected, thus providing a more informed attitude (Regan & Fazio, 1977).

# ☐ The Emotional Dimension

People can also mistakenly predict situations because some aspects of the situation simply cannot be anticipated. In particular, people do have only imperfect access to the emotional dimensions of situations that they will confront in the future. People cannot foresee completely how situations will make them feel, and then how those feelings will color their thoughts and shape their behaviors.

A thought experiment might illustrate this inability to anticipate the emotional aspects of situations. Suppose one morning you woke up and decided to take a shower. You walk into the bathroom, but upon pulling back the shower curtain you look down to see a four-foot alligator leering back at you in toothy expectation. In this situation, how would you feel, what would you be thinking, what would you do?

You probably have some insight into how you would react to this situation. You have some dim understanding that you would be surprised and scared. You might even have some expectation that you would yell and consider some efforts to leave the bathroom.

But that all said, the experience you can anticipate is probably just a pale shadow of the full Technicolor emotional experience you would have if you found an actual alligator lolling about in your morning bathtub. Your adrenaline is not pumping like it would in the actual situation, the fear you anticipate is not as full-bore as the visceral shock, utter confusion, and sheer panic that would be spilling out of you as you spotted the animal. You probably are not anticipating just how much your eyes are going to lock on and stay locked on that animal's seemingly smirking grin.

You cannot anticipate the intensity of your emotional reaction because many emotions are automatic reactions that kick in upon the actual sighting of an emotionally relevant stimulus (LeDoux, 1996). We cannot think our way into the emotions without the stimulus present (except, perhaps, a few of us who are highly trained actors). And this might be a good thing: If we had a full-blown emotional reaction every time we *thought* of an emotion-eliciting stimulus, it would be very tiring if not impossible to make it through the day.

Our inability to anticipate full-blown emotional reactions, however, leaves us ill equipped to perfectly predict how we will respond to emotionally laden situations. This deficiency leaves us unable to foresee just how profoundly and broadly the arousal of emotion will change our experience of a situation. First, there is all this emotion to contend with, which often brings with it tendencies toward action designed to deal with it (Fridja, 1986).

Second, emotions change the cognitive landscape of situations, influencing what situational features are salient. Emotional arousal, for example, causes people to care more about whether stimuli are basically positive or negative rather than looking beyond for descriptive meaning (Halberstadt & Niedenthal, 1997; Niedenthal, Halberstadt, & Innes-Ker, 1999). Emotional states inhibit attention to any information in the environment that is not emotionally relevant (Fox, Russo, & Bowles, 2001). Indeed, anxiety and fear have been shown to narrow visual attention to the most central aspects of the situation (Basso, Schefft, Ris, & Dember,

1996; Derryberry & Tucker, 1992). In addition, people seek out reasons for their feelings, producing further emphasis on the specific features of a situation that are potentially responsible for emotion (Barefoot & Straub, 1971; Dutton & Aron, 1974; Reisman, Insko, & Valins, 1970; Valins, 1966).

Third, emotions also prompt people to reach different assumptions about the situation, altering their behavior in predictable ways. Make people fearful, for example, and they are more likely to assume that a situation is out of their control, leading to overall pessimism and risk-aversion. But make people angry, and they assume they are in control and thus more likely to take risks (Lerner & Keltner, 2001). In one telling national survey, respondents were asked about the terrorist attacks of September 11, 2001. Some were asked about the aspects of the attacks that had made them fearful; others were asked about what had made them angry. Those talking about their fear were more likely to say the United States was at risk for suffering another terrorist attack than those discussing their anger (Lerner, Gonzalez, Small, & Fischhoff, 2003).

Several research examples demonstrate that people cannot completely anticipate how changes in emotion, as well as related visceral states such as hunger, will produce changes in their preferences and behavior. Instead, their current emotional or visceral state has a biasing influence on their predictions of future behavior even when people know at some intellectual level that their state will change. Read and van Leeuwen (1998), for example, approached office workers around Amsterdam when those workers were likely to be hungry (i.e., the late afternoon) or when they were not (i.e., right after lunch). Respondents were told that the experimenters would return in about a week with some snacks, some of which were healthy, such as apples and bananas, and some of which were not, such as Mars or Snickers bars. What snack would the respondent want? Importantly, respondents were told that the experimenters would be returning right after lunch (a nonhungry situation) or late in the afternoon (a more hungry circumstance).

The respondents demonstrated some awareness that they would be hungrier late in the afternoon than right after lunch. Roughly 60% stated that they would want a junk food snack late in the afternoon, but only 41% wanted such a snack immediately after lunch. That said, their predictions were colored by their current state of hunger. Roughly 67% approached in the late afternoon, when hunger pangs were at their peak, said they would want an unhealthy snack; indeed, a majority wanted that snack even if it were to be delivered right after they ate a lunch. In contrast, of those making predictions right after a filling lunch, only 34% wanted an unhealthy snack—and only 42% wanted such a snack even if they knew it would be delivered during a typically hunger-laden late afternoon time period (for similar data, see Gilbert, Gill, & Wilson, 2002).

Other work affirms the observation that current emotional or visceral states color predictions of the future. People are more likely to predict that they and other people would be bothered by thirst on a mountain hike if they are surveyed just after they complete a rigorous workout at the gym rather than just before they begin their workout (Van Boven & Loewenstein, 2003). College-aged men are more likely to predict that they would be less sexually aggressive on a date if they are in a "cool" emotional state rather than in a sexually aroused one brought on by watching a sexually explicit video (Loewenstein, Nagin, & Paternoster, 1997).

## Fear, Embarrassment, and Social Inhibition

Together with Leaf Van Boven and George Loewenstein, I have been involved in a research program showing how the inability to anticipate the impact of emotions leads to mistaken predictions in social settings. People often believe that they will be assertive beings in the future, actively taking risks and meeting whatever challenges are out there in the social world. People think that they will ask that attractive woman or man out at the first opportunity, that they will volunteer to give that important speech to their coworkers, and that they will tell that jerk a thing or two about his behavior. However, when the moment comes to act, their courage melts away into a placid tableau of nonaction. We never muster the courage to ask that person out, we sit idly by while the boss beseeches someone to volunteer to give the speech, and we quietly pretend not to notice as that jerk mistreats yet another person in our presence.

People suffer an *illusion of courage*, thinking they will take socially risky actions when they, in fact, do not. This illusion of courage persists because people cannot anticipate how much fear and anxiety they will feel when the moment to act arrives. They fail to appreciate just how much the potential for embarrassment will loom large for them.

And embarrassment matters. Fear of embarrassment, it can be argued, has a wide and deep influence on the behavior of people (Sabini, Cosmas, Siepmann, & Stein, 1999). It can prevent us, for example, from asking the auto mechanic to explain just once more what the problem is with the car. It can hold even more consequential implications. It can prevent people from intervening in emergencies (Latané & Darley, 1970), as well as inhibit lovers from insisting on using contraception (Herold, 1981). It can even contribute to copilots failing to take over airplane controls when the pilot is apparently incapacitated (Harper, Kidera, & Cullen, 1971).

In several studies, we have shown that people overestimate their courage in social situations. In one example, we asked college students whether they would, for $2, tell a joke at the end of the week to classmates in their research methods class. With the joke-telling task 5 days away, 16% of the class volunteered. However, when the end of the week came, only 5% went through with it, even though everyone had a joke in hand that they could tell.

In another classroom of about 250 students, we split the class into two groups. The first group was asked a hypothetical question about whether they would volunteer, for $5, to go up to the front of the class and dance to the classic funk tune *Superfreak* by Rick James for as long as the experimenter wanted. A full 31% of group indicated they would. If asked, on average, how much we would have to pay them to get them to the front of the class, respondents across the group indicated that we would have to pay them just under $21. For the second group, the question was not hypothetical; it was real. In this group, only 8% actually volunteered to do the dance, and on average the group stated that it would take nearly $53 to get them to do so (Van Boven, Loewenstein, Welch, & Dunning, 2003).

Such failures of courage should not be surprising, for they have been observed in other corners of psychological literature. Consider the plight of women, even in the contemporary world, who must deal with a range of issues from sexist comments to full-blown sexual harassment. Potential sufferers of sexism tend to overestimate how quickly, directly, and effectively they will confront it. Swim and Hyers (1999) asked male and female college students to work together on a group task, one in which they decided selected individuals who could best survive on a desert island. Unbeknownst to the female participants, one of the male group members was a plant who at one point kept making sexist remarks, suggesting, for example, that more women were needed on the island " to keep the men on the island satisfied." Only 45% of female group members acknowledged any of his remarks, and only 16% directly confronted the confederate over what he said. This reluctance to take a social risk occurred even though 81% of women said they would confront the confederate when the situation was presented to them hypothetically.

Perhaps the reason for this reluctance was revealed in another experiment on reactions to sexual harassment. Woodzicka and LaFrance (2001) asked college-aged women how they would react to a 30-something job interviewer who sprinkled the interview with inappropriate questions (e.g., *Do people find you desirable?*). A full 68% said they would refuse to answer at least one of the inappropriate questions, with 16% saying they would leave the interview. However, when a different group of college-aged women went through an actual interview, which they were told was for a research assistant job, everyone answered every question and no one left. To be sure, interviewees at times did respond to the questions by inquiring why it was being asked or by asking the interviewer to clarify the question—but in general interviewees were not as direct or as confrontational as they said they would be when responding to the situation hypothetically.

One key factor that may have produced different reactions between the hypothetical and the actual was emotional in nature. When thinking about hypothetical sexual harassment, respondents tended to predict that they would feel more angry than fearful. However, after the real interviews, participants reported the opposite. A full 40% of participants expressed some degree of fear after the interview; only 16% did the same with anger.

Two notes must be made about people's imperfect understanding of their capacity to take social risks. First, this lack of insight does arise because of the emotional gulf that exists between thinking about a situation hypothetically versus having to live it in actuality. Making people emotionally aroused as they consider a hypothetical chance to take a social risk causes them to make more accurate predictions. Consider people's predictions about whether they would volunteer to tell a joke to their classmates. If people are first shown an ominous and scary 2-minute film clip from a horror film (Stanley Kubrick's *The Shining*), they make more accurate predictions about whether they would be willing to tell a joke. Importantly, it appears that *any* type of emotional arousal is crucial for causing people to provide more accurate self-predictions. When people are shown movie clips designed to make them feel angry, or even amused, they provide more accurate assessments about whether they would like to perform in front of their peers than when they are not emotionally aroused (Van Boven, Loewenstein, Welch, & Dunning, 2003).

Second, people not only mistakenly predict their own social courage but also the social courage of others. Recall the previous experiment in which participants were asked hypothetically if they would dance to *Superfreak* in front of their classmates for $5. Although only 8% of participants would do it if the offer were for real, participants tended to think that 30% of their classmates would take the offer. On average, they thought that their classmates would require roughly $13 to do the dance (when people in the actual condition took roughly $52). Apparently, not feeling the threat of embarrassment themselves, participants were not able to infer how much the behavior of other people would be responsive to that fear (Van Boven, Loewenstein, & Dunning, 2003b).

Participants did have insights about how other people would respond to the offer once they were introduced to the situation for real. Participants facing a real decision realized that their peers would be quite reticent about dancing in front of their peers. They thought that only 16% of their peers would volunteer—a statistic much closer to the 8% truth—and that they, on average, would require roughly $19 to do the deed. Once introduced to the emotion of the event, participants garnered significantly more insight about how their peers would behave in the exact same situation.

## Emotions in the Long Term

Of course, all of this is not to say that people have no knowledge of the emotions they will feel when they experience emotional situations. People do have some awareness that they will feel a mixture of sadness, anger, and embarrassment if they were fired from their job. They just miss how profound those feelings will be at the moment they are escorted from their boss's office to collect their personal things from their desk.

But there is another error that people make about their emotional reactions. People may underestimate the immediate impact of such events as being fired, but paradoxically they then overestimate the long-term emotional impact of such events. It has long been observed in psychological literature that people adapt. It does not take long, after a life-altering event, for people to return to their normal level of emotional well-being (Helson, 1964). Office workers adapt to being fired. People come to terms with the death of a loved one. Lucky individuals win the lottery but progressively find that the vexing trials of quotidian life continue unabated. To be sure, these events do have an impact, but that impact is circumscribed to the short term.

The classic illustration of this return to normalcy comes from Brickman, Coates, and Janoff-Bulman (1978), who interviewed people who had been paralyzed within the last year, who had won the lottery within the same time frame (average winnings were around a half-million dollars), or who had had nothing particularly interesting happen to them. To the surprise of the researchers, and to a generation of readers who have scrutinized the research, lottery winners labeled themselves no happier than the control group who had not experienced any remarkable incidents. Those suffering paralysis described themselves as slightly less happy than the control group, but the difference was nowhere near as large as would be expected (see Schulz & Decker, 1985; and Wortman & Silver, 1987, for similar results).

People, however, do not seem to have an adequate understanding of the psychological mechanics of adaptation, believing that the emotional influence will be felt far longer than those effects actually are. College students overpredict how long they will be devastated by the breakup of their current romance. Young college professors overestimate how long they will find themselves distraught after being denied tenure. People voting for a losing gubernatorial candidate overrate how long they will be upset after the election (Gilbert, Pinel, Wilson, Blumberg, & Wheatley, 1998). Patients at a health clinic overestimate how anxious they will be several weeks after they are told they are HIV positive; those told they are HIV negative overestimate their relief (Sieff, Dawes, & Loewenstein, 1999).

This lack of appreciation for adaptation also leads to mistaken predictions of others. People tend to believe that others will be more affected by emotional events than those others actually are. Sackett and Torrance (1978) asked respondents how their quality of life would be affected if they had to undergo daily kidney dialysis. Respondents were asked to describe what they thought life would be on a scale that could range from 0 (just like death) to 1 (perfect health). The average projected rating was .39, which was far lower than the .56 given by patients actually undergoing dialysis. In a similar study, people hypothetically considering what life would be like after a colostomy projected that their life would rate about a .80, when actual colostomy patients rated their lives at around .92 (Boyd, Sutherland, Heasman, Tritcher, & Cummings, 1990).

# ☐ Misunderstanding Ownership

People's misunderstanding of their emotions extends to the simplest circumstances of human life. Suppose I knocked at your door and offered to sell you a really nice pen that commemorates this book. Not wanting to be selfish, I permit you to name your price. What is the most you would spend? Now let's change the situation just a touch in a second scenario: I give you the pen and wave goodbye—but 2 minutes later another person appears at your door asking whether you'd sell the pen. What's the lowest price you would ask to part with the pen?

The two scenarios obviously differ on one dimension—whether you own the pen in question as you are asked to name your price. In a sense, this variation should not make such a big difference in the price you name. The pen is, after all, the same one in each scenario, with the same feel in the hand, the same amount of ink, and the same attractive lettering on the barrel. In all, I think it is safe to stipulate that the pen possesses the same intrinsic value in either scenario, which should be reflected in pretty much the same price.

However, a good deal of research suggests that these two scenarios are very different psychologically. The simple act of owning an object can have a dramatic influence on the value people place on it. For example, Kahneman, Knetsch, and Thaler (1991) walked into a room and handed coffee mugs to roughly half of the students assembled there. They turned to the remainder of the students and asked how much they were willing to pay to acquire their own mug. On average, students stated that they would pay, at most, $2.25. The researchers then turned back to students who received mugs and asked for the lowest price they would sell their mug for. The average was $5.25.

These rather high selling prices were not strategic posturing. A wealth of research suggests that the simple act of owning an object causes people to honestly view it as more valuable, a phenomenon known as the *endowment effect*. Knetsch (1989) gave three different groups of participants a choice between a coffee mug and a Swiss chocolate bar. In one group, participants were shown the mug and the chocolate bar and asked which one they preferred. Given the choice presented in this way, 56% preferred the mug. In another group, participants were handed the mug first and then were asked if they wanted to exchange the mug for the candy bar. Presented in this way, 89% chose to keep the mug. In the third group, however, participants were handed the chocolate bar first before being presented the choice. In this circumstance, only 10% gave up their chocolate bar for the mug. The endowment effect is a phenomenon that has been shown for objects as diverse as cold cup insulators (Beggan, 1992) to opinions about social policy (Hammond, Keeney, & Raiffa, 1999; Samuelson & Zackhauser, 1988). It even extends to the letters contained in one's name (Nuttin, 1985, 1987). In effect, people seem to be "hardwired" to prefer that which they already have.

Why would this be the case? A good deal of work in behavioral economics provides one clear answer. People are *loss averse*. They are more sensitive to potential losses in their environment than they are to gains (Kahneman & Tversky, 1979a). As an illustration, consider how enthusiastic you would be if I offered to flip a coin (you could call "heads" or "tails" yourself), with me giving you $50 if you win, but you giving me $50 if you lose. Very few people find themselves enthusiastic about this bet. The prospect of losing the $50 looms larger than the prospect of winning $50, even though both events are equivalent in objective terms. Indeed, sensitivity to losses looms so large that only a third of people will accept a coin flip in which they could win $200 if they call the coin right but would lose only $100 if they called it wrong (Tversky & Shafir, 1992). In objective terms, this bet is definitely one to take (to an economist, the expected value is a profit of $50), but the psychological aversion to losses makes it highly unattractive.

The transfer of the logic of loss aversion to the endowment effect is rather straightforward. The prospect of gaining some potentially useful item, like a coffee mug or a pen, is psychologically positive, but as a gain it does not excite the pleasure machine in all of us all that much. However, once we own the item and someone asks to buy it from us, giving it up represents a hated loss that the pleasure machine abhors. As a consequence, to give up the item and to compensate for our loss, we must be paid handsomely.

The endowment effect has to be considered one of the most simple and fundamental phenomena ever documented in psychological literature. The phenomenon is a simple outgrowth of the way we are hardwired to gain pleasure and even more so to avoid displeasure. And once made aware of it, one can see how the endowment effect influences behavior in all walks of life. The endowment effect, for example, explains why negotiations tend to be so difficult, why home sellers set such "unreasonable" prices for their homes (if you do not believe me, see Tyson & Brown, 1996, *Home buying for dummies*, pp. 210–211), and even why it is hard for little Danny to let littler Harry play with his toys.

However, although the endowment effect is ubiquitous, people do not seem to have an adequate understanding of it. People display some vague understanding that people who own an object will place a higher price on it than those who do not own it, but they systematically underrate the impact of ownership. People also do not seem to be able to anticipate the full impact of the endowment effect on their own preferences and behavior. Loewenstein and Adler (1995) showed Carnegie-Mellon and University of Pittsburgh students a handsome embossed mug and told them that they were going to be given their own mug in a few days. They were asked how much they would be willing to accept to sell the mug back to the researchers. Students, on average, predicted that they would sell the mugs for somewhere between $3.27 and $3.73 when the time came. However, when that time came, these same students demanded, on average, anywhere from $4.56 to $5.40 for their mugs.

People also underappreciate the impact of the endowment effect on others. In Van Boven, Dunning, and Loewenstein (2000), we repeated the classic endowment effect procedure and gave mugs to half the students in a classroom, randomly selected. When asked, students on average said they would sell their newly acquired mugs for nothing less than $5.40. Students not given a mug, however, said they would pay at most $1.56 to obtain one.

Of key interest, however, were estimates of owners and nonowners about what the other group would say. Owners had some understanding that nonowners would not value the mugs as much as they did, but this understanding was far from perfect. Mug owners thought that nonowners would be willing to pay $2.93 for the mugs, an estimate that is nearly double what the nonowners were actually willing to pay. Nonowners similarly revealed an imperfect understanding of the endowment effect, thinking that owners would not sell their mugs unless they were paid $3.96 for them. This estimate was certainly higher than what nonowners thought the mugs were worth, but it was also much lower than what the owners actually said they would accept (Van Boven et al., 2000). Follow-up studies confirmed that owners and nonowners mistakenly predicted each other's perceptions of the mug, even when both were paid money to come up with accurate estimates.

Our participants continued to underestimate the endowment effect even when this error cost them money. In one experiment, we again gave half of the participants a mug and offered the other half a deal. We deputized them to serve as "buyers' agents," with the job of trying to buy the mugs back for us. We told these buyers' agents that we were going to give them $10 to buy a mug back from one of the mug owners, randomly selected. They were to make one bid for that owner's mug. If the owner accepted the bid, the agent would pay the owner out of the $10 and then could keep the rest. If the mug owner refused to sell at the bid the agent made, the agent had to hand the entire $10 back to us. Obviously, given this setup, the agent had to determine the lowest amount of money the mug owner would accept. Make a bid too low, and the agent would end up with nothing. Make a bid too high, and the owner would accept it, but the agent would be left with less money than he or she could have made.

Even with the monetary incentive to estimate the mug owner's price accurately, our buyers' agents did not do too well. In one study, buyers' agents on average offered $4.93, but mug owners on average wanted $6.83. Only 25% of the agents made bids high enough to successfully pry the mug from the owner's hands and earn themselves some money. A strict economic analysis of buyers' agents' behavior revealed that if their bids had been completely optimal, they would have earned on average $2.15. In reality, they earned only $.75. In a second experiment, the success rate of buyer's agents (19%) was even worse (Van Boven, Dunning, & Loewenstein, 2000).

## ☐ Learning About Endowment, or Rather, Not

In a sense, this failure to anticipate the impact of the endowment effect is a surprising one. The influence the phenomenon would have on the preferences of owners is a simple one, and people should have learned throughout a lifetime of owning, buying, selling, and haggling about how owners differ from nonowners. Yet, in the experiments we ran, people held far from a perfect understanding of the effect. Why had people not learned?

There are probably a whole host of reasons why people fail to learn about the endowment effect. To begin, one can return to all the material in chapter 4 about how difficult it is to learn from the incomplete, haphazard, and indistinct feedback that life gives people. To continue, one can also mention that people are not completely clueless about the endowment effect. Nonowners do show some awareness that owners will value their possessions more; they just fail to understand just how *much* owners will value those possessions. Owners also show some understanding that nonowners value less those things they do not own. They just fail to understand completely just how much less nonowners would value those items.

That said, in our own research, we have uncovered a good deal of evidence that learning to appreciate the endowment effect is a hard lesson to learn. For example, in one of our studies (Van Boven, Dunning, & Loewenstein, 2000, Study 2) we accidentally ran across some students who had heard about the endowment effect a few weeks earlier in one of their psychology classes. Indeed, their instructor had exactly mentioned the original coffee mug studies (Kahneman, Knetsch, & Thaler, 1991) that had inspired our own research. Did these students show a better understanding of the endowment effect when they estimated how mug owners and nonowners would value a mug? To cut to the chase, the answer was "no." Students lectured on the endowment effect provided no more accurate estimates than students who had never heard of the phenomenon before.

People also fail to learn about the endowment effect even when given explicit and repeated experience with it (Van Boven, Loewenstein, & Dunning, 2003a). In one series of studies, we gave buyers' agents not one but *five* opportunities to buy a mug from various mug owners. This repeated experience did teach the agents something. On their first attempt to buy a mug, agents' bids tended to be only 75% of what the mug owners wanted. But on the fifth attempt, those bids had risen to about 88% of what the owners wanted.

So far so good, except that we next asked buyers' agents to bid for pens that we had given some students. Would their bids on this new item show some wisdom about endowment, prompting agents to make higher bids and to make those bids sooner? The answer was "no." Agents' first bids for the pens were 75% of what owners wanted, almost exactly where buyer's agents had started with the mugs. And buyers' agents' subsequent bids increased at almost exactly the same rate as they had increased for the mugs. In short, whatever they had learned from the experience with the mugs had not transferred over to their behavior bidding for pens (Van Boven, Loewenstein, & Dunning, 2003a).

But perhaps this lack of learning should not be surprising, for the circumstance our buyers' agents were in shares many of the features that prevent learning in the real world. Say you bid $5 for a mug and you find out that the owner wants $8 for it. What do you make of this fact? Is this the endowment effect in action? Does the owner really like the mug? Is the owner greedy? Does she need the money? Is the owner deluded?

The problem of learning about the endowment effect is that every time one meets up with it, there are so many other candidate explanations around that could also account for the owner's puzzling behavior. Indeed, the major problem is that one simple, easy candidate explanation looms larger than all others—and that is that an owner asking for so much, or a nonowner offering so little, is just greedy. Indeed, in one of our studies, when one young woman found out the typical price that mug owners assigned to their possession, she blurted out that "Those f——ing mug owners are the most f——ing greediest people I've ever seen!" (Dunning, Van Boven, & Loewenstein, 2001, p. 86). The outburst was surprising; equally surprising was the number of heads in the room nodding in agreement.

More formal data from one of our buyers' agents studies confirmed how much participants tended to attribute failed transactions to greed (Van Boven, Dunning, & Loewenstein, 2000, Study 4). In instances in which buyers' agents bid too low, both owners and agents were asked why the transaction had failed to consummate. Participants were asked to judge the plausibility of a number of possible explanations, including one focusing on greed and another describing the endowment effect. Both owners and agents assigned more plausibility to greed than to the endowment effect.

In all these studies aimed at "teaching" people about the endowment effect, only one has "worked." People might have a hard time appreciating the endowment effect intellectually, but if they are allowed to "feel" endowment, they might begin to understand it in others. That was the logic of one experiment (Van Boven et al., 2000, Study 5) in which we once again asked half our participants to play the role of buyers' agent. However, before making bids for a mug, half of the participants were given their own mug and asked how much they would ask for to sell it. Now in a position to project themselves into the shoes of a mug owner, we thought these participants might gain some insight into how much owners would demand for their mug. And, consistent with our prediction, these participants made significantly higher bids for the mugs than did a control group, or even a group asked to project themselves into the mug owner's shoes without the benefit of their own mug.

## ☐ Concluding Remarks

At the beginning of this book, I reviewed a good deal of research showing that people's impressions of their skill and character were often disconnected from reality. The rest of this book has chronicled what people might be missing when they judge themselves, but this specific chapter has raised the stakes. People at times may understand themselves pretty well, but even superlative self-understanding may not lead to accuracy if people misunderstand the situations they get themselves into. Climbers of Mount Everest might find the mountain to be higher, the air colder, the slope steeper, the fatigue to be more oppressive than they ever would have imagined.

To the extent that self-understanding fails to extend beyond the boundary of the self, people may make mistakes about their likely behaviors and probable life outcomes. The cruelest irony of self-insight is that the most critical components of self-knowledge may not reside in our internal natures but rather hide somewhere in the territory outside.

# Reflections on Self-Reflection

*Afterthoughts on the Vagaries of Self-Insight*

In Greek mythology, Narcissus was the son of the river god Cephissus and the nymph Leiriope. When he was born, his mother sought out the blind seer Tiresias to ask whether her son would live a long life. The seer responded that he would, provided he never came to know himself.

Narcissus grew to be a handsome young man—indeed, one of the most striking in the land, spurning many lovers along the way. One day, walking in a wood, he caught a glimpse of his reflection in a pond. Transfixed, he fell in love with the image. He was, sorrowfully, never able to touch this image without disturbing it, but, so enamored, neither was he able to tear himself away from the pond. As a consequence, he wasted away and thus proved Tiresias' prophecy to be true.

In this book, I have asked what people see when they look upon their self-reflections. When people pause and reflect before a psychic mirror, do they see someone beautiful or ugly? Does what they see please them, if not as extremely as it pleased Narcissus? Is what they see a complicated image or a simple one? And, most important, does the image they see resemble the one that the rest of the world sees?

What people see in the mirror does matter. A thousand decisions are made across a lifetime based on what people think of themselves and their potential. Teenagers try out for sports teams based on perceptions of their athleticism. Employees argue for raises based on their beliefs about job performance. Students choose which social groups to join based on assessments of their personality (Niedenthal, Cantor, & Kihlstrom, 1985). People choose cars, restaurants, and even types of psychotherapy based, in part, as a function of their self-image (Niedenthal & Mordkoff, 1991; Setterlund & Niedenthal, 1993). College undergraduates select their academic majors because of notions about their intellectual strengths and weaknesses (Lent, Brown, & Hackett, 1994) and decide to go on to careers in science, the arts, or writing based on an assessment of their talents (Fouad, Smith, & Zao, 2002).

In this book, I have discussed evidence suggesting that what people see in the mirror often bears only a modest, at best, resemblance to what the rest of the world sees. This chapter concludes this volume by focusing on two tasks. The first is to bring into focus some themes that tie together the disparate stories that have been presented in the various chapters of the book. The second is to address some questions that might linger in the minds of readers who have made it this far.

# ☐ Themes and Variations

The previous eight chapters can be read as a series of short stories, each somehow linked to the general topic about the quality of people's self-assessments in everyday life, but not connected by some overarching conceptual framework or theory. In part, the omission of an overarching theoretical structure was deliberate. Self-assessment is a complex enterprise, and until researchers have in hand a more comprehensive list of psychological processes that lead to accuracy or bias in self-judgment, it may be premature to articulate overarching theories.

That said, astute readers might have discerned some general themes have emerged across the chapters, although typically with a slight variation in each instance. Other themes are also present, but those themes lurk more implicitly underneath the material being discussed. Notably, I believe two general themes about self-assessment can be extracted from the previous material in the book, although careful readers will probably find others. One general theme focuses squarely on the inherent difficulty of achieving accurate self-judgment and questions whether accurate self-evaluations are even possible. The other general theme has to do with tools that people have at their disposal to evaluate themselves but that they tend to ignore.

# ☐ The Inherent Difficulty of Self-Judgment

In many respects, this book has been about how people judge their skills and character when left to their own devices, with no external agent or aid to guide them in their quest for accurate self-knowledge. Achieving accurate self-judgment would be a far easier enterprise if, after we made some set of decisions about ourselves, some deity parted the clouds from on high and reached down to hand us a report revealing whether our decisions were wise or foolish. Life, however, does not provide such clear-cut or authoritative answer sheets. Instead, people must gather whatever information they can get and use whatever savvy they carry around with them to draw up their own grading key. Therein lies the rub.

The material in this book reveals just how difficult, complicated, and tricky it is to reach accurate self-assessments on one's own. There are many arduous hurdles that people have to jump to achieve any semblance of self-insight. The title of the book, after all, does focus on "roadblocks and detours," and that title was not chosen haphazardly.

## The Information Environment

First, consider the *information environment* that people find themselves in whenever they evaluate themselves. By information environment, I refer to all the data and knowledge that people have available when they assess their decisions, evaluate their skill, or predict their future. The information environment that people are placed in is often simply not sufficient to allow people to reach accurate self-insights. People do not have all the data and erudition that they need.

Several examples of insufficient information environments abound in the book. First, as discussed in chapter 2, incompetent people, because they lack proper skill and knowledge, do not have all the know-how they need to appropriately appraise their performance or the performances of other people (Kruger & Dunning, 1999). More importantly, their very lack of competence also means they are not competent to recognize just how poorly they are performing.

As also discussed in the same chapter, people in general, whether incompetent or capable, lack crucial awareness of their errors of omission (Caputo & Dunning, in press). They are aware of solutions they have generated to problems but by definition are unaware of solutions they could have generated or missed. A military general, for example, knows what tactics he has considered before battle but is not aware of tactics, potentially superior ones, that he could have employed. Given this, that general, as well as people in general, cannot be expected to provide completely accurate judgments of their decisions and performances.

The information environment is also insufficient when it comes to the cues that people rely on to judge the suitability of their decisions. As discussed in chapter 3, these cues are not foolproof indicators of accuracy. Right decisions often have a coherent and reasoned rationale behind them, but so do wrong decisions. People rely on speed to decide whether their decisions are correct, but external forces can prompt incorrect conclusions to come to mind swiftly, too. People, in addition, can evaluate their decisions based on preconceived notions of their skill and erudition, but those preconceived notions tend to hold only a moderate relationship, at best, with objective performance.

People also suffer from an inadequate information environment when they try to predict their future behavior. They live in a complicated world where the situations presented to them are never exactly the same as ones they have confronted before. Every customer the salesperson meets behaves differently from the previous one. Every parent knows that the second child just does not respond the same as the first. As a consequence, how situations will unfold is unknowable until one gets there, as discussed in chapter 8. Without knowing the exact nature of a situation, one's prediction about how one will respond to it will be vulnerable to error.

As also discussed in that chapter, it is especially difficult to anticipate how our preferences and actions will change once we are emotionally aroused—unless we happened to be emotionally aroused at the time we make the prediction (Van Boven, Loewenstein, Welch, & Dunning, 2003). Without key pieces of information about situational details and influences, our predictions of future behavior are vulnerable to error and any confidence in those predictions is susceptible to being misplaced.

Inadequacy in the information environment is also not something that dissipates through time and experience. Life experience provides no assurance that people ultimately come to an adequate understanding of self. As discussed in chapter 4, the world often withholds vital feedback about our actions or provides feedback that is misleading or cloaked in a smog of ambiguity. As a consequence, although we have direct experience to draw upon to assess skill and character, as well as to make predictions about the future, the lessons we learn from that experience might be misguided through no fault of our own.

In addition, even if people have all the information they need to provide exacting self-evaluations, they face another stumbling block. Even if they have correct and concrete information about their specific strengths and weaknesses, people would still not have a guarantee that they would arrive at flawless self-assessments. As noted in chapter 2, success in many real-world tasks is ill defined. It is hard, if not hopeless, to define what perfect performance is, as well as the steps one has to take and the competencies one needs to develop to reach it. There are no algorithms for defining the perfect advertising campaign for a new mouthwash or what to do to best console a friend.

Indeed, the material in chapter 6 echoed this difficulty by asserting that the very definitions of common skills like *intelligence* or *leadership* are not set but are rather open to interpretation. Given this, how are people ever in a position to know if they are more intelligent than the next person over, for example, when the very definition of that trait is something that defies clear-cut delineation? Without sharply defined standards of perfection, it is difficult to expect that people will evaluate their performances with precise accuracy.

## Unburying the Lede: Blame the Task, Not the Person

The existence of so many of these roadblocks to accurate self-assessment leads me to articulate one important message to draw from this book, as well as one message not to draw. The message not to draw is that people are stupid—as one might read this book and decide that I am harping about just how small, incapable, and irrational people are. One could conclude that people just do not possess the "right stuff" necessary to identify or to face the truth of what their strengths and weaknesses really are.

To be sure, people do make mistakes that they could avoid, and this book has chronicled some of them, but the clearer message is that people hardly carry the entire blame for their failure to achieve perfect self-knowledge. Far from it, and let me make sure to unbury the lede of this book: Gaining adequate, much less perfect, self-knowledge is a horribly thorny task. There are many obstacles and roadblocks thrown in people's way by outside agents. People fail to know themselves because the job of gaining self-knowledge is just simply very, very hard.

As such, if anything is to be blamed for people's failures in self-insight, it should be the inherent difficulty of the task itself. It is not that people are thick; it is that the challenges they face in gaining self-insight are numerous and formidable. The outside world can foil even the most sincere and diligent individual when it comes to the task of knowing thyself. Thus, I would not like to blame the person as much as I would like to blame the Herculean task people face as they strive to gain an adequate education of who and what they exactly are.

## Judgment as an Arrogant Act

So, too, the reader should not attribute self-judgment errors to arrogance, even if the judgments people tend to reach about themselves tend to be conceited ones, given how those judgments compare with objective reality. People are just not in an information environment that could conclusively dispossess them of their overconfident self-views.

However, if the reader still wishes to find some evidence of arrogance in the assessments people make of themselves, it is still possible. One could reasonably claim that the arrogance people show is that they reach any self-judgments at all. How can people reach such certain self-assessments when the information environment is so deficient? How can they be so bold, for example, to decide that they are good or bad at any skill when they plainly lack all the evidence needed to reach such conclusions?

Thus, one could claim that reaching any opinion about the self is in itself an arrogant act, but perhaps that would be a step too far. People do need to reach conclusions about themselves. They need to come to some sort of self-assessment to guide them through their daily life, as well as to make the big decisions (e.g., career, marriage) that cannot be avoided. Chiding people for reaching conclusions about themselves is a little like accusing a jury of being arrogant because it elects to reach a verdict in a criminal case. Juries often face uncertain and contradictory evidence in criminal cases, and their decisions can ultimately prove erroneous, but they are required by the legal system to reach verdicts no matter how difficult. Life often forces just as heavy a mandate on each of us to reach verdicts about ourselves. To reach no decisions about ourselves would leave us helplessly tied to an armchair, uncertain about what to do with the rest of our lives.

That said, perhaps people could reach self-judgments a little less arrogantly. As the material in this book points out, there are many unknowns people should be wary of when they reach self-judgments, and perhaps they should take those unknowns into account as they evaluate themselves.

Several of those unknowns have been specified in this book. The material on self-judgment among the incompetent suggests that people should be wary that they may not be the best judge of their own performance, and so should seek out feedback or other information to test their self-impressions. The material on situational insight suggests that people should recognize that they may not know exactly how the relevant situation will play out when predicting future behavior, and thus they should dial back the confidence they imbue in their predictions or at least consider the possibility that they may act differently from what they presume.

Furthermore, the typical error people make, at least in the North American context (Heine, Lehman, Markus, & Kitayama, 1999), is to be overly optimistic. As a consequence, people could profitably consider the hypothesis that their skill or accomplishments may not be as superb as their intuitions tell them. Their intuitions might tell them that they are a terrific cook or a fine public speaker, but they should keep in the back of their heads the thought that the reality often falls significantly short of belief. In doing so, they need not try to modify their intuitions. Rather, they should leave their beliefs unaltered but predict that actual outcomes will not match what their intuition is telling them.

In short, this last strategy would be adopting one that successful businesses often use when mapping out future projects. Such businesses often adopt *cognitive repairs*, in that they ask their experts for a prediction and then modify those predictions by some pre-set correction factor to bring them closer to the truth (Heath, Larrick, & Klayman, 1998). Companies that build dams typically ask engineers how much concrete they will need to ensure its structural integrity. To guard against overoptimism, these companies then triple, and sometimes even octuple, the amount that engineers estimate. In a similar vein, Microsoft automatically adds an additional 30% to 50% to the amount of time that programmers estimate that it will take to develop a new piece of software.

# ☐ Neglected Sources of Wisdom

The other major recurrent theme in the book has to do with valuable pieces of information that people have at their disposal to achieve more accurate self-judgment but that they tend to neglect. The road to accurate self-insight can be cleared—people already have some valuable tools at their disposal—they just have to recognize those tools and put them to work.

## Data from the Past

For example, people often have data about past outcomes that could inform expectations about the present or the future. As described in chapter 7, one of the reasons people fall prey to the planning fallacy is because they ignore the times in the past when they have barely gotten projects done before the deadline, as well as those times when the deadline passed and they were still working. Instead, people adopt an inside view, almost exclusively focusing on the scenarios about how they will complete the current task well before the cutoff date.

People would provide more accurate predictions if they adopted a more "outside," data-driven perspective and factored past experience into their predictions, or at least modified their inside, scenario-driven forecasts by at least noting past data. For example, Lovallo and Kahneman (2003) told a story about a group of academics developing a new curriculum for a local high school. A year into the project, group members were asked how long it would take for them to complete their task, with the most pessimistic estimate being 30 months. However, when asked how long it has taken comparable groups to finish, one group member volunteered that he had never seen a group finish within 7 years, and that around 40% never finished at all. True to form, this curriculum development group finished its work 8 years later.

## Data from Others

Perhaps equally important, this book shows time and again that people ignore another source of information around them: other people. This neglect is revealed in many different ways and has a wide range of impacts on the validity of self-assessment.

### Thinking Others Are Not Relevant to the Self

One problem with self-assessment is that people think they are qualitatively different from others, that whatever rules apply to other people do not apply to one's self. This belief has deleterious consequences for self-insight. As chapter 7 revealed, when it comes to moral behavior, people appear to have rather accurate views about how other people would respond to morally tinged situations. However, when self-prediction is involved, people set aside these valuable insights about other people and predict their own behavior as though they were the exception to the rule, responsive to a separate psychology from their peers. As a result, although they make imperfect but largely decent predictions about the behavior of others, they mistakenly predict their own behavior dramatically. This belief in the discontinuity between self and others is revealed in other locations in the book. As chapter 5 revealed, people tend to believe that they have a more vivid and complicated internal life than their peers, leading people to believe that they themselves are especially emotional, inhibited, and complex.

People would hold more accurate self-perceptions if they conceded that their psychology is not different from the psychology of others, that their own actions are molded largely by the same situational forces that govern the behavior of other people. In doing so, they could more readily learn from the experiences of others, using data about other people's outcomes to help forecast their own.

They could also, if they could "trick" themselves into doing so, predict their own behavior by instead predicting the likely behavior of others. For example, if I wanted to predict when I would get my taxes done, instead of predicting myself, I could predict when I thought the typical person would be done and use that forecast as my self-prediction. This notion leads to an interesting hypothesis, as far as I know one that is unexplored. Perhaps survey researchers could explore this trick: If they wanted to estimate how much people would donate to a certain cause in the future, perhaps they would obtain more accurate forecasts if they asked respondents what they thought their *peers* would do rather than what they themselves would do. Would this work? To date, it is unclear, but it is a possibility suggested by the material in chapter 7.

## Not Thinking of Others at All

People also neglect their peers in other ways. As discussed in chapter 5, the problem for many judgments is not that people think of their peers incorrectly; it is that they fail to think of their peers at all. People suffer from egocentrism, myopically focusing on their own attributes and circumstances while ignoring the same in other people. As a consequence, they fail to imagine how much other people want to control events just as much as themselves. They fail to consider how others might have just as rich an interior life as the self. Following up, in chapter 6, people fail to consider how others might legitimately define traits differently from the way they personally define those traits, or that other people might achieve success through means different from those utilized by the self.

This neglect of others is more than puzzling, because many of the most important self-judgments that people reach involve comparisons with others. Thus, if people fail to factor other people into such comparisons, those comparisons cannot help but be faulty. This neglect leads to clearly erroneous patterns of self-belief. Recall the example of students playing poker during in an experimental laboratory. When the experimenter increased the number of wild cards in the deck, students thought they were more likely to win and bet accordingly—even though they were no more likely to win with wild cards because everybody in the room shared the same advantage (Windshitl, Kruger, & Simms, 2003).

Thus, in a paradoxical way, traveling the road to self-insight might require paying more attention to other people, using their experience as a guide; our intuitions about their behavior can serve as a clue to our own. Just thinking about other people seriously might lead us to make more accurate judgments about how we stack up against them.

## Using Others as a Crucial Source of Information

Other people might prove to be the royal road to self-insight in another sense. As this book suggests, it is intrinsically difficult to achieve accurate self-beliefs just left to our own devices. We need help, and other people might be in a position to offer that help. As chapter 1 discussed, at times, our peers might have more insight into our skill and behavior than we do ourselves, and so pointedly asking for feedback from others might be healthy therapy to rid ourselves of self-misconceptions.

To be sure, there are problems with asking for feedback (see chapter 4), but compared with the alternative—no feedback at all—asking for pointers from others provides more of a possibility of self-improvement. Data support this assertion. In organizational settings, managers who actively sought out feedback, specifically negative feedback, had a more accurate grasp of where they stood with superiors, subordinates, and peers. They also were held in higher esteem by these groups (Ashford & Tsui, 1991).

Other real-world examples show how gaining meaningful feedback from others helps people to better assess the quality of their beliefs and actions. In the business world, one of the recurrent problems facing CEOs is their tendency to acquire other businesses too optimistically. They pay good money for other companies, but the typical result is that the stock market does not reward these decisions by increasing the price of the stock of the CEO's company. Instead, when such acquisitions are announced to the public, the stock price of both companies goes *down*, which cannot be considered a vote of confidence for the CEO's judgment (Hayward & Hambrick, 1997; Malmendier & Tate, 2003).

Such overly optimistic acquisitions are mitigated, in part, when CEOs have other people around who provide outside perspectives on the decision to acquire (Hayward & Hambrick, 1997). CEOs who must justify their decisions in front of an independent chairman of the board as well as a board of directors who are not primarily tied to the company (that is, the board is not dominated by suppliers, buyers, or employees of the company) tend to make more cautious and prudent offers of acquisition.

More generally, submitting one's decisions to a review by others is a healthy, although at times anxiety-producing, way to assess the advisability of the decision. A study of successful microbiology labs revealed that successful labs held lab meetings in which researchers had to submit their ideas to potentially unconvinced colleagues for critique (Dunbar, 1995). It is Pentagon policy to present military combat plans to a "Murder Board" with the express purpose of exposing and preventing ill-planned missions before they are deployed to the field (Heath et al., 1998).

## ☐ Summary

Although there might be several ways to tie the various strands of this book into an overall tapestry, one information summation is to point out just how hard it is for people on their own to achieve accurate self-insight. The environment often does not provide the conclusive clues needed to guide people toward accurate views of self, and people should not be blamed for the inherent difficulty of the task.

That all said, people do not take advantage of all the information they do have. They could look to data rather than spin scenarios. They could consult data from the past rather than project hypothetically into the future. And they could take advantage of the one source of information they have around them—other people. They could refer to the action and outcomes of other people, using that data to inform beliefs about themselves. Perhaps more important, they can simply ask other people their opinion. If asked, other people might share observations that can prevent the most misguided of self-views.

# ☐ Lingering Questions

Beyond these general themes, the material so far obviously leaves open many lingering questions. Three are of obvious, central importance and thus require discussion before this book can be concluded. The first question centers on whether people's self-perceptions are condemned to be meager predictors, at best, of their performances and achievements. The second question centers on the potential costs, as well as benefits, of mistaken self-views. The third question focuses on what can be done to improve the accuracy of people's self-judgments.

# ☐ Is Self-Judgment Always So Inaccurate?

This book depicts self-perceivers to be prone to error and bias, even in situations of significant consequence. Yet, in the everyday world, people are left with the impression that they are rather accurate and unbiased individuals (Friedrich, 1996; Pronin, Lin, & Ross, 2002), that they see things and themselves the way they really are, an impression left by a great deal of evidence accumulated through years of living. How can the picture painted in this book square with the very different image people hold of themselves in the everyday world?

We have discussed throughout this book why people might believe they hold accurate opinions of themselves despite pervasive inclinations toward error, but might people's rather favorable self-impressions be based on fact—that is, evidence just not considered in the previous chapters? Put simply, people might frequently make errors, but perhaps they more frequently reach correct conclusions about the self, and these instances of accuracy might just not be reported in psychological litera-ture. After all, reporters on the human condition tend to write stories about surprising and provocative events, not situations that are unre-markable and a cause for complacency. We might still live in a world in which *man bites dog* is more likely to be reported than *dog bites man*, even in the staid and scholarly psychological literature from which the bulk of the material in this book has been drawn.

This reporting bias might very well exist, but establishing whether or not it exists really misses the point. Let me stipulate that there are a num-ber of areas in life where people can make precisely accurate predictions, if we just bothered to ask. I assume that if I asked you whether you would get up before 3 p.m. tomorrow, talk to a family member in the next 6 hours, start your car in the morning, or consume bottled water in the next 2 days, you could provide exquisitely accurate predictions. There are a myriad of repeated, mundane, routine behaviors for which we could make correct forecasts. The real question is whether we achieve adequate rates of accu-racy as conditions become more consequential, complex, or novel.

But even that is not the real question. There are undoubtedly some cir-cumstances in which people provide exceedingly accurate self-assess-ments. The data already suggest this. Although Mabe and West (1982) found that people's self-perceptions correlated with their actual perfor-mances, on average, only modestly (around .29), there were some studies in which those correlations ascended to impressive heights (e.g., around .70). What distinguishes such circumstances pulling for accuracy from those pulling for error? This is an understudied question, and one wor-thy of future empirical research.

## An Example of Accurate Self-Appraisal

As a promissory note, one can begin to address this question by con-sidering one corner of the psychological literature that has, on occasion, shown a remarkably close correspondence between self-perception and objective behavior. That literature centers on *self-efficacy* and examines how much a person's performance is anticipated and molded by an indi-vidual's beliefs about success (Bandura, 1977, 1997).

In one of the first studies on self-efficacy, Bandura, Adams, and Beyer (1977) identified people suffering from snake phobias so severe that they endured nightmares and could not bear to attend social and recreational activities that presented a chance, no matter how remote, that a snake might appear. Bandura and colleagues brought phobics into the labora-tory and asked them to perform a number of tasks involving a red-tailed boa constrictor. For example, they were asked to enter the room with the snake, to approach its glass cage, to touch it with a gloved hand, to touch it with a bare hand—leading to letting the snake crawl on their lap. Obviously, participants did not necessarily complete all of these activities.

Participants were then led through therapeutic exercises aimed at desensitizing them to snakes, presented with the same list of activities, and then asked to predict which ones they could now perform. Participants' predictions correlated over .80 with what they could actually do. Indeed, over 85% of their specific predictions later proved spot-on accurate (Bandura et al., 1977).

It is instructive to contemplate why snake phobics in this study were so accurate in their predictions, whereas the rest of us have been so prone to error elsewhere in this book. Specifying what it is about the Bandura et al. (1977) situation that led to accuracy might give us clues concerning when people will be more accurate in their self-perceptions.

There are several aspects of the Bandura et al. (1977) situation one can point to. First, the situation and task were very well defined for participants. There is no ambiguity about what it means to enter a room with a snake, or approach it in its glass cage, or what touching it with a bare hand means. The situation was further well defined for participants in that they possessed direct experience with the task before they made their predictions, allowing them to know what the situation would look like concretely (gee, the snake does not writhe all that much) and what their emotional reaction would feel like (gosh, I do not faint when I touch it).

Second, the actions participants were asked to perform were, in a sense, completely under their control. Each had the physical capability to walk toward the snake, extend their hand to its skin, and to grasp it sufficiently to pick it up out of the cage. To be sure, their emotions may run unchecked, but if they had made the prediction to perform some task they did have it within their physical capability to complete it.

Third, the predictions that participants made were specifically and concretely tailored to the tasks at hand. They were asked precise questions about rather concrete behaviors, such as whether they could touch the snake with their bare hand. They were not asked more vague and indirect questions, such as whether they would be a good snake handler.

The specificity of the questions asked of people matters. A long litany of research findings suggests that people tend to be much more accurate when they are asked concrete questions about precisely defined behaviors rather than when asked more global and abstract queries less specifically tailored to the particular task at hand (Bandura, 1986). For example, if it is crucial for a researcher to know whether someone will use contraception while having sex, it is better to ask them whether they intend to use contraception with their sexual partners rather than asking them some vague question about whether they have a positive or negative attitude toward birth control. Better yet would be to ask about specific forms of contraception (Fishbein & Ajzen, 1980). The more precisely the question is tailored to the circumstance at hand, the better its ability to anticipate an individual's subsequent behavior.

## Peeling Away the Advantages

With these observations in mind, it is easy to see why self-predictions achieved high levels of accuracy in Bandura et al. (1977), whereas in other situations self-predictions failed to anticipate behavior as well. Indeed, in the self-efficacy literature itself, as we move from the circumscribed situation facing Bandura's snake phobics to the type of complex, ill-defined, and novel cacophony of the real world, we find that self-efficacy judgments do a traditionally modest job at predicting behavior and performance. Students' academic self-efficacy in the first year of college predicts their professors' evaluations of performance only at a .35 correlational clip (Chemers, Hu, & Garcia, 2001). In work-related settings, self-efficacy judgments predict performance at a .38 clip. However, if one moves exclusively away from lab to workplace settings, and then concentrates on complex assignments rather simple ones, that correlation melts to .20 (Stajkovic & Luchins, 1998).

Indeed, if one conducts a careful comparison of real-world circumstances to the Bandura et al. (1977) setting, one begins to be struck not by how little people can evaluate their skill and predict their own behavior but by the fact that they can achieve any sort of accuracy at all.

## ☐ Is It So Bad to Hold Erroneous Views of Self?

Another question a reader might have is whether erroneous self-views are anything to worry about. People might hold mistaken ideas about what they are capable of, but most of them still make it through life okay. They hold down jobs, raise lovely families, and reach the end of every day at least in some sort of shape to face the next. Perhaps the fact that people misestimate themselves, or more specifically tend to overestimate what they can achieve, is not really a problem to worry about.

If one surveys recent psychological literature, one finds that the answer to whether such errors matter is a complex one. In particular, if one looks just at one specific error, overestimating one's skills and character, one finds that this error can plausibly be both beneficial as well as costly.

## A Stipulation About Optimism

Before beginning a close examination of the consequences of overrating one's self, I must provide one stipulation. Holding a positive and optimistic view of the self carries many benefits, at least for people in North America (the Asian case might be different; see Heine, Lehman, Markus, & Kitayama, 1999). People with confidence in their abilities persist longer in the face of challenging tasks (Jacobs, Prentice-Dunn, & Rogers, 1984), often leading to better performance (Cervone & Peake, 1986). Children who believe in their math skills persevere longer on math problems (Bouffard-Bouchard, Parent, & Larivee, 1991). Adults optimistic about their physical prowess display greater stamina and react to defeat with renewed effort (Weinberg, Gould, Yudelson, & Jackson, 1981). When two wrestlers go into overtime in their match, it is the wrestler with more self-efficacy who tends to win (Kane, Marks, Zaccaro, & Blair, 1996). People trying to lose weight succeed to the extent that they believe they can succeed (Chambliss & Murray, 1979). Children with positive self-views about their academic skills achieve higher grades and hold more ambitious aspirations (Zimmerman, Bandura, & Martinez-Pons, 1992). Adults with higher work self-efficacy perform better on the job (Eden & Zuk, 1995; Wood, Bandura, & Bailey, 1990). People imbued with optimism are less likely to suffer from depression (Aspinwall & Taylor, 1992). HIV-positive men who are optimistic about their future tend to cope with their situation actively and constructively while avoiding depression and denial (Taylor, Kemeny, Aspinwall, Schneider, Rodriguez, & Herbert, 1992). Optimistic people tend to be healthier (Peterson, 1988). They have more robust immune systems (Kamen-Siegel, Rodin, Seligman, & Dwyer, 1991; Segerstrom, Taylor, Kemeny, & Fahey, 1998) and are more likely to pursue health-promoting behavior (Schwarzer, 1999).

The fact that optimism about the self is better than negativism is beyond dispute. Virginia Woolf was correct when she observed that without self-confidence we are as babes in the cradle. However, what remains well within dispute is whether optimism that exceeds the limits of reality is beneficial or costly. Can people overdo self-confidence? When people hold unrealistic and unjustified views about their skills and character, are they better or worse off for it? Both a *yea* and *nay* case can be, and have been, made about whether unwarranted optimism and unjustified self-confidence are something to cultivate. A quick look at both cases is instructive.

## The "Yea" Case

Several arguments, with data, can be made that overrating one's self is a blessing. To begin, sometimes the error one makes is not as important as the error one avoids. If people overrate themselves, they may get into some trouble, but as they overestimate themselves they avoid the serious problems associated with undervaluing themselves. If optimism brings achievement, stamina, psychological adjustment, and health, then the flip side of optimism tends to bring failure, frailty, depression, and illness. Much work shows this connection: Those who are pessimistic suffer a measurable price in psychological, social, and physical aspects of their life (Armor & Taylor, 1998; Taylor & Brown, 1988). Perhaps optimism carries its own costs, but the benefits of avoiding pessimism might very well outweigh them.

Besides this optimism, recent scholarship hints at a few direct benefits of unwarranted self-confidence. First, people who overvalue themselves leave a good first impression with others. Paulhus (1998) brought college students into the laboratory to take part in a 20-minute group discussion. Those who overrated themselves (compared with what their friends said of them) were viewed by group members as more confident, entertaining, and intelligent than other group members.

Second, people who overestimate themselves have also been shown to achieve more. Wright (2000) identified students who overestimated their academic ability, relative to their academic achievement, and tracked how well they did the following semester. Relative to their more self-doubting peers, overestimaters achieved higher grades.

Overly confident individuals also show signs of enhanced mental health. People with overly inflated views of themselves tend to show superior psychological adjustment across a wide battery of mental health measures that assessed personal growth, purpose in life, depression, anxiety, and positive relations with others (Taylor, Lerner, Sherman, Sage, & McDowell, 2003b). They also tend to be happier than their peers (Taylor & Brown, 1988).

Overestimaters also adjust to adversity better. Women with optimistic views about the potential course of their breast cancer show better psychological adjustment later on, even when those views are unrealistic (Taylor, Lichtman, & Wood, 1984). In a sample of people coping with the aftermath of the civil war in Bosnia-Herzegovina, people who rated themselves more favorably than their friends did reported fewer psychological and physical problems. They also reported fewer social and adjustment problems, impressions confirmed by mental health experts who had dealt with them (Bonanno, Field, Kovacevic, & Kaltman, 2002). Among people who recently had a loved one die a violent death, those scoring high on a measure of self-deception suffered fewer post-traumatic stress disorder symptoms, as rated by mental health professionals, 14 and 25 months after their loss (Bonanno et al., 2002).

Although provocative, the studies demonstrating the link between self-confidence and mental health have proven to be controversial. One major issue is that measures of mental health and well-being tend to be based on self-report, leaving open the possibility that people classified as overraters are also overrating their happiness, adjustment, personal fulfillment, and relations with others. Possibly, their reports of enhanced adjustment are just another product of their self-delusion. Indeed, when researchers instead identify overraters by comparing self-ratings with evaluations provided by clinicians conducting formal assessments, the relationship between optimism and psychological health is diminished greatly (Shedler, Mayman, & Manis, 1993; although Taylor et al., 2003b, failed to replicate this result).

More intriguing, however, are data showing that self-overestimation is related to objective markers of physical health. Taylor and colleagues invited college students to the laboratory and put them through a number of stressful exercises, including counting backward from 9,095 by 7's and providing associations to phrases that contained threatening and sexual themes (Taylor, Lerner, Sherman, Sage, & McDowell, 2003b). Overestimaters responded with less physiological stress, as measured by heart rate, blood pressure, and cortisol production, relative to their more realistic peers. In a more real-life setting, among HIV-positive individuals, those with unrealistic views of their future tend to experience a less rapid course of illness (Reed, Kemeny, Taylor, & Visscher, 1999) and, finally, live longer than their more pessimistic peers (Reed, Kemeny, Taylor, Wang, & Visscher, 1994).

## But ...

However, there is one major caveat to the notion that ignoring reality and welcoming delusion is a good thing. If overrating is good, it is best only in small doses (Baumeister, 1990; Taylor & Brown, 1994). People should not overindulge and overrate themselves as much as humanly possible. Instead, overestimation should occur only at the margins and perhaps not much more. The best evidence that moderation in self-inflation is important is that the overheated views of self-importance and self-esteem associated with mania are still a cause for treatment and not for celebration. If self-overestimation were always beneficial, one would not treat mania with lithium. Instead, the pharmaceutical industry would be looking for pills that could produce mania's psychological effects for the segment of the general population that could afford them. Thus, common experience in the mental health domain shows that outsized views of one's worth and competence that are too detached from reality can be cause for severe and unacceptable risk.

A few shards of data also suggest that overestimation is best when taken in moderate quantities. Mothers who overestimate their ability to control their 5-month old infant to a moderate degree have a more compliant child 18 months later than both mothers with accurate self-views and mothers who grossly overestimate their control (Donovan, Leavitt, & Walsh, 2000). Among smokers trying to quit, those who moderately overestimate their self-efficacy to abstain after a relapse are more successful in their efforts than those with pessimistic beliefs as well as those who grossly overestimate their ability to abstain (Haaga & Stewart, 1992).

## The "Nay" Case

However, emerging alongside the research described is a companion set of findings that speak to a number of costs of overestimation. For example, people might like overly confident individuals at first, but over time their company wears thin. After several group discussions among college students, group members who overestimated themselves, although initially liked, were ultimately seen as more arrogant, bragging, hostile, defensive, and psychologically maladjusted than their more modest peers (Paulhus, 1998; see also John & Robins, 1994).

The mental health of overestimaters can also be called into question. Relative to their more humble counterparts, overestimaters are seen by others as less socially skilled, and more hostile, thin-skinned, anxious, and fearful, among many other traits indicating maladjustment (Colvin, Block, & Funder, 1995). Overestimators tend to be narcissistic (John & Robins, 1994), and overestimation among children has been linked to attention deficit disorder (Owens & Hoza, 2003).

In addition, optimistic people might persist, but they might carry on in ways that are counterproductive. They may not have the insight to adhere to the "serenity prayer," the one that states that people should possess the courage to change what they can, the poise to accept what they cannot, and the wisdom to know the difference. Overly optimistic people persist on problems that are unsolvable (Feather, 1961). Business owners who are confident in a given business strategy stick to it far longer than they should when economic conditions change (Audia, Locke, & Smith, 2000). Students given unrealistic feedback persist on tasks they are not good at, thus not taking advantage of their true competencies, relative to those provided with realistic feedback (Forsterling & Morgenstern, 2002).

High expectations can also lead to disappointment and disengagement. Students who overestimate their academic skill when they enter college are more disengaged from academics and suffer lower levels of well-being compared with their more modest peers, even though they perform just as well and graduate just as often as those peers (Robins & Beer, 2001). Type A individuals, who display a syndrome of high achievement needs, competitiveness, and hostility, tend to set unrealistic performance goals. When they fail to reach them, they evaluate their performances more negatively and experience more psychological distress (Ward & Eisler, 1987).

Overconfidence can also lead to complacency. People who underestimate the amount of fat in their diet perceive themselves to be relatively invulnerable to cancer risks and express less of a need to change their eating habits (O'Brien, Fries, & Bowen, 2000). People with highly positive views of their analytical skills become overconfident and then start making sloppy logical errors that detract from their overall performance (Vancouver, Thompson, Tischner, & Putka, 2002; Vancouver, Thompson, & Williams, 2001). People led to be overconfident expend less effort and pay less critical attention to the strategy they are following, thus performing more poorly, relative to those induced to be more pessimistic (Stone, 1994; see also Bandura & Jourden, 1991).

This pattern of complacency and optimism can lead people to endanger themselves. People who are unrealistically overconfident about their risk for heart attack remember less of the material they have been given about the risks of the disease, presumably because they approach that material with a defensive stance (Radcliffe & Klein, 2002). A sense of invulnerability causes people to pay less attention to information indicating that they are at risk of illness, as well as to discount that information (Menon, Block, & Ramanathan, 2002). Young drivers, overconfident in their ability to spot risks on the road, take risks that lead to a higher accident rates (Deery, 1999). People who take an unrealistically positive stance toward their future in earthquake zones tend not to take precautions for the inevitable danger (Lehman & Taylor, 1987). People displaying unrealistic biases about risk also fail to test for radon in their homes, even if they live in a high-risk area (Weinstein & Lydon, 1999).

At times, the endangerment is not physical but professional. Financial dealers prone toward illusions of control in the laboratory tend to post lower performances than their more cautious peers, based on money earned as well as evaluations from their boss (Fenton-O'Creevy, Nicholson, Soane, & Willman, 2003). Overconfident CEOs push for mergers that damage the price of their company's stock (Malmendier & Tate, 2003). Among managers who are at risk for "derailment," a polite term for being fired or having to quit, those who overestimate themselves tend to derail in far greater numbers than those who do not overestimate themselves (Shipper & Dillard, 2000).

## Reconciliation

In short, both upbeat and downbeat portraits can be drawn of unrealistic optimism about the self. Given this, what conclusion is one to draw about unrealistic optimism? Is it something to nurture or a thing to extinguish? Obviously, given the already complicated portrait being drawn, more work must be done to draw a more sophisticated and comprehensive picture of the role of erroneous self-views on life outcomes. As a few prominent researchers have noted, work on the consequences of mistaken self-impressions is only in its infancy, and there is a lot of research that needs to be done (Armor & Taylor, 1998; Weinstein & Klein, 1996).

That said, a few hazy and tentative themes and principles can be drawn out from the findings so far. First, overconfidence seems to be beneficial when people face the most extreme challenges. For example, overconfidence, much like self-efficacy, appears linked to psychological adjustment when people face severe challenges of HIV infection (Taylor, Kemeny, Aspinwall, Schneider, Rodriguez, & Herbert, 1992), breast cancer (Taylor, Lichtman, & Wood, 1984), or life after wartime (Bonanno, Field, Kovacevic, & Kaltman, 2002). Overconfidence appears beneficial if it spurs a person to useful effort that will improve their circumstances. Overconfidence is also helpful, in some sense, when it is unclear that people are actually being overconfident—that is, when "reality," in some sense, lies in the future and has yet to be written (Schneider, 2001). Of course, if people are to be overconfident, they should do so only to a moderate degree (Baumeister, 1990).

Beyond that, whether overconfidence is beneficial or costly depends on the interaction of two factors. The first factor is whether it spurs people on a path to effort and persistence on the one hand versus inaction and complacency on the other. The second factor is the relative payoff for the path taken. In some situations, effort is the more profitable path. In others, inaction is the more rewarding avenue.

As an example, consider two very different situations with very different payoff structures for action versus inaction. The first is marriage. People show tremendous overconfidence in their skill at maintaining a happy and stable marriage (Weinstein, 1980). This belief is likely to spur them to take the marriage vow. They may find, once the honeymoon is over, that marriage requires more sacrifice, effort, negotiation, patience, and tolerance than they ever would have imagined. That said, despite their overconfidence, and although clearly not all marriages succeed, marriages tend to have a remarkable impact on a person's health and well-being. Marriage leads to improvements in mental health (Marks & Lambert, 1998). It also tends to pull people out of poverty (McLanahan &

Sandefur, 1994). Married people are less likely to suffer long-term illnesses (Murphy, Glaser, & Grundy, 1997). They also live longer (Lillard & Waite, 1995). When all is said and done, if overconfidence leads to action, and that action produces benefits in health and well-being, then the effect of that overconfidence is positive.

Other settings, however, present much different payoff structures. Marriage, on average, is beneficial; gambling, in the long run, is not. Overconfident views of one's gambling ability will, as in the case of marriage, spur a person to action, but that action can come with a hefty price tag that starts with money and may end in ruined social relations. Optimistic views about gambling have been linked to persistence in gambling and to sloughing off losses (Gibson & Sanbonmatsu, 2004). Thus, in gambling, the action spurred on by overconfidence can hardly be considered beneficial over the long term, in that the odds always favor the house. In another setting, overconfidence about the hard task of dieting can lead people to lose weight, only to gain it back, to try to lose it again—leading to drastic cycles of weight loss and gain that can bring about harmful health problems (Polivy & Herman, 2002).

In short, to map out an adequate account of the advantages and disadvantages of overconfidence, future researchers will have to keep a close eye on the payoff structures associated with specific situations. Overconfidence might be beneficial to a client in therapy because effort helps. But overconfidence among doctors, investment bankers, military officers, and air traffic controllers might lead to tragedy. Researchers will have to pay attention to these situational contingencies if they wish to provide an adequate account of the sequelae of overconfidence.

## ☐ Correcting Erroneous Self-Views

Earlier in this chapter, I suggested that people pay a little more attention to what other people have to say about them, that obtaining feedback from others, although problematic, offered at least the possibility that people could improve themselves. The same is true the other way. If we can provide feedback to the individuals around us, we can help them to form more perfect self-impressions of skill and character, and perhaps motivate them to improve themselves.

However, as anyone who has ever tried to give another person his or her honest opinion, giving feedback is a tricky and risky business, which may bring effects (and affects) far from what was intended. Even in situations in which people receive formal feedback, the feedback they receive might not be helpful. In a comprehensive review of feedback programs in organizations, Kluger and DeNisi (1996) found that nearly 40% of them led to decreased performance rather than improvement.

But what is the best way for outside parties to provide feedback? It is difficult to provide a simple answer to this question. What works best in one situation may not apply in another (DeNisi & Kluger, 2000). That said, there is one general issue that people should be mindful of as they provide feedback to others.

## Self-Affirmation

The issue is that receiving feedback, especially negative feedback, can put a person's self-esteem squarely at risk. Receiving a grade on a final exam, being called into the boss's office, or having one's therapist start to make an observation are all situations that might affect, for better or worse, a person's sense of worth. In particular, when feedback comprises bad news, people might be quite aggressive in their attempts to dismiss or discount the criticism (Kunda, 1990)—or worse. Thus, how does one get around the potential for defensiveness, anger, withdrawal, or blow-back that negative feedback might induce?

There are several moves a person giving feedback might make to remove or diminish a person's defensiveness. One move is to include a self-affirmation exercise, bolstering a person's sense of self-worth before giving him or her the bad news (Steele, 1988). For example, Sherman, Nelson, and Steele (2000) showed college students an AIDS-awareness video designed to heighten how vulnerable people in general were to infection. Students were then asked to rate their own risk and then were given the opportunity to buy some condoms on their way out of the lab. Before seeing the video, roughly half of the participants were put in a self-affirmation exercise in which they identified some important value of theirs (e.g., the importance of their family and friend relations) and wrote an essay about an experience in which that value had made them feel proud. This group, relative to a control condition, rated themselves as much more at risk for AIDS after seeing the video and bought more condoms as a consequence.

Other research affirms the efficacy of self-affirmation when it comes to dealing with uncomfortable news. Students reminded of just how kind they tend to be toward others are more open to news about potentially important health risks, relative to a control group. They rate risk-confirming information as more persuasive and are less likely to show biased memory for such information a week later (Reed & Aspinwall, 1998). People who go through self-affirmation exercises are more likely to consider the arguments of people who disagree with their political attitudes and are more likely to critique the arguments of those who agree with them (Cohen, Aronson, & Steele, 2000). People who have just gone through a success experience are more likely to pay attention to information about their potential shortcomings to achieve a thriving career relative to those who go through a failure experience (Trope & Pomerantz, 1998).

## Specificity of Feedback

Paying attention to the specificity at which feedback is given can also circumvent self-esteem issues. Feedback can be given at a specific level that emphasizes a person's actions and the concrete goals that a person should reach (e.g., your unit is producing only 35 widgets an hour; you should find a way to increase that to 40). Feedback can also be given at a broader and more abstract level (e.g., you really aren't the best work unit manager, are you?). Guess which type of feedback is more effective.

A comprehensive meta-analysis of feedback interventions finds that feedback at the specific level is more helpful than feedback aimed at a broader level (Kluger & DeNisi, 1996). By specific, I mean feedback that focuses on concrete behaviors and goals connected to a task. By broad, I mean feedback that aims, whether explicitly or implicitly, at the person's worth, personality, overall competence, or future job prospects. Broad feedback can also lower motivation and performance—for both children (Mueller & Dweck, 1998) and adults (Kluger & DeNisi). Likewise, any feedback that threatens self-esteem and presents discouraging assessments of the person's aptitude and personal make-up might do the same (Kluger & DeNisi).

Broad feedback runs the risk of reducing drive and accomplishment because it distracts people away from executing the task. That is, what they end up managing is their image rather than their skill. The person becomes involved with maintaining a positive sense of self and expends effort bolstering this self-impression rather than turning that effort toward better performance (DeNisi & Kluger, 2000). In addition, people stop worrying about improving themselves and turn toward just demonstrating that they already possess the relevant skill in question. They may quit sooner when they face impending failure or choose not to challenge themselves in the first place (Dweck & Leggett, 1988).

People also engage in more constructive self-criticism when feedback is concentrated at the task-specific level rather than at a more global and personal level. Kurman (2003) asked college students to complete a number of difficult geometric problems. She told some students that the test focused on their specific skills at shape perception; the rest were told the test assessed their global intelligence. Given the difficulty of the problems, and the fact that the experimenter told participants they had scored in the bottom 30%, students tended to think of their performance as a failure. However, those told that the test focused specifically on shape perception were subsequently more likely to have fewer negative emotional reactions to the failure. They were also more likely to practice on the task and improve their performance on a second go-round with similar problems. The performance of participants who were told that the task measured intelligence actually went down.

A couple of caveats are necessary about providing such feedback at the level of the task. First, it is possible to be too specific, to focus on the mechanics of achieving a goal rather than focusing on the goal itself. For example, suppose a bank manager wanted her tellers to provide more friendly service to customers. If the manager focuses too much on how tellers should smile more, she might focus her employees on this small subtask at the expense of all the actions they could take to make customers more comfortable and satisfied (DeNisi & Kluger, 2000).

Second, not only should a task-specific goal be given but concrete ways to achieve that goal should be provided as well. People obviously perform better when given hints about how to improve their behavior. In addition, after feedback is given, a follow-up assessment should be taken to see if the person has really improved. Without such a follow-up, the individual may never know if they have expanded their skills and enhanced their performance (DeNisi & Kluger, 2000).

## Focusing on the Malleability of Skills

Acceptance of feedback also depends on telling people that performance is malleable. If people believe performance and ability are stable and unchangeable aspects of a person, they tend to become defensive and self-serving under demanding circumstances (Dunning, 1995). Much scholarship over the past 15 years has shown that people react differently to challenge and failure if they think skills are immutable qualities given by genetics or God rather than attributes that can be changed and improved upon with effort. People who consider skills as absolutes react to failure by withdrawing from the challenge and engaging in psychic self-protection. People who think of skills as improvable are more likely to redouble their efforts after a challenge (Dweck, 1999; Dweck, Chiu, & Hong, 1995; Dweck & Leggett, 1988).

One study in particular shows that the theory of malleability people attach to skills has a significant impact on how they respond to setbacks. College students took a quick intelligence test and were told that their performance was either satisfactory or exceptionally substandard. They were then given an opportunity to complete a remedial exercise or some other unrelated task. Next, they were asked if they would like to complete an easy or difficult version of the test they had just taken (Hong, Chiu, Dweck, Lin, & Wan, 1999).

Importantly, before all this, participants read an article purportedly from *Psychology Today* about recent research on intelligence. For some, the article described intelligence as immutably 88% genetic. For others, the article described intelligence as mostly changeable and environmentally driven. This article had a noticeable impact on their choices after failure. Those who had posted a substandard performance wanted to see the remedial exercise more if they had read the article describing intelligence as changeable rather than fixed. Indeed, they requested the remedial exercise at the same rate as participants achieving satisfactory performances. Afterward, they also opted to take a more challenging version of the intelligence test than did their peers who were led to believe that intelligence was predetermined (Hong et al., 1999).

## ☐ Summary

In short, a quick summary of this chapter would have to conclude that there is much more insight that psychological researchers need to gain about self-insight. At times, people might possess quite insightful beliefs about their strengths and limitations, and researchers have yet to pin down when those circumstances might be. Whether deficiencies in self-awareness are something to approve or disapprove of is also open to question. At times, self-delusion might be helpful. At other times, it might be damning, and research has yet to draw a complete map containing the boundary between the former situation and the latter. Finally, there is much work to be done about how to introduce people to themselves more successfully, providing them with more veridical notions about their strong points as well as their weak ones. As such, there exists a long theoretical and empirical journey for psychological researchers to travel.

## ☐ Minor Everests

But for each of us meandering through our own personal lives, a parallel journey exists, with each individual encountering data every day that could be applied to the task of gaining self-knowledge. The material in this book suggests that this journey is a difficult one. Self-insight is neither a commodity that is easily obtained nor a destination easily reached. True self-awareness requires a long journey of experience and self-reflection of which there is no guarantee of success.

But perhaps the journey is the goal in itself. Life presents many challenges, strewn like hills and mountains in our path. Acquiring self-insight might just be one of those peaks, one that is more rugged and steep than it looks from afar. Perhaps this challenge might not be as extreme as conquering Everest, but its slopes and climbs are still formidable. In any event, although the challenge is daunting, it may very well likely represent a challenge wise to accept. From its peak, one does not know what the view of the psychological terrain might look like, but I assume that most people would be quite curious to take a glimpse of this view.

# References

Alicke, M. D. (1985). Global self-evaluation as determined by the desirability and controllability of trait adjectives. *Journal of Personality and Social Psychology, 49,* 1621–1630.

Alicke, M. D. (1993). Egocentric standards of conduct evaluation. *Basic and Applied Social Psychology, 14,* 171–192.

Alicke, M. D., LoSchiavo, F. M., Zerbst, J., & Zhang, S. (1997). The person who outperforms me is a genius: Maintaining perceived competence in upward social comparison. *Journal of Personality and Social Psychology, 72,* 781–789.

Allison, S. T., Messick, D. M., & Goethals, G. R. (1989). On being better but not smarter than others: The Muhammad Ali effect. *Social Cognition, 7,* 275–295.

Allport, F. H. (1924). *Social psychology.* Boston: Houghton Mifflin.

Anderson, C. A., & Sechler, E. S. (1986). Effects of explanation and counterexplanation on the development and use of social theories. *Journal of Personality and Social Psychology, 50,* 24–34.

Anderson, N. H. (1968). Likableness ratings of 555 personality-trait words. *Journal of Personality and Social Psychology, 9,* 272–279

Arkes, H. R. (1993). Some practical judgment and decision-making research. In N. J. Castellan, Jr. (Ed.), *Individual and group decision making: Current issues* (pp. 3–18). Hillsdale, NJ: Erlbaum.

Arkes, H. R., Boehm, L. E., & Xu, G. (1991). Determinants of judged validity. *Journal of Experimental Social Psychology, 27,* 576–605.

Armor, D. A., & Taylor, S. E. (1998). Situated optimism: Specific outcome expectancies and self-regulation. In M. Zanna (Ed.), *Advances in experimental social psychology* (vol. 30, pp. 309–379). San Diego: Academic Press.

Arnold, L., Willoughby, T. L., & Calkins, E. V. (1985). Self-evaluation in undergraduate medical education: A longitudinal perspective. *Journal of Medical Education, 60,* 21–28.

Ashford, S. J. (1989). Self-assessment in organizations: A literature review and integrative model. In L. L. Cummings & B. M. Staw (Eds.), *Research in Organizational Behavior* (vol. 11, pp. 133–174). Greenwich, CT: JAI Press.

Ashford, S. J., & Tsui, A. S. (1991). Self-regulation for managerial effectiveness: The role of active feedback-seeking. *Academy of Management Journal, 34,* 251–280.

Aspinwall, L. G., & Taylor, S. E. (1992). Modeling cognitive adaptation: A longitudinal investigation of the impact of individual differences and coping on college adjustment and performance. *Journal of Personality and Social Psychology, 63,* 989–1003.

Audia, P. G., Locke, E. A., & Smith, K. G. (2000). The paradox of success: An archival and a laboratory study of strategic persistence following radical environmental change. *Academy of Management Journal, 43,* 837–853.

Babcock, L., & Loewenstein, G. (1997). Explaining bargaining impasse: The role of self-serving biases. *Journal of Economic Perspectives, 11,* 109–126.

Babinski, M. J. (1914). Contribution à l'etude dés troubles mentaux dans l'hémiplégie organique cérébrale (anosognosie) [Contribution to the study of mental disturbance in organic hemiplegia (anosognosias)]. *Revue Neurologique (Paris), 12,* 845–848.

Bacon, F. T. (1979). Credibility of repeated statements: Memory for trivia. *Journal of Experimental Psychology: Human Learning and Memory, 5,* 241–252.

Baddeley, A. D., & Longman, D. J. A. (1978). The influence of length and frequency of training session on the rate of learning to type. *Ergonomics, 21,* 627–635.

Baillargeon, J., & Danis, C. (1984). Barnum meets the computer. *Journal of Personality Assessment, 48*, 415–419.

Balcetis, E. (2003). *Feeling "holier than thou" produces extreme and erroneous inferences about others*. Unpublished manuscript, Cornell University.

Bandura, A. (1977). Self-efficacy: Toward a unifying theory of behavioral change. *Psychological Review, 84*, 191–215.

Bandura, A. (1986). *Social foundations of thought and action: A social cognitive theory*. Englewood Cliffs, NJ: Prentice Hall.

Bandura, A. (1997). *Self-efficacy: The exercise of control*. New York: Freeman.

Bandura, A., Adams, N. E., & Beyer, J. (1977). Cognitive processes mediating behavioral change. *Journal of Personality and Social Psychology, 35*, 125–139.

Bandura, A., & Jourden, F. J. (1991). Self-regulatory mechanisms governing the impact of social comparison on complex decision making. *Journal of Personality and Social Psychology, 60*, 941–951.

Barefoot, J. C., & Straub, R. B. (1971). Opportunity for information search and the effect of false heart-rate feedback. *Journal of Personality and Social Psychology, 17*, 154–157.

Bass, B. M., & Yammarino, F. J. (1991). Congruence of self and others' leadership ratings of Naval officers for understanding successful performance. *Applied Psychology, 40*, 437–454.

Basso, M., Schefft, B. K., Ris, M. D., & Dember, W. N. (1996). Mood and global-local visual processing. *Journal of the International Neuropsychological Society, 2*, 249–255.

Baumeister, R. F. (1990). The optimal margin of illusion. *Journal of Social and Clinical Psychology, 8*, 176–189.

Baumeister, R. F., & Newman, L. S. (1994). Self-regulation of cognitive inference and decision processes. *Personality and Social Psychology Bulletin, 20*, 3–19.

Baumeister, R. F., Stillwell, A. M., & Wotman, S. R. (1990). Victim and perpetrator accounts of interpersonal conflict: Autobiographical narratives about anger. *Journal of Personality and Social Psychology, 90*, 994–1005.

Bazinska, R., & Wojciszke, B. (1996). Drawing inferences on moral and competence-related traits from the same behavioural information. *Polish Psychological Bulletin, 27*, 293–299.

Beauregard, K. S., & Dunning, D. (1998). Turning up the contrast: Self-enhancement motives prompt egocentric contrast effects in social judgments. *Journal of Personality and Social Psychology, 74*, 606–621.

Beauregard, K. S., & Dunning, D. (2001). Defining self worth: Trait self-esteem moderates the use of self-serving trait definitions in social judgment. *Motivation and Emotion, 25*, 135–162.

Beggan, J. K. (1992). On the social nature of non-social perception: The mere ownership effect. *Journal of Personality and Social Psychology, 62*, 229–237.

Ben-Zeev, T. (1998). Rational errors and the mathematical mind. *Review of General Psychology, 2*, 366–383.

Benjamin, A. S., & Bjork, R. A. (1996). Retrieval fluency as a metacognitive index. In L. M. Reder (Ed.), *Implicit memory and metacognition: The twenty-seventh Carnegie symposium on cognition* (pp. 309–338). Hillsdale, NJ: Erlbaum.

Benjamin, A. S., Bjork, R. A., & Schwartz, B. L. (1998). The mismeasure of memory: When retrieval fluency is misleading as a metamnemonic index. *Journal of Experimental Psychology: General, 127*, 55–68.

Berkowitz, A. (1997). From reactive to proactive prevention: Promoting an ecology of health on campus. In P. C. Rivers & E. R. Shore (Eds.) *Substance abuse on campus: A handbook for college and university personnel* (pp. 119–139). Westport, CT: Greenwood Press.

Berkowitz, A. D. (2003). Application of social norms theory to other health and social justice issues. In H. W. Perkins (Ed.), *The social norms approach to preventing school and college age substance abuse: A handbook for educators, counselors, and clinicians* (pp. 259–279). San Francisco, CA: Jossey-Bass.

Beyer, S. (1990). Gender differences in the accuracy of self-evaluations of performance. *Journal of Personality and Social Psychology, 59*, 960–970.

Beyer, S., & Bowden, E. M. (1997). Gender differences in self-perceptions: Convergent evidence from three measures of accuracy and bias. *Personality and Social Psychology Bulletin, 23*, 157–172.

Bjork, R. A. (1999). Assessing our own competence: Heuristics and illusions. In D. Gopher and A. Koriat (Eds.), *Attention and peformance XVII. Cognitive regulation of performance: Interaction of theory and application* (pp. 435–459). Cambridge, MA: MIT Press.

Blalock, S. J., DeVellis, B. M., & Afifi, R. A. (1990). Risk perceptions and participation in colorectal cancer screening. *Health Psychology, 9*, 792–806.

Blanton, H., Pelham, B. W., DeHart, T., & Carvallo, M. (2001). Overconfidence as dissonance reduction. *Journal of Experimental Social Psychology, 37*, 373–385.

Boehm, L. E. (1994). The validity effect: A search for mediating variables. *Personality and Social Psychology, 20*, 285–293.

Bonanno, G. A., Field, N. P., Kovacevic, A., & Kaltman, S. (2002). Self-enhancement as a buffer against extreme adversity: Civil war in Bosnia and traumatic loss in the United States. *Personality and Social Psychology Bulletin, 28*, 184–196.

Borkenau, P., & Liebler, A. (1993). Convergence of stranger ratings of personality and intelligence with self-ratings, partner ratings, and measured intelligence. *Journal of Personality and Social Psychology, 65*, 546–553.

Bouffard-Bouchard, T., Parent, S., & Larivee, S. (1991). Influence of self-efficacy on self-regulation and performance among junior and senior high-school age students. *International Journal of Behavioral Development, 14*, 153–164.

Boyd, N., Sutherland, H. J., Heasman, K. Z., Tritcher, D. L., & Cummings, B. (1990). Whose utilities for decision analysis? *Medical Decision Making, 10*, 58–67.

Boyer-Pennington, M. E., Pennington, J., & Spink, C. (2001). Students' expectations and optimism toward marriage as a function of parental divorce. *Journal of Divorce and Remarriage, 34*, 71–87.

Bradley, M. J. (1981). Overconfidence in ignorant experts. *Bulletin of the Psychonomic Society, 17*, 82–84.

Brehm, J. W. (1956). Post-decision changes in desirability of alternatives. *Journal of Abnormal and Social Psychology, 52*, 384–389.

Brenner, L. (2000). Should observed overconfidence be dismissed as a statistical artifact? Critique of Erev, Wallsten, & Budescu (1994). *Psychological Review, 107*, 943–946.

Brickman, P., Coates, D., & Janoff-Bulman, R. (1978). Lottery winners and accident victims: Is happiness relative? *Journal of Personality and Social Psychology, 36*, 917–927.

Brown, I. D., Groeger, J. A., & Biehl, B. (1988). Is driver training contributing enough towards road safety? In J. A. Rothengatter & R. A. de Bruin (Eds.), *Road users and traffic safety* (pp. 135–156). Wolfeboro, NH: Van Gorcum.

Brownstein, A. L. (2003). Biased predecision processing. *Psychological Bulletin, 129*, 545–568.

Brunner, B. (2002). Everest Trivia. Factmonster.com. Retrieved February 21, 2004 at http://factmonster.com/spot/everest-facts1.html

Budescu, D. V., & Bruderman, M. (1995). The relationship between the illusion of control and the desirability bias. *Journal of Behavioral Decision Making, 8*, 109–125.

Buehler, R., Griffin, D., & MacDonald, H. (1997). The role of motivated reasoning in optimistic time predictions. *Personality and Social Psychology Bulletin, 23*, 238–247.

Buehler, R., Griffin, D., & Ross, M. (1994). Exploring the "planning fallacy": Why people underestimate their task completion times. *Journal of Personality and Social Psychology, 67*, 366–381.

Caputo, D., & Dunning, D. (in press). What you do not know: The role played by errors of omission in imperfect self-assessment. *Journal of Experimental Social Psychology.*

Carlson, K. A., & Russo, J. E. (2001). Biased interpretation of evidence by mock jurors. *Journal of Experimental Psychology: Applied, 7*, 91–103.

Carroll, D., & Huxley, J. A. A. (1994). Cognitive, dispositional, and psychophysiological correlates of dependent slot machine gambling in young people. *Journal of Applied Social Psychology, 24*, 1070–1083.

Carpenter, W. T., Strauss, J. S., & Bartko, J. J. (1973). Flexible system for the diagnosis of schizophrenia: Report from the WHO International pilot study of schizophrenia. *Science, 182*, 1275–1278.

Ceci, S. J., & Liker, J. (1986). A day at the races: IQ, expertise, and cognitive complexity. *Journal of Experimental Psychology: General, 115*, 255–266.

Cervone, D., & Peake, P. K. (1986). Anchoring, efficacy, and action: The influence of judgmental heuristics on self-efficacy judgments and behavior. *Journal of Personality and Social Psychology, 50,* 492–501.

Chambliss, C. A., & Murray, E. J. (1979). Efficacy attribution, locus of control, and weight loss. *Cognitive Therapy and Research, 3,* 349–353

Chapman, L. J., & Chapman, J. P. (1967). The genesis of popular but erroneous psychodiagnostic observations. *Journal of Abnormal Psychology, 72,* 193–204.

Chapman, L. J., & Chapman, J. P. (1969). Illusory correlation as an obstacle to the use of valid psychodiagnostic signs. *Journal of Abnormal Psychology, 27,* 271–280.

Chemers, M. M., Hu, L., & Garcia, B. F. (2001). Academic self-efficacy and first-year college student performance and adjustment. *Journal of Educational Psychology, 93,* 55–64.

Chi, M. T. H. (1978). Knowledge structures and memory development. In R. Siegler (Ed.), *Children's thinking: What develops?* (pp. 73–96). Hillsdale, NJ: Erlbaum.

Chi, M. T. H., Glaser, R., & Rees, E. (1982). Expertise in problem solving. In R. Sternberg (Ed.), *Advances in the psychological of human intelligence* (vol. 1, pp. 17–76). Hillsdale, NJ: Erlbaum.

Christensen, P., & Glad, A. (1996). Mandatory course of driving on slippery roads does not reduce the accident risk. *Nordic Road and Transport Research, 8,* 22–23.

Christensen-Szalanski, J. J. J., & Bushyhead, J. B. (1981). Physicians' use of probablistic information in a real clinical setting. *Journal of Experimental Psychology: Human Perception and Performance, 7,* 928–935.

Christensen-Szalanski, J. J. J., Willham, F. C. (1991). The hindsight bias: A meta-analysis. *Organizational Behavior and Human Decision Processes, 48,* 147–158.

Christie, R. (2001) *The effectiveness of driver training as a road safety measure: A review of the literature.* Noble Park, Victoria, Australia: Royal Automobile Club of Victoria.

Cialdini, R. B., Reno, R. R., & Kallgren, C. A. (1990). A focus theory of normative conduct: Recycling the concept of norms to reduce littering in public places. *Journal of Personality and Social Psychology, 58,* 1015–1026.

Clotfelter, C. T., & Cook, P. J. (1989). *Selling hope: State lotteries in America.* Cambridge, MA: Harvard University Press.

Cohen, G. L., Aronson, J., & Steele, C. M. (2000). When beliefs yield to evidence: Reducing biased evaluation by affirming the self. *Personality and Social Psychology Bulletin, 26,* 1151–1164.

Cohen, M. D., & March, J. G. (1974). *Leadership and ambiguity: The American college president.* New York: McGraw-Hill.

College Board. (1976–1977). *Student descriptive qustionnaire.* Princeton, NJ: Educational Testing Service.

Colvin, C. R., & Block, J. (1994). Do positive illusions foster mental health? An examination of the Taylor and Brown formulation. *Psychological Bulletin, 116,* 3–20.

Colvin, C. R., Block, J., & Funder, D. (1995). Overly positive self-evaluations and personality: Negative implications for mental health. *Journal of Personality and Social Psychology, 68,* 1152–1162.

Cooper, A. C., Woo, C. Y., & Dunkelberg, W. C. (1988). Entrepreneurs' perceived chances for success. *Journal of Business Venturing, 3,* 97–108.

Costermans, J., Lories, G., & Ansay, C. (1992). Confidence level and feeling of knowing in question answering: The weight of inferential processes. *Journal of Experimental Psychology: Learning, Memory, and Cognition, 18,* 142–150.

Crosby, R. A., & Yarber, W. L. (2001). Perceived versus actual knowledge about correct condom use among U.S. adolescents. *Journal of Adolescent Health, 28,* 415–420.

Cross, P. (1977). Not can but *will* college teaching be improved? *New Directions for Higher Education, 17,* 1–15.

D'Amasio, A. R. (1994). *Descartes' error: Emotion, reason, and the human brain.* New York: Putnam.

Dawes, R. M. (1988). *Rational choice in an uncertain world.* San Diego, CA: Harcourt Brace Jovanovich.

Dawes, R. M., & Mulford, M. (1996). The false consensus effect and overconfidence: Flaws in judgment, or flaws in how we study judgment? *Organizational Behavior and Human Decision Processes, 65,* 201–211.

Dawson, E., Gilovich, T., & Regan, D. T. (2002). Motivated reasoning and performance on the Wason selection task. *Personality and Social Psychology Bulletin, 28*, 1379–1387.

Deery, H. A. (1999). Hazard and risk perception among young novice drivers. *Journal of Safety Research, 30*, 225–236.

DeJong, W., & Langford, L. A. (2002). Typology for campus-based alcohol prevention: Moving toward environmental management strategies. *Journal of Studies on Alcohol Supplement, 14*, 140–147.

DeJong, W., & Linkenbach, J. (1999). Telling it like it is: Using social norms marketing campaigns to reduce student drinking. *American Association for Higher Education Bulletin, 32*, 11–16.

DeJoy, D. M. (1989). The optimism bias and traffic accident risk perception. *Accident Analysis and Prevention, 21*, 333–340.

Dempster, F. N. (1990). The spacing effect: A case study in the failure to apply the results of psychological research. *American Psychologist, 43*, 627–634.

Dempster, F. N. (1996). Distributing and managing the conditions of encoding and practice. In E. L. Bjork & R. A. Bjork (Eds.), *Handbook of Perception and Cognition* (vol. 10; pp. 317–344). New York: Academic Press.

DeNisi, A. S., & Kluger, A. N. (2000). Feedback effectiveness: Can 360-degree appraisals be improved? *Academy of Management Executive, 14*, 129–139.

DePaulo, B. M. (1994). Spotting lies: Can humans learn to do better? *Current Directions in Psychological Science, 3*, 83–86.

DePaulo, B. M., & Bell, K. L. (1996). Truth and investment: Lies are told to those who care. *Journal of Personality and Social Psychology, 71*, 703–716.

DePaulo, B. M., Charlton, K., Cooper, H., Lindsay, J. J., & Muhlenbruck, L. (1997). The accuracy-confidence correlation in the detection of deception. *Personality and Social Psychology Review, 1*, 346–357.

DePaulo, B. M., Stone, J. I., & Lassiter, G. D. (1985). Deceiving and detecting deceit. In B. R. Schlenker (Ed.), *The self in social life* (pp. 323–370). New York: McGraw-Hill.

Derryberry, D., and Tucker, D. (1992). Neural mechanisms of emotion. *Journal of Consulting and Clinical Psychology, 60*, 329–337.

Dickson, D. H., & Kelly, I. W. (1985). The "Barnum effect" in personality assessment: A review of the literature. *Psychological Reports, 57*, 367–382.

Dies, R. R. (1972). Personal gullibility of pseudodiagnosis: A further test of the "fallacy of personal validation." *Journal of Clinical Psychology, 28*, 47–50.

Ditto, P. H., & Lopez, D. F. (1992). Motivated skepticism: Use of differential decision criteria for preferred and nonpreferred conclusions. *Journal of Personality and Social Psychology, 63*, 568–584.

Ditto, P. H., Scepansky, J. A., Munro, G. D., Apanovitch, A. M., & Lockhart, L. K. (1998). Motivated sensitivity to preference-inconsistent information. *Journal of Personality and Social Psychology, 75*, 53–69.

Donovan, W. L., Leavitt, L. A., & Walsh, R. O. (2000). Maternal illusory control predicts socialization strategies and toddler compliance. *Developmental Psychology, 36*, 402–411.

Drew, P. (1987). Po-faced receipts of teases. *Linguistics, 25*, 219–253.

Duffin, J. M., & Simpson, A. P. (1993). Natural, conflicting, and alien. *Journal of Mathematical Behavior, 12*, 313–328.

Dun & Bradstreet. (1967). *Patterns of success in managing a business*. New York: Dun & Bradstreet.

Dunbar, K. (1995). How scientists really reason: Scientific reasoning in real-world laboratories. In R.J. Sternberg & J. Davidson (Eds.), *Mechanisms of insight* (pp. 365–395). Cambridge, MA: MIT Press.

Dunlosky, J., & Nelson, T. O. (1992). Importance of the kind of cue for judgments of learning (JOL) and the delayed-JOL effect. *Memory and Cognition, 20*, 374–380.

Dunning, D. (1995). Trait importance and modifiability as factors influencing self-assessment and self-enhancement motives. *Personality and Social Psychology Bulletin, 21*, 1297–1306.

Dunning, D. (1999). A newer look: Motivated social cognition and the schematic representation of social concepts. *Psychological Inquiry, 10*, 1–11.

Dunning, D. (2000). Social judgment as implicit social comparison. In J. Suls & L. Wheeler (Eds.), *Handbook of social comparison: Theory and research* (pp. 353–378). New York: Kluwer Academic/Plenum.

Dunning, D. (2001). On the motives underlying social cognition. In N. Schwarz & A. Tesser (Eds.), *Blackwell handbook of social psychology: Volume 1: Intraindividual processes* (pp. 348–374). New York: Blackwell.

Dunning, D. (2003). Self-perceived versus actual knowledge about sexually transmitted diseases. Unpublished data, Cornell University.

Dunning, D., & Beauregard, K. S. (2000). Regulating impressions of others to affirm images of the self. *Social Cognition, 18,* 198–222.

Dunning, D., & Cohen, G. L. (1992). Egocentric definitions of traits and abilities in social judgment. *Journal of Personality and Social Psychology, 63,* 341–355.

Dunning, D., Griffin, D. W., Milojkovic, J. H., & Ross, L. (1990). The overconfidence effect in social prediction. *Journal of Personality and Social Psychology, 58,* 568–592.

Dunning, D., & Hayes, A. F. (1996). Evidence for egocentric comparison in social judgment. *Journal of Personality and Social Psychology, 71,* 213–229.

Dunning, D., Johnson, K., Ehrlinger, J., & Kruger, J. (2003). Why people fail to recognize their own incompetence. *Current Directions in Psychological Science, 12,* 83–86.

Dunning, D., Leuenberger, A., & Sherman, D. A. (1995). A new look at motivated inference: Are self-serving theories of success a product of motivational forces? *Journal of Personality and Social Psychology, 59,* 58–68.

Dunning, D., & McElwee, R. O. (1995). Idiosyncratic trait definitions: Implications for self-description and social judgment. *Journal of Personality and Social Psychology, 68,* 936–946.

Dunning, D., Meyerowitz, J. A., & Holzberg, A. D. (1989). Ambiguity and self-evaluation: The role of idiosyncratic trait definitions in self-serving assessments of ability. *Journal of Personality and Social Psychology, 57,* 1082–1090.

Dunning, D., & Parpal, M. (1989). Mental addition and subtraction in counterfactual reasoning: On assessing the impact of actions and life events. *Journal of Personality and Social Psychology, 57,* 5–15.

Dunning, D., Perie, M., & Story, A. L. (1991). Self-serving prototypes of social categories. *Journal of Personality and Social Psychology, 61,* 957–968.

Dunning, D., & Perretta, S. (2002). Automaticity and eyewitness accuracy: A 10- to 12-second rule for distinguishing accurate from inaccurate positive identifications. *Journal of Applied Psychology, 87,* 951–962.

Dunning, D., & Sherman, D. A. (1997). Stereotypes and tacit inference. *Journal of Personality and Social Psychology, 73,* 459–471.

Dunning, D., & Stern, L. B. (1994). Distinguishing accurate from inaccurate identifications via inquiries about decision processes. *Journal of Personality and Social Psychology, 67,* 818–835.

Dunning, D., & Story, A. L. (1991). Depression, realism, and the overconfidence effect: Are the sadder wiser when predicting future actions and events? *Journal of Personality and Social Psychology, 61,* 521–532.

Dunning, D., Van Boven, L., Loewenstein, G. (2001). Egocentric empathy gaps in social interaction and exchange. In S. Thye, E. J. Lawler, M. Macy, & H. Walker (Eds.), *Advances in Group Processes* (vol. 18; pp. 65–98), Stamford, CT: JAI.

Dutton, D. G., & Aron, A. P. (1974). Some evidence for heightened sexual attraction under conditions of high anxiety. *Journal of Personality and Social Psychology, 30,* 510–517.

Dweck, C.S. (1999). *Self-theories: Their role in motivation, personality and development.* Philadelphia, PA: Psychology Press.

Dweck, C. S., Chiu, C. Y., & Hong, Y. Y. (1995). Implicit theories and their role in judgments and reactions: A world from two perspectives. *Psychological Inquiry, 6,* 267–285.

Dweck, C. S., & Leggett, E. L. (1988). A social-cognitive approach to motivation and personality. *Psychological Review, 95,* 256–273.

Eccles, J. S. (1987). Gender roles and women's achievement-related decisions. *Psychology of Women Quarterly, 11,* 135–172.

Eden, D., & Zuk, Y. (1995). Seasickness as a self-fulfilling prophecy: Raising self-efficacy to boost performance at sea. *Journal of Applied Psychology, 80,* 628–635.

Ehrlinger, J., & Dunning, D. (2003). How chronic self-views influence (and potentially mislead) estimates of performance. *Journal of Personality and Social Psychology, 84*, 5–17.

Ehrlinger, J., Johnson, K., Banner, M., Dunning, D., & Kruger, D. (2004). *Why the unskilled are unaware: Further explorations of (absent) self-insight among the incompetent.* Unpublished manuscript, Cornell University.

Ekman, P., & O'Sullivan, M. (1991). Who can catch a liar? *American Psychologist, 46*, 913–920.

Epley, N., & Dunning, D. (2000). Feeling "holier than thou": Are self-serving assessments produced by errors in self or social prediction? *Journal of Personality and Social Psychology, 79*, 861–875.

Epley, N., & Dunning, D. (2004). *The mixed blessings of self-knowledge in behavioral prediction.* Unpublished manuscript, Harvard University.

Erev, I., Wallsten, T. S., & Budescu, D. V. (1994). Simultaneous over- and underconfidence: The role of error in judgment processes. *Psychological Review, 101*, 519–527.

Evans, J. B. T., & Wason, P. C. (1976). Rationalization in a reasoning task. *British Journal of Psychology, 67*, 479–486.

Falchikov, J. N., & Boud, D. (1989). Student self-assessment in higher education: A meta-analysis. *Review of Educational Research, 59*, 395–430.

Fatsis, S. (2001). *Word freak.* New York: Penguin Putnam.

Fazio, R. H., & Zanna, M. P. (1981). Direct experience and attitude-behavior consistency. In L. Berkowitz (Ed.), *Advances in experimental social psychology* (vol. 14, pp. 161–202). New York: Academic Press.

Feather, N. T. (1961). The relationship of persistence at a task to expectation of success and achievement related motives. *Journal of Abnormal and Social Psychology, 63*, 552–561.

Feather, N. T. (1968). Change in confidence following success or failure as a predictor of subsequent performance. *Journal of Personality and Social Psychology, 9*, 38–46.

Felson, R. B. (1981). Ambiguity and bias in the self-concept. *Social Psychology Quarterly, 44*, 64–69.

Fenton-O'Creevy, M., Nicholson, N., Soane, E., & Willman, P. (2003). Trading on illusions: Unrealistic perceptions of control and trading performance. *Journal of Occupational and Organisational Psychology, 76*, 53–68.

Fischhoff, B. (1975). Hindsight ≠ foresight: The effect of outcome knowledge on judgment under uncertainty. *Journal of Experimental Psychology: Human Perception and Performance, 1*, 288–299.

Fischhoff, B. (1977). Perceived informativeness of facts. *Journal of Experimental Psychology: Human Perception and Performance, 3*, 349–358.

Fischhoff, B., Slovic, P., & Lichtenstein, S. (1977). Knowing with certainty: The appropriateness of extreme confidence. *Journal of Experimental Psychology: Human Perception and Performance, 3*, 552–564.

Fishbein, M., & Ajzen, I. (1980). *Understanding attitudes and predicting social behavior.* New Jersey: Prentice Hall.

Fisher, C. D. (1979). Transmission of positive and negative feedback to subordinates: A laboratory investigation. *Journal of Applied Psychology, 64*, 533–540.

Forer, B. R. (1949) The fallacy of personal validation: A classroom demonstration of gullibility. *Journal of Abnormal Psychology, 44*, 118–121.

Forsterling, F., & Morgenstern, M. (2002). Accuracy of self-assessment and task performance: Does it pay to know the truth? *Journal of Educational Psychology, 94*, 576–585.

Fouad, N. A., Smith, P. L., & Zao, K. E. (2002). Across academic domains: Extensions of the social-cognitive career model. *Journal of Counseling Psychology, 49*, 164–171.

Fox, L. H., Benbow, C. P., & Perkins, S. (1983). An accelerated mathematics program for girls: A longitudinal evaluation. In C. P. Benbow & J. C. Stanley (Eds.), *Academic precocity: Aspects of its development* (pp. 133–139). Baltimore, MD: Johns Hopkins University Press.

Fox, E., Russo, R., & Bowles, R. (2001). Do threatening stimuli draw or hold visual attention in subclinical anxiety? *Journal of Experimental Psychology: General, 130*, 681–700.

Fridja, N. H. (1986). *The emotions.* Cambridge, England: Cambridge University Press.

Friedrich, J. (1996). On seeing oneself as less self-serving than others: The ultimate self-serving bias? *Teaching of Psychology, 23*, 107–109.

Frieze, I. H., Hymer, S., & Greenberg, M. S. (1987). Describing the crime victim: Psychological reactions to victimization. *Professional Psychology: Research & Practice, 18,* 299–315.

Fussell, S. R., & Krauss, R. M. (1991). Accuracy and bias in estimates of others' knowledge. *European Journal of Social Psychology, 21,* 445–454.

Fussell, S. R., & Krauss, R. M. (1992). Coordination of knowledge in communication: Effects of speakers' assumptions about what others know. *Journal of Personality and Social Psychology, 62,* 378–391.

Garb, H. N. (1989). Clinical judgment, clinical training, and professional experience. *Psychological Bulletin, 105,* 387–396.

Gibbs, N. (2001). The day of the attack. *Time.com.* Retrieved February 19, 2004 at http://www.time.com/time/world/article/0,8599,174655,00.html.

Gibson, B., & Sanbonmatsu, D. M. (2004). Optimism, pessimism, and gambling: The downside of optimism. *Personality and Social Psychology Bulletin, 30,* 149–160.

Gigerenzer, G. (1984). External validity of laboratory experiments: The frequency-validity relationship. *American Journal of Psychology, 97,* 185–195.

Gilbert, D. T., Gill, M. J., & Wilson, T. D. (2002). The future is now: Temporal correction in affective forecasting. *Organizational Behavior and Human Decision Processes, 88,* 430–444.

Gilbert, D. T., Pinel, E. C., Wilson, T. D., Blumberg, S. J., & Wheatley, T. P. (1998). Immune neglect: A source of durability bias in affective forecasting. *Journal of Personality and Social Psychology, 75,* 617–638.

Gill, M. J., Swann, W. B., Jr., & Silvera, D. H. (1998). On the genesis of confidence. *Journal of Personality and Social Psychology, 75,* 1101–1114.

Gilovich, T. (1983). Biased evaluation and persistence in gambling. *Journal of Personality and Social Psychology, 44,* 1110–1126.

Gilovich, T. (1991). *How we know what isn't so: The fallibility of human reason in everyday life.* New York: Free Press.

Gilovich, T., Kerr, M., & Medvec, V. H. (1993). The effect of temporal perspective on subjective confidence. *Journal of Personality and Social Psychology, 64,* 552–560.

Glenberg, A. M. (1992). Distributed practice effects. In L. R. Squire (Eds.), *Encyclopedia of learning and memory* (pp. 138–142). New York: Macmillan.

Glenberg, A. M., & Epstein, W. (1987). Inexpert calibration of comprehension. *Memory & Cognition, 15,* 84–93.

Goethals, G. R. (1986). Fabricating and ignoring social reality: Self-serving estimates of consensus. In J. Olson, C. P. Herman, & M. P. Zanna (Eds.), *Relative deprivation and social comparison: The Ontario symposium on social cognition* (vol. 4, pp. 135–157). Hillsdale, NJ: Erlbaum.

Goethals, G. R., Messick, D., & Allison, S. (1991). The uniqueness bias: Studies of constructive social comparison. In J. Suls & T. A. Wills (Eds.), *Social comparison: Contemporary theory and research* (pp. 149–176). Hillsdale, NJ: Erlbaum.

Greene, R. L. (1977). Student acceptance of generalized personality interpretations: A reexamination. *Journal of Consulting and Clinical Psychology, 45,* 965–966.

Greenwald, A. G., Carnot, C. G., Beach, R., & Young, B. (1987). Increasing voting behavior by asking people if they expect to vote. *Journal of Applied Psychology, 72,* 315–318.

Gregerson, N. P. (1996). What should be taught? Basic vehicle control skills or higher order skills? In H. Simpson (Ed.), *New to the road: Reducing the risks for young motorists* (pp. 103–114). Los Angeles, CA: Youth Enhancement Service, Brain Information Service.

Greve, W., & Wentura, D. (2003). Immunizing the self: Self-concept stabilization through reality-adaptive self-definitions. *Personality and Social Psychology Bulletin, 29,* 39–50.

Griffin, D. W., Dunning, D., & Ross, L. (1990). The role of construal processes in overconfident predictions about the self and others. *Journal of Personality and Social Psychology, 59,* 1128–1139.

Griffin, D. W., & Ross, L. (1991). Subjective construal, social inference, and human misunderstanding. In L. Berkowitz (Ed.), *Advances in experimental social psychology* (vol. 24, pp. 319–359). San Diego, CA: Academic Press.

Haaga, D. A., & Stewart, B. L. (1992). Self-efficacy for recovery from a lapse after smoking cessation. *Journal of Consulting and Clinical Psychology, 60,* 24–28.

Hacker, D. J., Bol, L., Horgan, D. D., & Rakow, E. A. (2000). Test prediction and performance in a classroom context. *Journal of Educational Psychology, 92*, 160–170.

Haines, M. P. (1996). *A social norms approach to preventing binge drinking at colleges and universities.* Newton, MA: The Higher Education Center for Alcohol and Other Drug Prevention.

Haines, M. P. (1998). Social norms in a wellness model for health promotion in higher education. *Wellness Management, 14*, 1–10.

Haines, M. P., & Spear S. F. (1996). Changing the perception of the norm: A strategy to decrease binge drinking among college students. *Journal of American College Health, 24*, 134–140.

Halberstadt, J. B., & Niedenthal, P. M. (1997). Emotional state and the use of stimulus dimensions in judgment. *Journal of Personality and Social Psychology, 72*, 1017–1033.

Hammond, J. S., Keeney, R. L., & Raiffa, H. (1999). *Smart choice: A practical guide to making better decisions.* New York: Random House.

Hampson, S. E., Gilmour, R., & Harris, P. L. (1978). Accuracy in self-perception: The "fallacy of personal validation." *British Journal of Social and Clinical Psychology, 17*, 231–325.

Hansen, G. L. (1987). Extradyadic relations during courtship. *Journal of Sex Research, 23*, 382–390.

Hansford, B. C., & Hattie, J. A. (1982). The relationship between self and achievement/performance measures. *Review of Educational Research, 52*, 123–142.

Harper, C. R., Kidera, C. J., & Cullen, J. F. (1971). Study of simulated airplane pilot incapacitation. *Aerospace Medicine, 42*, 946–948.

Harris, M. E., & Greene, R. L. (1984). Students' perception of actual, trivial, and inaccurate personality feedback. *Journal of Personality Assessment, 48*, 179–184.

Harris, M. M., & Schaubroeck, J. (1988). A meta-analysis of self-supervisor, self-peer, and peer-supervisor ratings. *Personnel Psychology, 41*, 43–62.

Harris, P., & Middleton, W. (1994). The illusion of control and optimism about health: On being less at risk but no more in control than others. *British Journal of Social Psychology, 33*, 369–386.

Harris, P. R. (1996). Sufficient grounds for optimism? The relationship between perceived controllabilitiy and optimistic bias. *Journal of Social and Clinical Psychology, 15*, 9–52.

Harrison, D. A., & Shaffer, M. A. (1994). Comparative examinations of self-reports and perceived absenteeism norms: Wading through Lake Wobegone. *Journal of Applied Psychology, 79*, 240–251.

Harvey, N., Garwood, J., & Palencia, M. (1987). Vocal matching of pitch intervals: Learning and transfer effects. *Psychology of Music, 15*, 90–106.

Hasher, L., & Chromiak, W. (1977). The processing of frequency information: An automatic mechanism? *Journal of Verbal Learning and Verbal Behavior, 16*, 173–184.

Hasher, L., Goldstein, D., & Toppino, T. (1977). Frequency and the conference of referential validity. *Journal of Verbal learning and Verbal Behavior, 16*, 107–112.

Hasher, L., & Zacks, R. T. (1984). Automatic processing of fundamental information: The case of frequency of occurrence. *American Psychologist, 39*, 1372–1388.

Hasher, L., Zacks, R. T., Rose, K. C., & Sanft, H. (1987). Truly incidental encoding of frequency information. *American Journal of Psychology, 100*, 69–91.

Haun, D. E., Zeringue, A., Leach, A., & Foley, A. (2000). Assessing the competence of specimen-processing personnel. *Laboratory Medicine, 31*, 633–637.

Hawkins, S. A., & Hastie, R. (1990). Hindsight-biased judgments of past events after the outcomes are known. *Psychological Bulletin, 107*, 311–327.

Hayes, A. F., & Dunning, D. (1997). Construal processes and trait ambiguity: Implications for self-peer agreement in personality judgment. *Journal of Personality and Social Psychology, 72*, 664–677.

Hayward, M. L. A., & Hambrick, D. C. (1997). Explaining the premiums paid for large acquisitions: Evidence of CEO hubris. *Administrative Science Quarterly, 42*, 103–127.

Heath, C., Larrick, R. P., & Klayman, J. (1998). Cognitive repairs: How organized practices can compensate for individual shortcomings. In B. M. Staw & L. L. Cummings (Eds.), *Research in Organizational Behavior, 20*, 1–37.

Heine, S. J., Lehman, D. R., Markus, H. R., & Kitayama, S. (1999). Is there a universal need for positive self-regard? *Psychological Review, 106*, 766–794.

Helson, H. (1964). *Adaptation-level theory: An experimental and systematic approach to behavior.* New York: Harper and Row.

Helweg-Larsen, M. (1999). (The lack of) optimistic biases in response to the Northridge earthquake: The role of personal experience. *Basic and Applied Social Psychology, 21,* 119–129.

Helweg-Larsen, M., & Shepperd, J. A. (2001). Do moderators of the optimistic bias affect personal or target risk estimates? A review of the literature. *Personality and Social Psychology Review, 5,* 74–95.

Henslin, J. M. (1967). Craps and magic. *American Journal of Sociology, 73,* 316–333.

Herold, E. S. (1981). Contraceptive embarrassment and contraceptive behavior among young single women. *Journal of Youth and Adolescence, 10,* 233–242.

Hertwig, R., Gigerenzer, G., & Hoffrage, U. (1997). The reiteration effect in hindsight bias. *Psychological Review, 104,* 194–202.

Hines, D., Saris, R. N., & Throckmorton-Belzer, L. (2002). Pluralistic ignorance and health risk behaviors: Do college students misperceive social approval for risky behaviors on campus and in media. *Journal of Applied Social Psychology, 32,* 2621–2640.

Hirschi, T. (1969). *Causes of delinquency.* Stanford, CA: University of California Press.

Hoch, S. J. (1985). Counterfactual reasoning and accuracy in predicting personal events. *Journal of Experimental Psychology: Learning, Memory, and Cognition, 11,* 719–731.

Hodges, B., Regehr, G., & Martin, D. (2001). Difficulties in recognizing one's own incompetence: Novice physicians who are unskilled and unaware of it. *Academic Medicine, 76,* S87–S89.

Holte, C. S., Jamruszka, V., Gustafson, J., Beaman, A. L., & Camp, G. C. (1984). Influence of children's positive self-perceptions on donating behavior in a naturalistic setting. *Journal of School Psychology, 22,* 145–153.

Hong, Y. Y., Chiu, C. Y., Dweck, C. S, Lin, D. M. S., & Wan, W. (1999). Implicit theories, attributions, and coping: A meaning system approach. *Journal of Personality and Social Psychology, 77,* 588–599.

Hoorens, V., & Buunk, B. P. (1993). Social comparison of health risks: Locus of control, the person-positivity bias, and unrealistic optimism. *Journal of Applied Social Psychology, 24,* 291–302.

Hoza, B., Pelham, W. E., Jr., Dobbs, J., Owens, J. S., & Pillow, D. R. (2002). Do boys with attention-deficit/hyperactivity disorder have positive illusory self-concepts? *Journal of Abnormal Psychology, 111,* 268–278.

Hsee, C. K. (1995). Elastic justification: How tempting but task-irrelevant factors influence decisions. *Organizational Behavior and Human Decision Processes, 62,* 330–337.

Hsee, C. K. (1996). Elastic justification: How unjustifiable factors influence judgments. *Organizational Behavior and Human Decision Processes, 62,* 330–337.

Ilgen, D. R. (1971). Satisfaction with performance as a function of initial level of expected performance and deviation from expectations. *Organizational Behavior and Human Performance, 6,* 345–361.

Ilgen, D. R., & Hamstra, B. W. (1972). Performance satisfaction as a function of difference between expected and reported performance and five levels of reported performance. *Organizational Behavior and Human Performance, 7,* 359–370.

Ilgen, D. R., & Knowlton, W. A., Jr. (1980). Performance attributional effects on feedback from supervisors. *Organizational Behavior and Human Performance, 25,* 441–456.

Jacobs, B., Prentice-Dunn, S., & Rogers, R. W. (1984). Understanding persistence: An interface of control theory and self-efficacy theory. *Basic and Applied Social Psychology, 5,* 333–347.

John, O. P., & Robins, R. W. (1994). Accuracy and bias in self-perception: Individual differences in self-enhancement and role of narcissism. *Journal of Personality and Social Psychology, 66,* 206–219.

Kahneman, D., Knetsch, J. L., & Thaler, R. H. (1991). The endowment effect, loss aversion, and status quo bias: Anomalies. *Journal of Economic Perspectives, 5,* 193–206.

Kahneman, D., & Lovallo, D. (1991). Bold forecasting and timid decisions: A cognitive perspective on risk taking. In R. Rumelt, P. Schendel, & D. Teece (Eds.), *Fundamental issues in strategy.* Cambridge, England: Cambridge University Press.

Kahneman, D., & Tversky, A. (1973). On the psychology of prediction. *Psychological Review, 80*, 313–327.

Kahneman, D., & Tversky, A. (1979a). Intuitive prediction: Biases and corrective procedures. *TIMS Studies in Management Science, 12*, 313–327.

Kahneman, D., & Tversky, A. (1979b). Prospect theory: An analysis of decision under risk. *Econometrica, 47*, 263–291.

Kahneman, D., & Tversky, A. (1982). The simulation heuristic. In D. Kahneman, P. Slovic, & A. Tversky (Eds.), *Judgment under uncertainty: Heuristics and biases* (pp. 509–520). Cambridge, England: Cambridge University Press.

Kamen, A. (2002, June 7). Tent rent: $10 a day. *Washington Post*, p. A25.

Kamen-Siegel, L., Rodin, J., & Seligman, M. E. P., & Dwyer, J. (1991). Explanatory style and cell-mediated immunity. *Health Psychology, 10*, 229–235.

Kane, T. D., Marks, M. A., Zaccaro, S. J., & Blair, V. (1996). Self-efficacy, personal goals, and wrestlers' self-regulation. *Journal of Sport and Exercise Psychology, 18*, 36–48.

Kaufman, M. (2003, October 11). Athletes, women a dangerous mix: Despite rookie initiation sessions conducted by all major pro sports, the scandals continue. *Ottawa Citizen*, F1.

Kelley, C. M., & Lindsay, D. S. (1993). Remembering mistaken for knowing: Ease of retrieval as a basis for confidence in answers to general knowledge questions. *Journal of Memory and Language, 32*, 1–24.

Keltner, D., Capps, L., Kring, A. M., Young, R. C., & Heerey, E. A. (2001). Just teasing: A conceptual analysis and empirical review. *Psychological Bulletin, 127*, 229–248.

Keltner, D., & Robinson, R. J. (1996). Extremism, power, and the imagined basis of social conflict. *Current Directions in Psychological Science, 5*, 101–105.

Keltner, D., Young, R. C., Heerey, E. A., Oemig, C., & Monarch, N. D. (1998). Teasing in hierarchical and intimate relations. *Journal of Personality and Social Psychology, 75*, 1231–1247.

Keren, G. B. (1987). Facing uncertainty in the game of bridge: A calibration study. *Organizational Behavior and Human Decision Processes, 139*, 98–114.

Keren, G. B. (1994). The rationality of gambling: Gamblers' conceptions of probability, chance and luck. In G. Wright & P. Ayton (Eds.), *Subjective probability* (pp. 485–499). New York: Wiley.

Keren, G. B., & Wagenaar, W. A. (1985). On the psychology of playing blackjack: Normative and descriptive considerations with implications for decision theory. *Journal of Experimental Psychology: General, 114*, 133–158.

Klar, Y., & Giladi, E. E. (1999). Are most people happier than their peers, or are they just happy? *Personality and Social Psychology Bulletin, 25*, 585–594.

Klayman, J., & Schoemaker, P. J. H. (1993). Thinking about the future: A cognitive perspective. *Journal of Forecasting, 12*, 161–168.

Klein, C. T. F., & Helweg-Larsen, M. (2002). Perceived control and the optimistic bias: A meta-analytic review. *Psychology and Health, 17*, 437–446.

Klein, W. M., & Kunda, Z. (1994). Exaggerated self-assessments and the preferences for controllable risks. *Organizational Behavior and Human Decision Processes, 59*, 410–427.

Kluger, A. N., & DeNisi, A. (1996). The effects of feedback interventions on performance: A historical review, a meta-analysis, and a preliminary feedback intervention theory. *Psychological Bulletin, 119*, 254–284.

Knetsch, J. L. (1989). The endowment effect and evidence of nonreversible indifference curves. *American Economic Review, 79*, 1277–1284.

Knox, R. E., & Inkster, J. A. (1968). Postdecision dissonance at post time. *Journal of Personality and Social Psychology, 8*, 319–323.

Koriat, A. (1976). Another look at the relationship between phonetic symbolism and the feeling of knowing. *Memory and Cognition, 4*, 244–248.

Koriat, A. (1993). How do we know that we know? The accessibility model of the feeling of knowing. *Psychological Review, 100*, 609–639.

Koriat, A. (1995). Dissociating knowing and the feeling of knowing: Further evidence for the accessibility model. *Journal of Experimental Psychology, 124*, 311–333.

Koriat, A., Lichtenstein, S., & Fischhoff, B. (1980). Reasons for confidence. *Journal of Experimental Psychology: Human Learning and Memory, 6*, 107–118.

Krueger, J., & Mueller, R. A. (2002). Unskilled, unaware, or both? The contribution of social-perceptual skills and statistical regression to self-enhancement biases. *Journal of Personality and Social Psychology, 82,* 180–188.

Kruger, J. (1999). Lake Wobegone be gone! The "below-average effect" and the egocentric nature of comparative ability judgments. *Journal of Personality and Social Psychology, 77,* 221–232.

Kruger, J. M., & Dunning, D. (1999). Unskilled and unaware of it: How difficulties in recognizing one's own incompetence lead to inflated self-assessments. *Journal of Personality and Social Psychology, 77,* 1121–1134.

Kruger, J., & Dunning, D. (2002). Unskilled and unaware —But why? A reply to Krueger and Mueller. *Journal of Personality and Social Psychology, 82,* 189–192.

Kruger, J., & Gilovich, T. (2004). Actions and intentions in self-assessment: The road to self-enhancement is paved with good intentions. *Personality and Social Psychology Bulletin, 30,* 328–339.

Kruger, J., Gordon, C., & Kuban, J. (in press). Intentions in teasing: When "just kidding" just isn't good enough. *Journal of Personality and Social Psychology.*

Kunda, Z. (1987). Motivated inference: Self-serving generation and evaluation of causal theories. *Journal of Personality and Social Psychology, 53,* 37–54.

Kunda, Z. (1990). The case for motivated reasoning. *Psychological Bulletin, 108,* 480–498.

Kunda, Z., Fong, G. T., Sanitioso, R., & Reber, E. (1993). Directional questions direct self-perceptions. *Journal of Experimental Social Psychology, 29,* 63–86.

Kurman, J. (2003). The role of perceived specificity level of failure events in self-enhancement and in constructive self-criticism. *Personality and Social Psychology Bulletin, 29,* 285–294.

Lambert, T. A., Kahn, A. S., & Apple, K. J. (2003). Pluralistic ignorance and hooking up. *Journal of Sex Research, 40,* 129–133.

Langenderfer, J. (1996). Lotteries and education: The mediating effect of illusion of control. In R. P. Hill & C. R. Taylor (Eds.), *Marketing and public policy conference proceedings* (vol. 6, pp. 190–198). Chicago: American Marketing Association.

Langer, E. J. (1975). The illusion of control. *Journal of Personality and Social Psychology, 32,* 311–328.

Langer, E. J., & Roth, J. (1975). Heads I win, tails it's chance: The effects of sequence of outcomes in a chance task on the illusion of control. *Journal of Personality and Social Psychology, 32,* 951–955.

LaPiere, R. T. (1934). Attitudes vs. action. *Social Forces, 13,* 230–237.

Larson, J. R., Jr. (1986). Supervisors' performance feedback to subordinates: The impact of subordinate performance valence and outcome dependence. *Organizational Behavior and Human Decision Processes, 37,* 391–408.

Larwood, L. (1978). Swine flu: A field study of self-serving biases. *Journal of Applied Social Psychology, 8,* 283–289.

Larwood, L., & Whittaker, W. (1977). Managerial myopia: Self-serving biases in organizational planning. *Journal of Applied Psychology, 62,* 194–198.

Latané, B., & Darley, J. M. (1970). *The unresponsive bystander: Why doesn't he help?* Englewood Cliffs, NJ: Prentice Hall.

Lau, R. R., & Russell, D. (1980). Attributions in the sports pages. *Journal of Personality and Social Psychology, 39,* 29–38.

Laumann, E. O., Gagnon, J. H., Michael, R. T., & Michaels, S. (1994). *The social organization of sexuality: Sexual practices in the United States.* Chicago: University of Chicago Press.

LeDoux, J. (1996). *The emotional brain.* New York: Simon & Schuster.

Lehman, D. R., & Taylor, S. E. (1987). Date with an earthquake: Coping with a probable, unpredictable disaster. *Personality and Social Psychology Bulletin, 23,* 546–555.

Lent, R. W., Brown, S. D., & Hackett, G. (1994). Toward a unifying social cognitive theory of career and academic interest, choice, and performance. *Journal of Vocational Behavior, 45,* 79–122.

Lerner, J. S., Gonzalez, R. M., Small, D. A., & Fischhoff, B. (2003). Effects of fear and anger on perceived risks of terrorism: A national field experiment. *Psychological Science, 14,* 144–150.

Lerner, J. S., & Keltner, D. (2001). Fear, anger, and risk. *Journal of Personality and Social Psychology, 81*, 146–159.

Levenberg, S. B. (1975). Professional training, psychodiagnostic skill, and kinetic family drawings. *Journal of Personality Assessment, 39*, 389–393.

Libby, R., Trotman, K. T., & Zimmer, I. (1987). Member variation, recognition of expertise, and group performance. *Journal of Applied Psychology, 72*, 81–87.

Liberman, N., & Trope, Y. (1998). The role of feasibility and desirability considerations in near and distant future decisions: A test of temporal construal theory. *Journal of Personality & Social Psychology, 75*, 5–18.

Lichtenstein, S., & Fischhoff, B. (1980). Training for calibration. *Organizational Behavior and Human Performance, 26*, 149–171.

Liebrand, W. B. G., Messick, D. M., & Wolters, F. J. M. (1986). Why we are fairer than others: A cross-cultural replication and extension. *Journal of Experimental Social Psychology, 22*, 590–604.

Lifton, R. J. (1986). *The Nazi doctors: Medical killing and the psychology of genocide*. New York: Basic Books.

Lillard, L. A., & Waite, L. J. (1995). Till death do us part: Marital disruption and mortality. *American Journal of Sociology, 100*, 1131–1156.

Lin, I. F., Spiga, R., & Fortsch, W. (1979). Insight and adherence to medication in chronic schizophrenics. *Journal of Clinical Psychology, 40*, 430–432.

Linkenbach, J., & Perkins, H. W. (2003). Most of us are tobacco free: An eight-month social norms campaign reducing youth initiation of smoking in Montana. In H. W. Perkins (Ed.), *The social norms approach to preventing school and college age substance abuse: A handbook for educators, counselors, and clinicians* (pp. 224–234), San Francisco: Jossey-Bass.

Littlepage, G. E., Robison, W., & Reddington, K., (1997). Effects of task experience and group experience on group performance, member ability, and recognition of expertise. *Organizational Behavior and Human Decision Processes, 69*, 133–147.

Loewenstein, G., & Adler, D. (1995). A bias in the prediction of tastes. *The Economic Journal, 105*, 929–937.

Loewenstein, G., Nagin, D., & Paternoster, R. (1997). The effect of sexual arousal on predictions of sexual forcefulness. *Journal of Crime and Delinquency, 32*, 443–473.

Loftus, E. F. (1979). *Eyewitness testimony*. Cambridge, MA: Harvard University Press.

Loftus, E. F., & Wagenaar, W. A. (1988). Lawyers' predictions of success. *Jurimetrics Journal, 29*, 437–453.

Longenecker, C. L., Sims, J. P., Jr., & Gioia, D. A. (1987). Behind the mask: The politics of employee appraisal. *Academy of Management Executive, 1*, 183–193.

Lord, C. G., & Lepper, M. R. (1999). Attitude representation theory. In M. P. Zanna (Ed.), *Advances in Experimental Social Psychology* (vol. 31, pp. 265–343). San Diego, CA: Academic Press.

Lord, C. G., Lepper, M. R., & Mackie, D. (1984). Attitude prototypes as determinants of attitude-behavior consistency. *Journal of Personality and Social Psychology, 46*, 1254–1266.

Lovallo, D., and Kahneman, D. (2003). Delusions of success: How optimism undermines executives' decision. *Harvard Business Review, 81*, 56–63.

Maass, A., Milesi, A., Zabbini, S., & Stahlberg, D. (1995). Linguistic intergroup bias: Differential expectancies or in-group protection. *Journal of Personality and Social Psychology, 68*, 116–126.

Maass, A., Salvi, D., Arcuri, L.,& Semin, G. (1989). Language use in intergroup contexts: The linguistic intergroup bias. *Journal of Personality and Social Psychology, 57*, 981–993.

Mabe, P. A., III, & West, S. G. (1982). Validity of self-evaluation of ability: A review and meta-analysis. *Journal of Applied Psychology, 67*, 280–286.

MacDonald, T. K., & Ross, M. (1999). Assessing the accuracy of predictions about dating relationships: How and why do lovers' predictions differ from those made by observers? *Personality and Social Psychology Bulletin, 25*, 1417–1429.

Maki, R. H., & Berry, S. L. (1984). Metacomprehension of text material. *Journal of Experimental Psychology: Learning, Memory, & Cognition, 10*, 663–679.

Maki, R. H., Jonas, D., & Kallod, M. (1994). The relationship between comprehension and metacomprehension ability. *Psychonomic Bulletin and Review, 1*, 126–129.

Malmendier, U., & Tate, G. (2003). *Who makes acquisitions? CEO overconfidence and the market's reaction.* Unpublished manuscript, Stanford University.

Marks, G., & Miller, N. (1987). Ten years of research on the false consensus effect: An empirical and theoretical review. *Psychological Bulletin, 102*, 72–90.

Marks, N., & Lambert, J. (1998). Marital status continuity and change among young and midlife adults: Longitudinal effects on psychological well-being. *Journal of Family Issues, 19*, 652–686.

Marottoli, R. A., & Richardson, E. D. (1998). Confidence in, and self-rating of, driving ability among older drivers. *Accident Analysis and Prevention, 30*, 331–336.

Marteau, T. M., Johnston, M., Wynne, G., & Evans, T. R. (1989). Cognitive factors in the explanation of the mismatch between confidence and competence in performing basic life support. *Psychology and Health, 3*, 173–182.

Marteau, T. M., Wynne, G., Kaye, W., & Evans, T. R. (1990). Resuscitation: Experience without feedback increases confidence but not skill. *British Medical Journal, 300*, 849–850.

Matza, D. (1964). *Delinquency and drift.* New York: Wiley.

May, E. R. (1973). *"Lessons" of the past: The use and misuse of history in American foreign policy.* New York: Oxford University Press.

Mayhew, D. R., & Simpson, H. M. (1996). *Effectiveness and role of driver education and training in a graduated licensing system.* Ottawa, Ontario: Traffic Injury Research Foundation.

McCall, M., & Nattrass, K. (2001). Carding for the purchase of alcohol: I'm tougher than other clerks are! *Journal of Applied Social Psychology, 31*, 2184–2194.

McCloskey, M., & Kohl, D. (1983). Naïve physics: The curvilinear impetus principles and its role in interactions with moving objects. *Journal of Experimental Psychology: Learning, Memory, and Cognition, 9*, 146–156.

McElwee, R. O., Dunning, D., Tan, P. L., & Hollmann, S. (2001). Evaluating others: The role of who we are versus what we think traits mean. *Basic and Applied Social Psychology, 23*, 123–136.

McFarland, C., & Miller, D. T. (1990). Judgments of self-other similarity: Just like other people, only more so. *Personality and Social Psychology Bulletin, 16*, 475–484.

McGlynn, S. M. (1994). Impaired awareness of deficits in a psychiatric context: Implications for rehabilitation. In J. Metcalfe & A. P. Shimamura (Eds.), *Metacognition: Knowing about knowing* (pp. 221–248). Cambridge, MA: MIT Press.

McGlynn, S. M., & Kaszniak, A. W. (1991). Unawareness of deficits in dementia and schizophrenia. In G. P. Prigatano & D. L. Schacter (Eds.), *Awareness of deficit after brain injury: Clincal and theoretical issue* (pp. 63–83). New York: Oxford University Press.

McKenna, F. P. (1993). It won't happen to me: Unrealistic optimism or illusion of control? *British Journal of Psychology, 84*, 39–50.

McLanahan, S., & Sandefur, G. (1994). *Growing up with a single parent: What hurts, what helps.* Cambridge, MA: Harvard University Press.

McPherson, S. L., & Thomas, J. R. (1989). Relation of knowledge and performance in boys' tennis: Age and expertise. *Journal of Experimental Child Psychology, 48*, 190–211.

Menon, G., Block, L. G., & Ramanathan, S. (2002). We're at as much risk as we are led to believe: Effects of message cues on judgments of health. *Journal of Consumer Research, 28*, 533–549.

Merrens, M. R., & Richards, W. S. (1973). Length of personality inventory and the evaluation of a generalized personality interpretation. *Journal of Personality Assessment, 37*, 83–85.

Messick, D. M., Bloom, S., Boldizar, J. P., & Samuelson, C. D. (1985). Why we are fairer than others. *Journal of Experimental Social Psychology, 21*, 480–500.

Metcalfe, J. (1998). Cognitive optimism: Self-deception or memory-based processing heuristics. *Personality and Social Psychology Review, 2*, 100–110.

Metcalfe, J., Schwartz, B. L., & Joaquim. S. G. (1993). The cue-familiarity heuristic in metacognition. *Journal of Experimental Psychology: Learning, Memory, and Cognition, 19*, 851–861.

Middleton, W., Harris, P., & Surman, M. (1996). Give 'em enough rope: Perception of health and safety risks in bungee jumpers. *Journal of Social and Clinical Psychology, 15*, 68–79.

Miller, D. T., & McFarland, C. (1987). Pluralistic ignorance: When similarity is interpreted as dissimilarity. *Journal of Personality and Social Psychology, 53*, 298–305.

Miller, D. T., & Nelson, L. (2002). Seeing approach motivation in the avoidance behavior of others: Implications for an understanding of pluralistic ignorance. *Journal of Personality and Social Psychology, 83*, 1066–1075.

Miller, R. L., Brickman, P., & Bolen, D. (1975). Attribution versus persuasion as a means for modifying behavior. *Journal of Personality and Social Psychology, 31*, 430–441.

Miner, C. F. (1984). Group versus individual decision making: An investigation of performance measures, decision strategies, and process losses/gains. *Organizational Behavior and Human Performance, 33*, 112–124.

Miyazaki, A. D., Brumbaugh, A. M., & Sprott, D. E. (2001). Promoting and countering consumer misconceptions of random events: The case of perceived control and state-sponsored lotteries. *Journal of Public Policy & Marketing, 20*, 254–267.

Moore, D. A., & Kim, T. G. (2003). Myopic social prediction and the solo comparison effect. *Journal of Personality and Social Psychology, 85*, 1121–1135.

Mueller, C. M., & Dweck, C. S. (1998). Praise for intelligence can undermine children's motivation and performance. *Journal of Personality and Social Psychology, 75*, 33–52.

Murphy, M., Glaser, K., & Grundy, E. (1997). Marital status and long term illness in Great Britain. *Journal of Marriage and the Family, 59*, 156–164.

National Research Council: Committee on Women in Science and Engineering. (1991). *Women in science and engineering: Increasing their numbers in the 1990s*. Washington, DC: National Academy Press.

National Science Foundation (2000). *Women, minorities, and persons with disabilities in science and engineering*. Arlington, VA: National Science Foundation.

National Science Foundation (2002). *Science and engineering indicators —2002*. Arlington, VA: National Science Foundation.

Neale, M. A., & Bazerman, M. H. (1983). The role of perspective-taking ability in negotiating under different forms of arbitration. *Industrial and Labor Relations Review, 36*, 378–88.

Nelson, T. O., & Dunlosky, J. (1991). When people's judgments of learning (JOLs) are extremely accurate at predicting subsequent recall: The delayed-JOL effect. *Psychological Science, 2*, 267–270.

Newby-Clark, I. R., Ross, M., Buehler, R., Koehler, D. J., & Griffin, D. (2000). People focus on optimistic and disregard pessimistic scenarios while predicting their task completion times. *Journal of Experimental Psychology: Applied, 6*, 171–182

Newell, A. (1969). Heuristic programming: Ill-structured problems. In J. Aronofsky (Ed.), *Progress in operations research* (vol. 3; pp. 360–414). New York: Wiley.

Nickerson, R. S., Baddeley, A., & Freeman, B. (1987). Are people's estimates of what other people know influenced by what they themselves know? *Acta Psychologica, 64*, 245–259.

Niedenthal, P. M., Cantor, N., & Kihlstrom, J. F. (1985). Prototype matching: A strategy for social decision-making. *Journal of Personality and Social Psychology 48*, 575–584.

Niedenthal, P. M., Halberstadt, & Innes-Ker, A. H. (1999). Emotional response categorization. *Psychological Review, 106*, 337–361.

Niedenthal, P. M., & Mordkoff, J. T. (1991). Prototype distancing: A strategy for choosing among threatening situations. *Personality and Social Psychology Bulletin, 17*, 483–493.

Nisbett, R. E., & Kunda, Z. (1985). Perceptions of social distributions. *Journal of Personality and Social Psychology, 48*, 297–311.

Nisbett, R. E., & Ross, L. (1980). *Human inference: Strategies and shortcomings of social judgment*. Englewood Cliffs, NJ: Prentice-Hall.

Nuttin, J. M. (1985). Narcissism beyond Gestalt and awareness: The name letter effect. *European Journal of Social Psychology, 15*, 353–361.

Nuttin, J. M. (1987). Affective consequences of mere ownership: The name letter effect in twelve European languages. *European Journal of Social Psychology, 17*, 381–402.

Obermiller, C., & Spangenberg, E. R. (2000). Improving telephone fund-raising by use of self-prophecy. *International Journal of Non-Profit and Voluntary Sector Marketing, 5*, 365–372.

O'Brien, A., Fries, E., & Bowen, D. (2000). The effect of accuracy of perceptions of dietary-fat intake on perceived risk and intentions to change. *Journal of Behavioral Medicine, 23,* 465–473.

Odean, T. (1998). Volume, volatility, price, and profit when all traders are above average. *Journal of Finance, 8,* 1887–1934.

O'Dell, J. W. (1972). P. T. Barnum explores the computer. *Journal of Consulting and Clinical Psychology, 38,* 270–273.

O'Gorman, H. J., & Garry, S. L. (1977). Pluralistic ignorance: Replication and extension. *Public Opinion Quarterly, 40,* 449–458.

Oksam, J., Kingma, J., & Klasen, H. J. (2000). Clinicians' recognition of 10 different types of distal radial fractures. *Perceptual and Motor Skills, 91,* 917–924.

Ono, K. (1987). Superstitious behavior in humans. *Journal of the Experimental Analysis of Behavior, 47,* 261–271.

Oskamp, S. (1965). Overconfidence in case-study judgments. *Journal of Clinical Psychology, 29,* 261–265.

Owens, J. S., & Hoza, B. (2003). The role of inattention and hyperactivity/impulsivity in the positive illusory bias. *Journal of Consulting and Clinical Psychology, 71,* 680–691.

Paulhus, D. L. (1998). Interpersonal and intrapsychic adaptiveness of trait self-enhancement: A mixed blessing. *Journal of Personality and Social Psychology, 74,* 1197–1208.

Perkins, H. W. (2002). Social norms and the prevention of alcohol misuse in college contexts. *Journal of Studies on Alcohol,* supplement no. 14.

Peterson, C. (1988). Explanatory style as a risk factor for illness. *Cognitive Therapy and Research, 12* 119–132.

Petty, R. E., Fleming, M. A., & Fabrigar, L. R. (1999). The review process at PSPB: Correlates of interreviewer agreement and manuscript acceptance. *Personality and Social Psychology Bulletin, 25,* 188–203.

Polivy, J., & Herman, C. P. (2002). If at first you don't succeed: False hopes of self-change. *American Psychologist, 57,* 677–689.

Prentice, D. A., & Miller, D. T. (1993). Pluralistic ignorance and alcohol use on campus: Some consequences of misperceiving the social norm. *Journal of Personality and Social Psychology, 64,* 243–356.

Pronin, E., Lin, D. Y., & Ross, L. (2002). The bias blind spot: Perceptions of bias in self versus others. *Personality and Social Psychology Bulletin, 28,* 369–381.

Pyszczynski, T., & Greenberg, J. (1987). Toward an integration of cognitive and motivational perspectives on social inference: a biased hypothesis-testing model. *Advances in Experimental Social Psychology, 20,* 297–340.

Radcliffe, N. M., & Klein, W. M. P. (2002). Dispositional, unrealistic, and comparative optimism: Differential relations with the knowledge and processing of risk information and beliefs about personal risk. *Personality and Social Psychology Bulletin, 28,* 836–846.

Read, D., & van Leeuwen, B. (1998). Time and desire: The effects of anticipated and experienced hunger and delay to consumption on the choice between healthy and unhealthy snack food. *Organizational Behavior and Human Decision Processes, 76,* 189–205.

Read, S. J. (1987). Constructing causal scenarios: A knowledge structure approach to causal reasoning. *Journal of Personality and Social Psychology, 52,* 288–302.

Reckless, W. C. (1961). A new theory of delinquency and crime. *Federal Probation, 25,* 42–46.

Reder, L. M. (1987). Strategy selection in question answering. *Cognitive Psychology, 19,* 111–138.

Reder, L. M., & Ritter, F. E. (1992). What determines initial feeling of knowing? Familiarity with question terms, not with the answer. *Journal of Experimental Psychology: Learning, Memory, and Cognition, 13,* 435–451.

Redlich, F. C., & Dorsey, J. F. (1945). Denial of blindness by patients with cerebral disease. *Archives of Neurology and Psychiatry, 53,* 407–417.

Reed, G. M., Kemeny, M. E., Taylor, S. E., & Visscher, B. R. (1999). Negative HIV-specific expectancies and AIDS-related bereavement as predictors of symptom onset in asymptomatic HIV-positive gay men. *Health Psychology, 18,* 354–363.

Reed, G. M., Kemeny, M. E., Taylor, S. E., Wang, H.-Y. J., & Visscher, B. R. (1994). Realistic acceptance: as a predictor of decreased survival time in gay men with AIDS. *Health Psychology, 13,* 299–307.

Reed, M. B., & Aspinwall, L. G. (1998). Self-affirmation reduces biased processing of health risk information. *Motivation & Emotion, 22,* 99–132.

Regan, D. R., & Fazio, R. (1977). On the consistency between attitudes and behavior: Look to the method of attitude formation. *Journal of Experimental Social Psychology, 13,* 28–45.

Reisman, S., Insko, C. A., & Valins, S. (1970). Triadic consistency and false heart-rate feedback. *Journal of Personality, 38,* 629–640.

Reitman, W. R. (1964). Heuristic decision procedures, open constraints, and the structure of ill-defined problems. In M. W. Shelley & G. L. Bryan (Eds.), *Human judgments and optimality* (pp. 282–315). New York: Wiley.

Riggio, R. & Friedman, H.S. (1983). Individual differences and cues to deception. *Journal of Personality and Social Psychology, 45,* 899–915.

Riggio, R. E., Widaman, K. F., & Friedman, H. S. (1985). Actual and perceived emotional sending and personality correlates. *Journal of Nonverbal Behavior, 9,* 69–83.

Risucci, D. A., Tortolani, A. J., & Ward, R. J. (1989). Ratings of surgical residents by self, supervisors and peers. *Surgical Gynecology and Obstetrics, 169,* 519–526.

Robins, R. W., & Beer, J. S. (2001). Positive illusions about the self: Short-term benefits and long-term costs. *Journal of Personality and Social Psychology, 80,* 340–352.

Robinson, R. J., Keltner, D., Ward, A., & Ross, L. (1995). Actual versus assumed differences in construal: "Naïve realism" in intergroup perception and conflict. *Journal of Personality and Social Psychology, 68,* 404–417.

Rolfhus, E. L., & Ackerman, P. L. (1999). Assessing individual differences in knowledge: Knowledge, intelligence, and related traits. *Journal of Educational Psychology, 91,* 511–526.

Rosenthal, R., & Fode, K. L. (1963). The effect of experimenter bias on the performance of the albino rat. *Behavioral Science, 8,* 183–189.

Rosenthal, R., & Jacobsen, L. (1968). *Pygmalian in the classroom: Teacher expectation and pupil's intellectual development.* Holt, Rinehart & Winston.

Ross, L. D., Greene, D., and House, P. (1977). The "false consensus effect": An egocentric bias in social perception and attribution processes. *Journal of Experimental Social Psychology, 13,* 279–301.

Rothbart, M., & Snyder, M. (1970). Confidence in prediction and postdiction of an uncertain outcome. *Canadian Journal of Behavioral Science, 2,* 38–43.

Rotter, J. (1966). Generalized expectancies for internal versus external control of reinforcement. *Psychological Monographs: General and Applied, 80,* whole no. 609.

Russo, J. E., Medvec, V. H., & Meloy, M. G. (1996). The distortion of information during decisions. *Organizational Behavior and Human Decision Processes, 66,* 102–110.

Russo, J. E., Meloy, M. G., & Medvec, V. H. (1998). Predecisional distortion of product information. *Journal of Marketing Research, 35,* 438–452.

Russo, J. E., Meloy, M. G., & Wilks, T. J. (2000). Predecisional distortion of information by auditors and salespersons. *Management Science, 46,* 13–26.

Rutter, D. R., Quine, L., & Albery, I. P. (1998). Perceptions of risk in motorcyclists: Unrealistic optimism, relative realism and predictions of behaviour. *British Journal of Psychology, 89,* 681–696.

Sabini, J., Cosmas, K., Siepmann, M., & Stein, J. (1999). Underestimates and truly false consensus effects in estimates of embarrassment and other emotions. *Basic and Applied Social Psychology, 21,* 233–241.

Sackett, D. L., & Torrance, G. W. (1978). The utility of different health states as perceived by the general public. *Journal of Chronic Diseases, 31,* 697–704.

Samuelson, W., & Zackhauser, R. (1988). Status quo bias in decision making. *Journal of Risk and Uncertainty, 1,* 7–59.

Sanderson, C. A., Darley, J. M., & Messinger, C. S. (2002). "I'm not as thin as you think I am": The development and consequences of feeling discrepant from the thinness norm. *Personality and Social Psychology Bulletin, 28,* 172–183.

Schacter, D. L., McLachlan, D. R., Moscovitch, M., & Tulving, E. (1986). Monitoring of recall performance by memory-disordered patients. *Journal of Clinical and Experimental Neuropsychology Abstracts, 8*, 130.

Schanck, R. L. (1932). A study of community and its group institutions conceived of as behavior of individuals. *Psychological Monographs, 43*, 1–133.

Schkade, D. A., & Kahneman, D. (1998). Does living in California make people happy? A focusing illusion in judgments of life satisfaction. *Psychological Science, 9*, 340–346.

Schneider, S. L. (2001). In search of realistic optimism: Meaning, knowledge, and warm fuzziness. *American Psychologist, 56*, 250–263.

Schneider, W. (1985). Training high-performance skills: Fallacies and guidelines. *Human Factors, 27*, 285–300.

Schoenfeld, A. H. (1988). When good teaching leads to bad results: The disasters of "well-taught" mathematics courses. *Educational Psychologist, 23*, 145–166.

Schulz, R., & Decker, S. (1985). Long-term adjustment to physical disability: The role of social support, perceived control, and self-blame. *Journal of Personality and Social Psychology, 48*, 1162–1172.

Schuman, H., & Johnson, M. P. (1976). Attitudes and behavior. *Annual Review of Sociology, 2*, 161–207.

Schwartz, B. L., & Metcalfe, J. (1992). Cue familiarity but not target retrievability enhances feeling-of-knowing judgments. *Journal of Experimental Psychology: Learning, Memory, and Cognition, 18*, 1074–1083.

Schwarzer, R. (1999). Self-regulatory processes in the adoption and maintenance of health behaviors: The role of optimism, goals, and threats. *Journal of Health Psychology, 4*, 115–127

Sclabassi, S. E., & Woelfel, S. K. (1984). Development of self-assessment skills in medical students. *Medical Education, 84*, 226–231.

Segerstrom, S. C., Taylor, S. E., Kemeny, M. E., & Fahey, J. L. (1998). Optimism is associated with mood, coping, immune change in response to stress. *Journal of Personality and Social Psychology, 74*, 1646–1655.

Setterlund, M. B., & Niedenthal, P. M. (1993). "Who am I? Why am I here?": Self-esteem, self-clarity, and prototype matching. *Journal of Personality and Social Psychology, 65*, 769–780.

Seymour, E. (1992). "The problem iceberg" in science, mathematics, and engineering education: Student explanations for high attrition rates. *Journal of College Science Teaching, 21*, 230–232.

Shapiro, J. P., Baumeister, R. F., & Kessler, J. W. (1991). A three-component model of children's teasing: Aggression, humor, and ambiguity. *Journal of Social and Clinical Psychology, 10*, 459–472.

Shaughnessy, J. J. (1979). Confidence judgment accuracy as a predictor of test performance. *Journal of Research in Personality, 13*, 505–514.

Shaw, J. (1996). Increases in eyewitness confidence resulting from postevent questioning. *Journal of Experimental Psychology: Applied, 2*, 126–146.

Shedler, J., Mayman, M., & Manis, M. (1993). The illusion of mental health. *American Psychologist, 48*, 1117–1131.

Shepherd, J. A., Carroll, P., Grace, J., & Terry, M. (2002). Exploring the cause of comparative optimism. *Psychologica Belgica, 42*, 65–98.

Sherman, D. A. K., Nelson, L. D., & Steele, C. M. (2000). Do messages about health risks threaten the self? Increasing the acceptance of threatening health messages via self-affirmation. *Personality and Social Psychology Bulletin, 26*, 1046–1058.

Sherman, D. K., Nelson, L. D., & Ross, L. (2003). Naïve realism and affirmative action: Adversaries are more similar than they think. *Basic and Applied Social Psychology, 25*, 275–289.

Sherman, S. J. (1980). On the self-erasing nature of errors of prediction. *Journal of Personality and Social Psychology, 39*, 211–221.

Shimamura, A. P., & Squire, L. R. (1986). Memory and metamemory: A study of the feeling-of-knowing phenomenon in amnesic patients. *American Journal of Psychiatry, 136*, 918–922.

Shipper, F., & Dillard, J. E., Jr. (2000). A study of impending derailment and recovery of middle managers across career stages. *Human Resource Management, 39,* 331–345.

Shrauger, J. S., & Rosenberg, S. E. (1970). Self-esteem and the effects of success and failure feedback on performance. *Journal of Personality, 38,* 404–417.

Shrauger, J. S., & Terbovic, M. L. (1976). Self-evaluation and assessments of performance by self and others. *Journal of Consulting and Clinical Psychology, 44,* 564–572.

Sieff, E. M., Dawes, R. M., & Loewenstein, G. (1999). Anticipated versus actual reaction to HIV test results. *American Journal of Psychology, 112,* 297–311.

Simon, D. A., & Bjork, R. A. (2001). Metacognition in motor learning. *Journal of Experimental Psychology: Learning, Memory, and Cognition, 27,* 907–912.

Simon, H. A. (1973). The structure of ill-structured problems. *Artificial Intelligence, 4,* 181–201.

Sinkavich, F. J. (1995). Performance and metamemory: Do students know what they don't know? *Instructional Psychology, 22,* 77–87.

Skinner, B. F. (1948). "Superstition" in the pigeon. *Journal of Experimental Psychology, 38,* 168–172.

Smedlund, J. (1963). The concept of correlation in adults. *Scandinavian Journal of Psychology, 4,* 165–173.

Snyder, C. R., Shenkel, R. J., & Lowery, C. R. (1977). Acceptance of personality interpretations: The "Barnum effect" and beyond. *Journal of Consulting and Clinical Psychology, 45,* 104–114.

Snyder, M., & Cantor, N. (1979). Testing hypotheses about other people: The use of historical knowledge. *Journal of Experimental Social Psychology, 15,* 330–342.

Spangenberg, E. R. (1997). Increasing health club attendance through self-prophecy. *Marketing Letters, 8,* 23–31.

Spangenberg, E. R., & Obermiller, C. (1996). To cheat or not to cheat: Reducing cheating by requesting self-prophecy. *Marketing Education Review, 6,* 95–103.

Sparks, P., & Shepherd, R. (1994). Public perceptions of the potential hazards associated with food production and food consumption: An empirical study. *Risk Analysis, 14,* 799–806.

Sporer, S. L. (1992). Post-dicting eyewitness accuracy: Confidence, decision times and person descriptions of choosers and non-choosers. *European Journal of Social Psychology, 22,* 157–180.

Sporer, S. L. (1993). Eyewitness identification accuracy, confidence, and decision times in simultaneous and sequential lineups. *Journal of Applied Psychology, 78,* 22–33.

Sprott, D. E., Brumbaugh, A. M., & Miyazaki, A. D. (2001). Motivation and ability as predictors of play behavior in state-sponsored lotteries: An empirical assessment of psychological control. *Psychology & Marketing, 18,* 973–983.

Sprott, D. E., Spangenberg, E. R., & Fisher, R. (2003). The importance of normative beliefs to the self-prophecy effect. *Journal of Applied Psychology, 88,* 423–431.

Sprott, D. E., Spangenberg, E. R., & Perkins, A. W. (1999). Two more self-prophecy experiments. In L. Scott & E. J. Arnould (Eds.), *Advances in consumer research* (vol. 25, pp. 621–626). Provo, UT: Association for Consumer Research.

Stajkovic, A. D., & Luchins, F. (1998). Self-efficacy and work-related performance: A meta-analysis. *Psychological Bulletin, 124,* 240–261.

Steele, C. M. (1988). The psychology of self-affirmation: Sustaining the integrity of the self. In L. Berkowitz (Ed.), *Advances in Experimental Social Psychology* (vol. 21, pp. 261–302), San Diego, CA: Academic Press.

Stone, D. N. (1994). Overconfidence in initial self-efficacy judgments: Effects on decision processes and performance. *Organizational Behavior and Human Decision Processes, 59,* 452–474.

Story, A. L. (1998). Self-esteem and memory for favorable and unfavorable personality feedback. *Personality and Social Psychology Bulletin, 24,* 51–64.

Story, A. L. (2003). Similarity of trait and construal and consensus in interpersonal perception. *Journal of Experimental Social Psychology, 39,* 364–370.

Story, A. L., & Dunning, D. (1998). The more rational side of self-serving prototypes: The effects of success and failure performance feedback. *Journal of Experimental Social Psychology, 34,* 513–529.

Strecher, V. J., Kreuter, M. W., & Kobrin, S. C. (1995). Do cigarette smokers have unrealistic perceptions of their heart attack, cancer, and stroke risks? *Journal of Behavioral Medicine, 18,* 45–54.

Strenta, A., & DeJong, W. (1981). The effect of a pro-social label on helping behavior. *Social Psychology Quarterly, 44,* 142–147.

Stuart, M. R., Goldstein, H. S., & Snope, F. C. (1980). Self-evaluation by residents in family medicine. *Journal of Family Practice, 10,* 639–642.

Suls, J., Lemos, K., & Stewart, H. L. (2002). Self-esteem, construal, and comparisons with the self, friends, and peers. *Journal of Personality and Social Psychology, 82,* 252–261.

Suls, J., & Wan, C. K. (1987). In search of the false-uniqueness phenomenon: Fear and estimates of social consensus. *Journal of Personality and Social Psychology, 52,* 211–217.

Swann, W. B., Jr., & Gill, M. J. (1997). Confidence and accuracy in person perception: Do we know what we think we know about our relationship partners? *Journal of Personality and Social Psychology, 73,* 747–757.

Swann, W. B., Jr., & Read, S. J. (1981a). Acquiring self-knowledge: The search for feedback that fits. *Journal of Personality and Social Psychology, 41,* 1119–1128.

Swann, W. B., Jr., & Read, S. J. (1981b). Self-verification processes: How we sustain our self-conceptions. *Journal of Experimental Social Psychology, 17,* 351–372.

Swann, W. B., Jr., Rentfrow, P. J., & Guinn, J. (2002). Self-verification: The search for coherence. In M. Leary and J. Tagney (Eds.), *Handbook of self and identity.* Guilford, New York.

Swann, W. B., Jr., Stein-Seroussi, A., & Giesler, B. (1992). Why people self-verify. *Journal of Personality and Social Psychology, 62,* 392–401.

Swann, W. B., Jr., Stein-Seroussi, A., & McNulty, S. E. (1992). Outcasts in a white-lie society: The enigmatic worlds of people with negative self-conceptions. *Journal of Personality and Social Psychology, 62,* 618–624.

Swann, W. B., Jr., Wenzlaff, R. M., Krull, D. S., & Pelham, W. B. (1992). Allure of negative feedback: Self-verification strivings among depressed persons. *Journal of Abnormal Psychology, 101,* 293–306.

Swim, J. K., & Hyers, L. L. (1999). Excuse me —what did you just say?!: Women's public and private responses to sexist remarks. *Journal of Experimental Social Psychology, 35,* 68–88.

Taris, T. W. (1999). Describing behaviors of self and others: Self-enhancing beliefs and language abstraction level. *European Journal of Social Psychology, 29,* 391–396.

Taylor, S. E., & Brown, J. D. (1988) Illusion and well-being: A social psychological perspective on mental health. *Psychological Bulletin, 103,* 193–210.

Taylor, S. E., & Brown, J. D. (1994). Positive illusions and well-being revisited: Separating fact from fiction. *Psychological Bulletin, 116,* 21–27.

Taylor, S. E., Kemeny, M. E., Aspinwall, L. G., Schneider, S. G., Rodriquez, R., & Herbert, M. (1992). Optimism, coping, psychological distress, and high-risk sexual behavior among men at risk for acquired immunodeficiency syndrome (AIDS). *Journal of Personality and Social Psychology, 63,* 460–473.

Taylor, S. E., Lerner, J. S., Sherman, D. K., Sage, R. M., & McDowell, N. K. (2003a). Are self-enhancing cognitions associated with healthy or unhealthy biological profiles? *Journal of Personality and Social Psychology, 85,* 605–615.

Taylor, S. E., Lerner, J. S., Sherman, D. K., Sage, R. M., & McDowell, N. K. (2003b). Portrait of the self-enhancer: Well-adjusted and well-liked or maladjusted and friendless? *Journal of Personality and Social Psychology, 84,* 165–176.

Taylor, S. E., Lichtman, R. R., & Wood, J. V. (1984). Attributions, beliefs about control, and adjustment to breast cancer. *Journal of Personality and Social Psychology, 46,* 489–502.

Tesser, A., & Rosen, S. (1975) The reluctance to transmit bad news. In L. Berkowitz (Ed.) *Advances in Experimental Social Psychology* (vol. 8 pp. 193–232). New York: Academic Press.

Tesser, A., Rosen, S., & Conlee, M. C. (1972). News valence and available recipient as determinants of news transmission. *Sociometry, 35,* 619–628.

Tesser, A., Rosen, S., & Tesser, M. (1971). On the reluctance to communicate undesirable messages (the MUM effect): A field study. *Psychology Reports, 29,* 651–654.

Time.com. (2001). The numbers: The remains of the day. Retrieved February 19, 2004 at http://www.time.com/time/covers/1101020909/anumbers.html

Tittle, C. K. (1986). Gender research and education. *American Psychologist, 41*, 1161–1168.

Toneatto, T. (1999). Cognitive psychopathology of problem gambling. *Substance Use and Misuse, 34*, 1593–1604.

Toppino, T. C., & Luipersbeck, S. M. (1993). Generality of the negative suggestion effect in objective tests. *Journal of Educational Research, 86*, 357–362.

Tracey, J. M., Arroll, B., Richmond, D. E., & Barham, P. M. (1997). The validity of general practitioners' self-assessment of knowledge: Cross sectional study. *British Journal of Medicine, 315*, 1426–1428.

Trope, Y., & Liberman, N. (2000). Temporal construal and time-dependent changes in preference. *Journal of Personality and Social Psychology, 79*, 876–889.

Trope, Y., & Liberman, N. (2003). Temporal construal. *Psychological Review, 110*, 403–422.

Trope, Y., & Pomerantz, E. M. (1998). Resolving conflicts among self-evaluative motives: Positive experiences as a resource for overcoming defensiveness. *Motivation & Emotion, 22*, 53–72.

Trotman, K. T., Yetton, P. W., & Zimmer, I. R. (1983). Individual and group judgments of internal control systems. *Journal of Accounting Research, 21*, 286–292.

Tversky, A., & Shafir, E. (1992). The disjunction effect in choice under uncertainty, *Psychological Science, 3*, 305–309.

Tyler, T. R., & Cook, F. L. (1984). The mass media and judgments of risk: Distinguishing impact on personal and societal level judgments. *Journal of Personality and Social Psychology, 47*, 693–708.

Tyson, E., & Brown, R. (1996). *Home buying for dummies*. Foster City, CA: IDG Books.

Valins, S. (1966). Cognitive effects of false heart-rate feedback. *Journal of Personality and Social Psychology, 4*, 400–408.

Vallone, R. P., Griffin, D. W., Lin, S., & Ross, L. (1990). Overconfident prediction of future actions and outcomes by self and others. *Journal of Personality and Social Psychology, 58*, 582–592.

Van Boven, L. (2000). Political correctness and pluralistic ignorance: The case of affirmative action. *Political Psychology, 21*, 267–276.

Van Boven, L., Dunning, D., & Loewenstein, G. (2000). Egocentric empathy gaps between owners and buyers: Misperceptions of the endowment effect. *Journal of Personality and Social Psychology, 79*, 66–76.

Van Boven, L., & Loewenstein, G. (2003). Projection of transient visceral states. *Personality and Social Psychology Bulletin, 29*, 1159–1168.

Van Boven, L., Loewenstein, G., & Dunning, D. (2003a). Biased predictions of others' tastes: Underestimation of owners' selling prices by "buyer's agents." *Journal of Economic Behavior and Organization, 51*, 351–365.

Van Boven, L., Loewenstein, G., & Dunning, D. (2003b). *The illusion of courage in social predictions: Underestimating the impact of fear of embarrassment on other people.* Unpublished manuscript, University of Colorado.

Van Boven, L., Loewenstein, G., Welch, E., & Dunning, D. (2003). *The illusion of courage: Underestimating fear of embarrassment in public performance decisions.* Unpublished manuscript, University of Colorado.

Vancouver, J. B., Thompson, C. M., Tischner, E. C., & Putka, D. J. (2002). Two studies examining the negative effect of self-efficacy on performance. *Journal of Applied Psychology, 87*, 506–516.

Vancouver, J. B., Thompson, C. M., & Williams, A. A. (2001). The changing signs in the relationships between self-efficacy, personal goals and performance. *Journal of Applied Psychology, 86*, 605–620.

Van der Velde, F. W., Hooykaas, C., & van der Pligt, J. (1992). Risk perception and behavior: pessimism, realism, and optimism about AIDS-related health behavior. *Psychology and Health, 6*, 23–38.

Van Lange, P. A. (1991). Being better but not smarter than others: The Muhammad Ali effect at work in interpersonal situations. *Personality and Social Psychology Bulletin, 17(6)*, 689–693.

Van Lange, P. A. M. (1999). Why authors believe that reviewers stress limiting aspects of manuscripts: The SLAM effect in peer review. *Journal of Applied Social Psychology, 29,* 2550–2566.

Van Lange, P. A., & Sedikides, C. (1998). Being more honest but not necessarily more intelligent than others: Generality and explanations for the Muhammad Ali effect. *European Journal of Social Psychology, 28,* 675–680.

VanLehn, K. (1986). Arithmetic procedures are induced from examples. In J. Jiebert (Ed.), *Conceptual and procedural knowledge: The case of mathematics* (pp. 133–179). Hillsdale, NJ: Erlbaum.

VanLehn, K. (1990). *Mind bugs: The origins of procedural misconceptions.* Cambridge, MA: MIT Press.

Van Putten, T., Crumpton, E., & Yale, C. (1976). Drug refusal in schizophrenia and the wish to be crazy. *Archives of General Psychiatry, 33,* 1443–1446.

Vorauer, J. D., & Ratner, R. K. (1996). Who's going to make the first move? Pluralistic ignorance as an impediment to relationship formation. *Journal of Social and Personal Relationships, 13,* 483–506.

Viega, J. F. (1988). Face your problem subordinates now! *Academy of Management Executive, 2,* 145–152.

Wagenaar, W. A., & Keren, G. B. (1985). Calibration of probability assessments by professional blackjack dealers, statistical experts, and lay people. *Organizational Behavior and Human Decision Processes, 36,* 406–416.

Ward, C. H., & Eisler, R. M. (1987). Type A behavior, achievement striving, and a dysfunctional self-evaluation system. *Journal of Personality and Social Psychology, 53,* 318–326.

Ward, M., Gruppen, L., & Regehr, G. (2002). Measuring self-assessment: Current state of the art. *Advances in Health Sciences Education, 7,* 63–80.

Ward, W. C., & Jenkins, H. M. (1965). The display of information and the judgment of contingency. *Canadian Journal of Psychology, 19,* 231–241.

Wason, P. C. (1960). On the failure to eliminate hypotheses in a conceptual task. *Quarterly Journal of Experimental Psychology, 12,* 129–140.

Wason, P. C. (1966). Reasoning. In B. M. Foss (Ed.), *New horizons in psychology* (pp. 135–151). Baltimore: Penguin Press.

Wechsler, H., Nelson, T., Lee, J. E., Seibring, M., Lewis, C., & Keeling, R. (2003). Perception and reality: A national evaluation of social norms marketing interventions to reduce college student's heavy alcohol use. *Journal of Studies on Alcohol, 64,* 484–494.

Weinberg, R. S., Gould, D., Yudelson, D., & Jackson, A. (1981). The effect of preexisting and manipulated self-efficacy on a competitive muscular endurance task. *Journal of Sport Psychology, 4,* 345–354.

Weinstein, N. D. (1980). Unrealistic optimism about future life events. *Journal of Personality and Social Psychology, 58,* 806–820.

Weinstein, N. D. (1987). Unrealistic optimism about susceptibility to health problems: Conclusions from a community-wide sample. *Journal of Behavioral Medicine, 10,* 481–500.

Weinstein, N. D. (1989). Optimistic biases about personal risks. *Science, 246,* 1232.

Weinstein, N. D., & Klein, W. M. (1996). Unrealistic optimism: Present and future. *Journal of Social and Clinical Psychology, 15,* 1–8.

Weinstein, N. D., & Lachendro, E. (1982). Egocentrism as a source of unrealistic optimism. *Personality and Social Psychology Bulletin, 8,* 195–200.

Weinstein, N. D., & Lydon, J. E. (1999). Mindset, optimistic bias about personal risk and health-protective behavior. *British Journal of Health Psychology, 4,* 289–300.

Weiss, H., & Sherman, J. (1973). Internal-external control as a predictor of task effort and satisfaction subsequent to failure. *Journal of Applied Psychology, 57,* 132–136.

Wells, G. L., Ferguson, T. J., & Lindsay, R. C. L. (1981). The tractability of eyewitness confidence and its implications for triers of fact. *Journal of Applied Psychology 66,* 688–696.

Wicker, A. W. (1969). Attitudes versus actions: The relationship of verbal and overt behavioral responses to attitude objects. *Journal of Social Issues, 25,* 41–78.

Wilde, G. J. S. (1994). *Target risk: Dealing with the danger of death, disease and damage in everyday decisions.* Toronto, Canada: PDE Publications.

Wilde, G. J. S. (1998). Targeting risk. *Recovery, 9,* 18–19.

Williams, S. S., Kimble, D. L., Covell, N. H., Weiss, L. H., Newton, K. J., Fisher, J. D., & Fisher, W. A. College students use implicit personality theory instead of safer sex. *Journal of Applied Social Psychology, 22,* 921–933.

Wilson, T. D., Dunn, D. S., Bybee, J. A., Hyman, D. B., & Rotondo, J. A. (1984). Effects of analyzing reasons on attitude-behavior consistency. *Journal of Personality and Social Psychology, 47,* 5–16.

Wilson, T. D., & LaFleur, S. J. (1995). Knowing what you'll do: Effects of analyzing reasons on self-prediction. *Journal of Personality and Social Psychology, 68,* 21–35.

Wilson, T. D., Lisle, D., Schooler, J., Hodges, S. D., Klaaren, K. J., & LaFleur, S. J. (1993). Introspecting about reasons can reduce post-choice satisfaction. *Personality and Social Psychology Bulletin, 19,* 331–339.

Wilson, T. D., & Schooler, J. W. (1991). Thinking too much: Introspection can reduce the quality of preferences and decisions. *Journal of Personality and Social Psychology, 60,* 181–192.

Wilson, T. D., Wheatley, T., Meyers, J. M., Gilbert, D. T., & Axsom, D. (2000). Focalism: A source of durability bias in affective forecasting. *Journal of Personality and Social Psychology, 78,* 821–836.

Windshitl, P. D., Kruger, J., & Simms, E. (2003). The influence of egocentism and focalism on people's optimism in competitions. *Journal of Personality and Social Psychology, 85,* 389–408.

WNBC.com. (2001). Who looted ground zero? Retrieved February 19, 2004 at http:// www.wnbc.com/News/1406989/detail.html

Wojciszke, B., Bazinska, R., & Jaworski, M. (1998). On the dominance of moral categories in impression formation. *Personality and Social Psychology Bulletin, 24,* 1251–1263.

Wojciszke, B., & Klusek, B. (1996). Moral and competence-related traits in political perception. *Polish Psychological Bulletin, 27,* 319–324.

Wood, R. E., Bandura, A., & Bailey, T. (1990). Mechanisms governing organizational performance in complex decision-making environments. *Organizational Behavior and Human Decision Processes, 46,* 181–201.

Wood, G. (1978). The I-knew-it-all-along effect. *Journal of Experimental Psychology: Human Perception and Performance, 4,* 345–343.

Woodzicka, J. A., & LaFrance, M. (2001). Real versus imagined gender harassment. *Journal of Social Issues, 57,* 15–30.

Wortman, C., & Silver, R. (1987). Coping with irrevocable loss. In G. R. Vanden Bos & B. K. Bryant (Eds.), *Cataclysms, crises and catastrophes: Psychology in action* (pp. 189–235). Washington, DC: American Psychological Association.

Wright, S. S. (2000). Looking at the self in a rose-colored mirror: Unrealistically positive self-views and academic performance. *Journal of Social and Clinical Psychology, 19,* 451–462.

Yetton, P. W., & Bottger, P. C. (1982). Individual versus group problem solving: An empirical test of a best member strategy. *Organizational Behavior and Human Performance, 29,* 307–321.

Zacks, R. T., Hasher, L., & Sanft, H. (1982). Automatic encoding of event frequency: Further findings. *Journal of Experimental Psychology: Learning, Memory, and Cognition, 8,* 106–110.

Zaragoza, M. S., & Mitchell, K. J. (1996). Repeated exposure to suggestion and the creation of false memories. *Psychological Science, 7,* 294–300.

Zimmerman, B. J., Bandura, A., & Martinez-Pons, M. (1992). Self-motivation for academic attainment: The role of self-efficacy beliefs and personal goal-setting. *American Educational Research Journal, 29,* 663–676.

Zukier, H. (1986). The paradigmatic and narrative modes in goal-guided inference. In R. M. Sorrentino & E. T. Higgins (Eds.), *Handbook of motivation and cognition: foundations of social behavior* (pp. 465–502). New York: Guilford Press.

# Author Index

# Subject Index